OXFORD SURVEYS IN EVOLUTIONARY BIOLOGY

Volume 1
1984

OXFORD SURVEYS IN EVOLUTIONARY BIOLOGY

EDITED BY

R. DAWKINS AND M. RIDLEY

Volume 1
1984

OXFORD UNIVERSITY PRESS
1984

Oxford University Press, Walton Street, OX2 6DP

London New York Toronto
Delhi Bombay Calcutta Madras Karachi
Kuala Lumpur Singapore Hong Kong Tokyo
Nairobi Dar es Salaam Cape Town
Melbourne Auckland
and associated companies in
Beirut Berlin Ibadan Mexico City Nicosia

Oxford is a trade mark of Oxford University Press

Published in the United States
by Oxford University Press, New York

© Oxford University Press, 1984

ISSN 0265-072X

ISBN 0 19 854158 9

Typeset by Oxford Print Associates
Printed in Great Britain
at the University Press, Oxford
by David Stanford
Printer to the University

Contents

List of contributors

John Tyler Bonner: Princeton University, Princeton, New Jersey 08544, USA

Lynn Margulis and Dorion Sagan: Department of Biology, Boston University, Boston, Massachusetts 02215, USA

James E. Lloyd: Department of Entomology and Nematology, University of Florida, Gainesville, Florida 32611, USA

Daniel H. Janzen: Department of Biology, University of Pennsylvania, Philadelphia, Pennsylvania 19104, USA

Otto T. Solbrig and Dorothy J. Solbrig: Department of Organismic and Evolutionary Biology, Harvard University, 22 Divinity Avenue, Cambridge, Massachusetts 02138, USA and Postgrado de Ecologia Tropical, Facultad de Ciencias, Universidad de los Andes, Merida, Venezuela

Michael T. Clegg: Department of Botany and Plant Sciences, University of California, Riverside, California 92521, USA

Niles Eldredge: Department of Invertebrates, The American Museum of Natural History, Central Park West at 79th Street, New York, New York 10024, USA

Stanley N. Salthe: Department of Biology, Brooklyn College, Brooklyn, New York 11210, USA

Michael T. Ghiselin: Department of Invertebrates, California Academy of Sciences, Golden Gate Park, San Francisco, California 94118, USA

The evolution of chemical signal-receptor systems (from slime moulds to man)

JOHN TYLER BONNER

If one considers how natural selection affects organisms there is the obvious fact that the phenotype immediately receives the effects of selection; it is the structure that competes for successful reproduction. Yet the only significant result of this selection, from the point of view of evolution, is the determination of what genes are preserved, or what new genetic variants persist, and what ones disappear after numerous generations. This simple statement neglects the fact that the phenotype is not merely an adult, but a life cycle, and therefore one is not concerned solely with the genes that affect adults, but with those that affect the whole of development as well. And a further complication is that in nature these life cycles overlap in time and combine in families and other kinds of social groups, and that there is an interaction between organisms of the same species which may play an important role in their evolution. Finally, any one species of organism may interact in a variety of ways with other species, through competition, or parasitism, or symbiosis, and so forth (see Dawkins 1982). These complications should not be dismissed for fear that they might cloud the central issue; instead they should become the frame for considering how natural selection does its work.

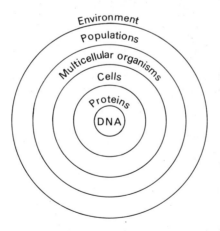

As a beginning let us think of organisms in terms of a series of hierarchical levels (Fig. 1). We will put DNA at the core, and follow this by the proteins for which the DNA code. The next level would be cells, followed by multicellular organisms, populations, and lastly the environment, which includes all the other organisms that may surround any one individual.

The most striking feature of these levels is that not only are there all sorts of chemical communication systems at any one level, but also between levels. For instance, a steroid hormone produced in a cell will directly affect the transcription of the DNA of another cell, or the production of a pheromone of one multicellular individual will directly affect the direction of development of another, or the toxic substances from a population of one species of animal or plant could prevent various other species from growing in their immediate vicinity. It is even possible for the top level, the environment, to affect the DNA directly as is shown by heat shock and other forms of environmental stress that initiate transcription in the heat shock genes, a set of genes that appear to be common to all organisms. The list of examples could be greatly extended, but the principle involved is immediately clear.

We now ask the question: what is the basis of this chemical communication? One of the fundamental properties of living organisms is their ability to respond to signals with some sort of receptor system. Organisms often produce their own species-specific signals, although signals may come from the environment, either as some chemical or physical non-uniformity, or as a chemical signal emitted by some other species of animal or plant. Since receptor systems, and especially chemical signal-receptor systems, are so universal I would like here to focus specifically on their relation to evolution. How have they been affected by natural selection; what is their relation to the different hierarchical levels (Fig. 1)? They are present at all levels, and because they are the means of communication within and between levels, they must represent a key part of the phenotype that is especially prone to small changes in structure, the kind of changes that allows natural selection to produce significant evolutionary progress. Perhaps if we viewed evolution from the point of view of changes in signal-receptor systems we might gain a fresh insight into how change is mediated through natural selection.

I will begin with a discussion of chemical receptor systems in motile bacteria. This will introduce the general principle involved. Next will be an examination of the more important instances where both the receptor system and the signal are generated by the organism: this is the crucial aspect for our consideration of evolution. The discussion will be subdivided into those changes in signal-response systems that result in the separation or isolation of populations, and those changes that result in the increased coordination and internal integration within multi-cellular organisms. From this it will be evident that signal-receptor systems are highly opportunistic and ultimately are involved in both external and internal diversity.

BACTERIAL CHEMORECEPTOR SYSTEMS

Perhaps the best known of all receptor systems are those of motile bacteria, such as *Escherichia coli* and *Salmonella* that orient in chemical gradients. They move by the rotation of each of their flagella, and if they are going up a gradient of a substance to which they respond with positive chemotaxis, their flagella will continue their motion uninterrupted, but should they be moving in the direction of decreasing concentration they will momentarily reverse the direction of rotation of each of their flagella, causing a change in direction of the entire cell. Although this direction change may be haphazard, the net result of repeated such 'tumblings' will be the accumulation of the bacteria where the concentration of the attractant is highest (review: Hazelbauer 1981).

Much is known about the molecular aspects of this response system. There are approximately 20 different kinds of receptor proteins on the surface that attach to specific molecules, such as simple sugars, or amino acids. Some of the receptors respond negatively to repellents, for instance phenol, and ultimately cause the cells to swim down the gradient instead of up. From the work of J. Adler and others it is clear that once the receptor protein has combined with the external attractant or repellent, it stimulates a change in the methylation of another protein which in turn passes the signal on to the rotor at the base of the flagellum and in some way effects a reversal of its direction. Through mutant analysis we have a considerable amount of information about the genetic control of this remarkable receptor system, and there has been rapid progress in identifying the key proteins involved in the whole chain of events.

This system is the simplest type in the sense that the organism only produces receptors; the signals are substances that happen to be in the environment. There are, among prokaryotes, examples where an organism produces the signal as well as the receptor system. Responses to signals of their own makings are found in the aggregation chemotaxis of swarming myxobacteria cells, although the molecular details are obscure (review: Kaiser *et al.* 1979). Fortunately we do know quite a bit about the convergent cellular slime moulds and the molecular basis of their signal-receptor system, a subject to be discussed presently.

ISOLATING MECHANISMS

One way of producing diversity has been to devise variation in signal-receptor systems that results in the isolation of populations. Instances of this can be found among both unicellular organisms and multi-cellular organisms of a wide range of complexity. One very good example, to which I confess a special fondness, is found in a group of soil amoebae known as the cellular slime moulds. First let me briefly describe their asexual life history, and then discuss their isolating mechanisms. The asexual life cycle of the cellular slime moulds is first characterized by a feeding stage where the amoebae feed on bacteria within the soil (Fig. 2). After feeding is completed and starvation sets in, in the amoebae, which may be genetically identical, aggregate into multicellular masses that ultimately form small fruiting bodies consisting of a delicately tapered stalk (made up of dead cells encased in a cellulose sheath that they have secreted) and a terminal mass of spores, each containing a single amoeba. From our point of view

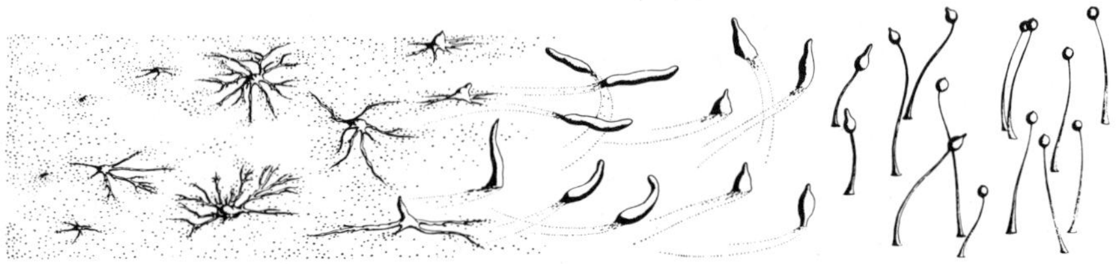

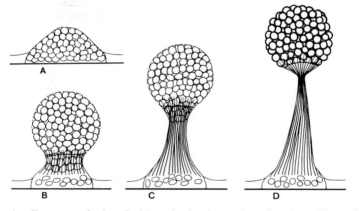

Fig. 2. The development of the cellular slime mould *Dictystelium discoideum* from the feeding stage (left), through aggregation, migration, and the final culmination stage. (Drawing by Patricia Collins from J. T. Bonner, *Scientific American* (June, 1969), pp. 82–83).

the important phase is aggregation. As starvation takes hold the cells start synthesizing three key components: a signal substance, a receptor protein specific for that substance, and an important new feature: an enzyme that inactivates the signal substance. In some of the best known species, the signal substance is cyclic AMP, and the inactivating enzyme is a cyclic AMP phosphodiesterase. Both are secreted by the amoebae, and in various ways external gradients are set up that attract the cells to central collection points. There are many interesting details to the process (reviews: Newell 1981; Devreotes 1982) but they are not directly relevant here.

The first question to ask concerning the cellular slime moulds is why they aggregate to become multicellular; what are the supposed selective advantages of such a life history. There is considerable evidence that aggregation has arisen independently more than once among amoebae (Olive 1975) and it is prevalent among myxobacteria (Thaxter 1892 *et seq.*). It has even been discovered in a species of ciliate protozoan that aggregates to form a small, raised fruiting body containing encysted individuals (Fig. 3; Olive 1978). Therefore, on the basis of convergence

Fig. 3. A diagram of the fruiting body formation in the ciliate *Sorogena stoianovitchae* that results after the aggregation of the ciliate cells. (From Olive, 1978).

alone one could argue that small fruiting bodies are under positive selection in small, soil and humus organisms. If one looks for examples that have arisen by means other than aggregation, the number is vastly increased, for all the moulds and mildews have similar small, erect spore bearing bodies. The assumption is that the reason for this special kind of primitive multicellularity lies in spore dispersal; the spreading of propagules is more effectively achieved when they are placed in a group on a pedestal than when they are spread separately as cysts in the soil. Some species of amoebae, and many species of bacteria and fungi (yeasts) do form solitary or isolated spores; what we would like to understand is what ecological circumstances favour multicellular, stalked spore masses, and what ones favour separate, unicellular propagules.

Cellular slime moulds are one of the main constituents of the soil fauna. One can estimate that in a gram of soil there may be thousands of amoebae that feed on millions of bacteria that lie in that same gram. In a sense amoebae are the prime grazers in the soil, where bacteria might be considered equivalent to grass. And of those thousands of amoebae a very high percentage will be cellular slime moulds, and specifically a group of cellular slime moulds called dictyostelids (Olive 1975; Raper 1984).

Largely through the work of K. B. Raper, and his student J. C. Cavender, and others, we know a lot about the distribution of dictyostelids in the soil (review: Raper 1984). Cavender (1973, 1978) has examined their worldwide diversity, and as can be seen from Fig. 4 they obey the general principle of being more abundant in tropical than in colder climes. It may also be estimated from their work that as many as five to eight species may coexist in one bit (e.g. a few grams) of soil in some of the more favourable habitats.

The interesting question here is why is there more than one species in any one place; how is this possible? There is no reason to assume that the problem of diversity of these primitive amoebae is any different from that

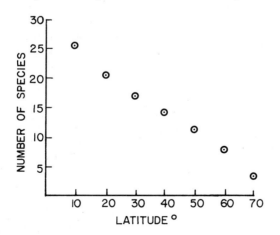

Fig. 4. Species diversity (number of cellular slime mould species) at different latitudes. (From Cavender 1978).

of vertebrates or angiosperms: natural selection is the driving force underlying the diversity. In both cases it is also the driving force for species formation, admitting the likelihood that what is meant by a 'species' might well be different for amoebae in contrast to higher animals and plants.

We must look, then, to competition to see if we can understand coexistence. The first study along these lines was done by E. G. Horn (1971) who showed that in a plot of ground in Princeton four species of dictyostelids coexisted and if he isolated the bacteria from the same plot and tested in different ways each slime mould with the various strains of bacteria, there was a clear indication that each species of slime mould had preferences for different strains of bacteria. Therefore, even though the slime mould species existed side-by-side, they lessened competition by partitioning the food resources.

This brings us to the next question: how did the different species arise? If gene mutations occurred that led to food preferences, then why do not the amoebae of different strains co-aggregate and each generation blur the genetic differences between the cells? Even if one assumes that two slime mould populations were separated geographically and by successive mutations became genetically different, when reunited in the same bit of soil they again might co-aggregate. In order to avoid losing the genetic differences that may be important in avoiding competition for food, it is necessary to have isolating mechanisms so that cells of different species will not join in the same fruiting body.

In the early paper Raper and Thom (1941) made clear that there were two mechanisms involved. They mixed various species, one of which was marked in some way. In one such mixture (*Dictyostelium discoideum* with *D. mucoroides*) the amoebae did co-aggregate, but at the centre of the aggregation the cells of the two species sorted out producing two adjacent fruiting bodies, each containing the spores of only one of the species (Fig. 5A). In the other case (*D. discoideum* mixed with *Polysphondylium violaceum*) there was no co-aggregation; the cells went to separate centres, even though the aggregation streams overlapped (Fig. 5B). We now have a molecular understanding of both these cases, although it is still relatively crude in the first instance. There the motile cells of the two species differ in their adhesive properties and as a result they sort out probably by differential adhesion (Forman and Garrod 1977; Sternfeld 1979). What is not known are the molecular details of the differences between the surface of the cells of different species. In the second case the difference between the two species is that they have a different signal-receptor system. Here the chemical identity of the attractants (or acrasins) is known: one is cyclic AMP and the other is a dipeptide called glorin (review: Bonner 1983).

This latter case is the one of central interest to us here. In these two species (*D. discoideum* and *P. violaceum*) not only is the acrasin a radically different chemical, but in order for the system to work there must be different protein receptors at the cell surface, as well as different inactivating enzymes, or acrasinases. It is difficult to estimate how many different basic proteins (and their genes) might be involved for each acrasin, but four would be a minimal and most conservative estimate.

A: *Dictyostelium discoideum* and *D. mucoroides* with *Serratia marcescens*

B: *D. discoideum* and *Polysphondylium violaceum* with *Escherichia coli*

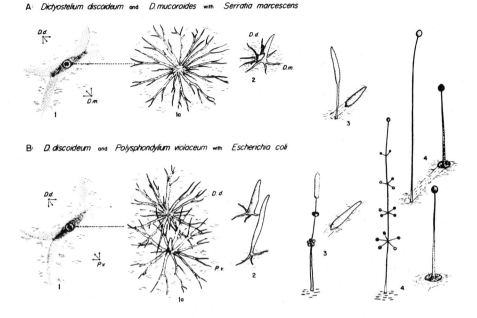

Fig. 5. Diagrams to show: (A) Two species that coaggregate but whose tips subsequently separate at the centre of the aggregate. (The pigment from *S. marcesens* is only retained by *D. discoideum* and therefore the cells of the two species can be identified). (B) Two species that have separate acrasins and aggregate with overlapping streams to their individual centres. (From Raper and Thom 1941).

If one now looks to other species of dictyostelids there is further evidence for acrasin diversity. It has been known for some time that most dictyostelids also respond chemotactically to gradients of folic acid and pterin derivatives (Pan *et al.* 1972, 1975). There is some evidence that for many species this response is especially strong during the feeding or vegetative stage, and therefore perhaps involved in finding food, for bacteria exude folic acid. However, recently Konijn and his colleagues in Leiden have shown that two other species are known to use different folic acid derivatives for their respective acrasins (*D. lacteum* and *D. minutum*) (Van Haastert *et al.* 1982; DeWit and Konijn 1983).

This means that we have a good idea of the identity of four different acrasins, and some evidence for the existence of four more (Bonner, 1982). Undoubtedly more exist and will be discovered when all the 50 species have been analyzed. In other words, evolving new signal-receptor systems has been a major factor in producing and maintaining diversity in the cellular slime moulds.

If this is so, then how do new aggregation chemotaxis systems arise? Since at least four and probably even more specific proteins are involved it is inconceivable that an equivalent number of new genes could have simultaneously appeared by new gene mutation. A more reasonable hypothesis is that cellular slime mould amoebae have more than one signal-receptor system and just one of these is used in aggregation. Consider the case of *D. discoideum* where the cells have folate receptors and a folic acid deaminase that removes extra-cellular folate. This system is not used for aggregation, but, as mentioned earlier, possibly for food seeking. Devreotes (1983) suggests an additional function: that folic acid might also potentiate, that is, enhance the sensitivity to acrasin.

Another excellent source of a primitive signalling system may be found in a phenomenon described for separate, feeding amoebae (Keating and Bonner 1977; Bonner 1977; Kakebeeke *et al.* 1978). It has been shown that they repel one another, a phenomenon thought perhaps to be a mechanism for more efficient grazing of the bacteria by spreading the feeding amoebae evenly over the substratum. So not only are vegetative amoebae attracted to food, but they are repelled by one another. In this latter case we do not know the signal molecular or molecules involved, but they could certainly be mobilized for aggregation chemotaxis in descendants. In any event they are, as my colleague Henry Horn has pointed out to me, an excellent candidate for the most primitive self-produced signalling substance in early, ancestral eukaryotes.

To continue our argument on how one acrasin system could evolve into another, consider the one found in *D. discoideum* that is centred around cyclic AMP. Let us now make the assumption that this kind of cellular slime mould is primeval, and that somehow mutations appear that shift the acrasin from the cyclic AMP system to the folate system. This would mean, provided the acrasin remained specific – either cyclic AMP or a folate derivative – the mutant strain would not coaggregate with the ancestral strain. (It is equally possible that the reverse might have happened: that the ancestor used a folic acid derivative as its acrasin, as in *D. minutum* and *D. lacteum*.) There are many problems with these hypothetical arguments, but I cannot help but feel that they are properly directed, although the details are, and may always remain, uncomfortably vague.

The puzzle is increased by the discovery of glorin which is a dipeptide consisting of glumatic acid and ornithine with some side groups (Shimomura *et al.* 1982) that serves as the acrasin for *P. violaceum*. This substance was totally unknown heretofore. What might its other functions be? In the case of folic acid and cyclic AMP we know them as common constituents of cells, and all that need be added to make them acrasins is to provide specificity. But glorin has, so far as we know, no such common function. One possibility is that it is common, but so far undescribed; another is that it is a special invention for *Polysphondylium*. If the latter is true, then we have the problem of how it arose: how its synthesis was devised, as well as that of its acrasinase and its receptor. This would appear to be a formidable set of novelties unless parts were borrowed from other bits of the cell machinery. In the case of neuropeptides, as we shall see, it is true that they can be traced back to direct gene products, but for glorin that is not possible because ornithine is not an amino acid found in proteins or coded for by DNA.

Before leaving the subject of isolating mechanisms, I would like to mention one other whole class of mechanisms that apply to both simple unicellular organisms and complex multicellular ones. They are mating reactions which are a basic form of a signal-receptor system. For instance, among a number of single-cell algae, such as *Chlamydomonas*, and many multicellular algae, simple fungi, and protozoa, there are opposite mating types and they must be brought together in order for fertilization to take place. These mating reactions, in general, involve surface receptors in which a chemical from the surface of one sex must combine with receptors of another in order for the mating reaction to take place. In some instances there is evidence for diffusable factors as well, as in the chemotropic reactions found in phycomycetes that bring the hyphae of the opposite mating types together (review: Gooday 1981). But not all of the latter are species specific, while the surface contact reactions invariably are. As a result these mating reactions tend to isolate genetically distinct populations and can even be instrumental in species formation. In those cases where specificity is important we know little about the particular contact surface signals but, because they are so highly specific, it is quite possible that they are large molecules, proteins or glycoproteins, which would account for their immobility.

If we think of the evolution of multicellular animals and plants it is clear that their ancestors had an ingenious mating chemical signal-receptor system which they inherited and continue to use as an effective isolating mechanism.

INTEGRATING MECHANISMS

Signal-receptor systems play an even more conspicuous role in evolution as a means of integrating groups of cells into multicellular organisms, or integrating organisms into social groups. They do this in three different ways, although the borderlines between the three are somewhat blurred. The first is that development itself is controlled by signal-receptor systems; the second is that adults are to some extent controlled and integrated by hormonal systems; and third, adult animals, above a certain level of elaboration, are integrated by a nervous system that is in large part regulated by neurotransmitters, the ultimate among signal-receptor systems. Note that this sequence also represents a time sequence: developmental signals and responses are the slowest, hormonal ones may be equally slow or somewhat more rapid depending upon the example, and neurotransmitters are characterized by their rapidity of action.

DEVELOPMENTAL (INCLUDING HORMONAL) SIGNAL-RESPONSE SYSTEMS

Let me begin by pointing out that cellular slime moulds, in their development, are replete with integrating signal-response systems. Not only does the aggregating acrasin system qualify, for it is an integrating as well as an isolating mechanism, but also all the later stages of slime mould development are integrated by such signal-response systems. There is clear evidence for signals involved in the differentiation of stalk cells and spores, including their constant ratio, or proportions, although we are only at the threshold of understanding their molecular characteristics (reviews: MacWilliams and Bonner 1979; Morrissey 1982, 1983). The same can be said for the study of the development of many other organisms; in fact, the recognition of the basic chemical signalling nature of development has spawned a great interest in the mathematical modelling of these signal systems. There are many ingenious practitioners of this thriving industry, and I cannot list them all; but as an excellent example see Meinhardt (1983) one who has done so much to analyze reaction-diffusion models that apply in detail to signal-response systems. But modelling is rather like philosophy of science; its rate of progress is somewhat limited by our progress in the discovery of new facts. The models have been very helpful in ordering and guiding our search for those facts, but ultimately we must know the molecular details of the signals and the receptor systems in order to understand how the development really works.

Certainly the greatest advance in developmental biology in this century was Spemann's (review: 1938) discovery of embryonic induction. Although this is a perfect example of a signal-receptor system, the biochemistry of induction has had a long and tortuous history, and remains partially shrouded and obscure. In general those examples that can be truly classified as embryonic induction do not seem to involve freely diffusable chemical signals, but cell contact is necessary. And as soon as one enters the realm of contact signals, the biochemistry becomes enormously difficult.

If one turns to the actions of hormones during development, then our understanding of the molecular aspects has made great strides. Let me briefly remind the reader that steroid hormones pass right through the cell membrane, combine with a receptor protein inside the cell and the complex passes into the nucleus and initiates transcription in a specific site on the genome. Non-steroid hormones, on the other hand, are bound to receptors on the cell membrane surface; and this complex activates a subsequent series of reactions within the cell many of which are well known (review: Alberts et al. 1982).

· The principal point to emphasise here is that there has been during the course of evolution a proliferation of both inductors and hormones in development, that is, an increase in internal diversity of these signal-receptor systems. This is especially obvious when we compare extremes: mammals with coelenterates, or angiosperms with phycomycetes. The question of how this diversity arose and how new signal-response systems came into being during the course of evolution is totally speculative. We are faced with the same problems we examined in our discussion of new cellular slime mould acrasins, and some of the speculations there might apply here as well.

There is one aspect of the internal diversity of the signal-receptor systems that is particularly important. It is true for both complex plants and animals that if the signal is a freely diffusing, small molecule, its distribution throughout the organism may be quite general; there is a relatively small amount of pattern that is dependent upon the localization of the signal. On the other hand, cells containing the receptor for a specific signal will tend to be beautifully segregated during the course of development. Therefore elaborate pattern is achieved not only by the proliferation of new signal-receptor systems, but by the localization or regionalization of the cells containing the different receptors.

NEURAL SIGNAL-RECEPTOR SYSTEMS

The ultimate in efficient signalling systems is found in the nervous system of animals. Because impulses can be carried down the axons of nerves, great rapidity of communicatioon can be achieved. But there is also selectivity that is achieved at the synapse; by the production of excitatory and inhibitory signal-receptor systems at the synaptic junctions between neurons it is possible not only to pass different information from one nerve to the next, but because the signal substance is released from one side of the junction only, and the receptors are found only on the other side of the gap, the synapse serves as a one way valve for the passage of information. One of the exciting features of current neurobiology is the realization that there are many different signal substances or neurotransmitters in the nervous system with the corresponding result that there may be many different ways in which information is processed throughout the polarized neuronal network.

Since the prime function of the nervous system is to allow the animal to respond rapidly and effectively to external stimuli, some neurons are specialized sensory receptors, and others are connected directly to the muscle effectors. As the size of the brain increases at successive stages of animal evolution there arises an increasing number of interneurons that coordinate and modulate the information between the receptors and the effectors. If we add signal-receptor systems to this elementary picture, there are, in the first place, receptor proteins on the receptor neurons that may be quite general or specific, depending on what kinds of molecules or physical stimuli they receive. But, as before, we are more interested in the self-produced signals and their receptor systems that lie entirely between the synaptic connections.

The extraordinary richness of different neurotransmitter substances that are being discovered at a rapid pace can be classified as either excitatory or inhibitory. The differences between them are often ones of degree, that is affecting the strength or rapidity of excitation or inhibition. They seem to come under the general category of fine tuning responses and effects, although part of their modulatory role involves their ability to select certain pathways in the neuronal network and block others. The complexity of the neurotransmitter system of synapses is tightly bound to the architecture of the neural net and its polarity which results in the signal-receptor systems serving as one way valves. Finally it is well understood that any one neuron may possess more than one neurotransmitter and correspondingly, more than one receptor protein.

Now we return to our central question: how did this profusion of neuro signal-receptor systems arise? What are the selective forces that influenced the population of cells within the organism? The general answer to this question seems simple and straightforward. Selection is culling so that those animals best integrated and coordinated to cope with the environment and competitors will survive, and this selection pressure for increased locomotor and response efficiency leads directly to increased control and modulation within the nervous system. It is somewhat more difficult to see how this proliferation of signal-receptor systems came into being. It is the very same problem we considered with cellular slime moulds: how does one go from a single signal-receptor system to one that involves multiple transmitters?

Unfortunately, as with slime moulds, this can only be dealt with at the level of total speculation. It is an easy assumption that the rise in the number of transmitters parallels the rise in the number of neurons and the accompanying complexity of their interrelations. If one considers a hypothetical ancestral organism with a very few, relatively undifferentiated nerves, it is quite possible to imagine that there was only one neurotransmitter and one specific receptor for it. This transmitter would be stimulatory, giving an all-or-none response. But if a population of such a hypothetical lowly invertebrate were, by genetic change, to evolve an additional inhibitory transmitter, then it would be able to produce more controlled responses to the external stimuli and for this reason be successful in competition and therefore successful in reproduction. This might ultimately have led to qualitatively different responses to the same 'message'.

If one examines this kind of an origin of multiple transmitters from a molecular point of view, the problems seem formidable, as they did with the cellular slime moulds. The difficulty comes back to the problem of so many biochemical steps having to be invented at the same time in order for a new signal-receptor system to work. Again one could assume that the neurotransmitters are part of the cell's existing machinery which are borrowed for a new signal-receptor role. This would perhaps be a possible explanation of some of the non-peptide signal substances such as adrenalin or acetycholine, but there must be a limit to how many potential signalling molecules exist in a cell as part of its normal metabolism.

Most neurotransmitters that are now known to exist in a complex multicellular animal are small peptides. Furthermore, there is strong evidence that many of them are direct gene products or, more often, fragments of proteins. Therefore by using peptides as signal substances, one can have an easy way of devising a large number of different ones. If one then asks how so many different, appropriate receptor proteins work, one could argue that once a generalized peptide receptor protein is synthesized, specificity for different peptides is a matter of small genetic changes. The business of supplying new enzymes to inactivate the peptide is probably unnecessary because non-specific peptidases, which are common, could well serve such a purpose.

BEHAVIOUR SIGNALS

There are signal receptor systems at an even higher level between multi-cellular animals which involve the nervous system. This is the subject of behaviour where one finds a rich variety of signalling between individuals in all forms of social activities. Some of those signals are visual, some auditory, some tactile, some electrical, and a significant number are chemical. A deer will mark its territory with secretions from a special gland, or a female fox in oestrus will give off a scent that is a powerful attractant to males, to give two of a plethora of possible examples. In all these cases the communication system involves the same kind of signal-receptor system found at lower hierarchical levels and they serve to integrate the family or the social group presumably so that the individuals in that group have a better chance for survival and reproductive success.

However, such social communication serves another purpose as well, which brings us back to the subject of the previous main section. In the case of higher vertebrates, mammals especially, the elaborate brain makes it possible to have individual recognition, and as every dog owner knows, that recognition can be by odour. Once such a behavioural recognition has been established it is again possible for signal-receptor systems to serve as isolating mechanisms at this social level. Animals can recognize individuals such as kin, or their pack, or whatever is the constitution of the larger social group. In this way they can identify and reject foreign individuals of the same species, serving as the beginning of an isolating mechanism. Here the isolation is not by inventing new signal receptor systems, but by having such an efficient receptor system that it can recognize subtle differences between individuals, and this recognition is then learned. By such a learning procedure mammals have gone beyond the need for always inventing new signal-receptor systems as their only means of progress in the evolution of integration and isolation.

Conclusion

Signal-receptor systems are a basic part of the phenotype that have led, by selection, in both internal (integrative) and external (isolating) directions. The combination of these two results of natural selection has been a key element in producing the extraordinary variety of plants and animals that exist on earth today. Evolutionary progress seems to involve two complementary strategies: one is to integrate into well coordinated units and produce an internal diversity; the other is to isolate those units to produce an external diversity. In the former case competition is met straight on by internal improvement; in the latter, competition is avoided. The result of both competition and its avoidance is an increase in the number of signal-response systems.

One can trace an evolution of the chemical signal-receptor systems themselves; they form a continuum from primitive single-celled organisms to complex vertebrates. First we described a response system sensitive to external stimuli, then cells that produced their own signals to which they responded. In the simplest case cells repelled their own kind with a chemical signal of their own making and perhaps this evolved to systems where they could produce signals that could attract genetically identical cells and ignore cells of others. During the course of evolution these chemical signal-receptor systems led to that curious dualism where the opposites, isolating and integration, together led to the complexity of vertebrates and angiosperms. Only animals, because of their delicate nervous systems and brains, were able to take the process one step further and use the signal-response system to build the capacity to learn and with learning they have achieved new levels of subtlety in mechanisms of isolation and integration.

Acknowledgements

I am once again enormously indebted to Henry S. Horn, this time for his penetrating and constructive criticism of the first draft. I also wish to thank Ruth Bonner for key help in editing the final draft and Linda Karanewsky for typing all the drafts.

References

Alberts, B., Bray, D., Lewis, J., Raff, M., Roberts, K., and Watson, J. D. (1983). *The Molecular Biology of the Cell*. New York: Garland Publishing.

Bonner, J. T. (1977). Some aspects of chemotaxis using the cellular slime moulds as an example. *Mycologia*, **49**, 443–459.

Bonner, J. T. (1982). Evolutionary strategies and developmental constraints in the cellular slime moulds. *American Naturalist*, **119**, 530–552.

Bonner, J. T. (1983). Chemical signals of social amoebae. *Scientific American* (March), 106–112.

Cavender, J. C. (1973). Geographical distribution of the Acrasieae. *Mycologia*, **65**, 1044–1054.

Dawkins, R. (1982). *The Extended Phenotype*. San Francisco: Freeman Publishing.

Devroetes, P. N. (1982). Chemotaxis. In *The Development of Dictyostelium discoideum* (ed. W. F. Loomis). New York: Academic Press.

Devroetes, P. N. (1983). The effect of folic acid on cAMP-elicited cAMP production in Dictyostelium discoideum. *Developmental Biology*, **95**, 154–162.

De Wit, R. J. W. and Konijn, T. M. (1983). Identification of the acrasin of *Dictyostelium minutum* as a derivative of folic acid. *Cell Differentiation*, **12**, 205–210.

Forman, D. and Garrord, D. R. (1977). Pattern formation in *Dictostelium discoideum*. II. Differentiation and pattern formation in non-polar aggregates. *Journal of Embryology and Experimental Morphology*, **40**, 229–243.

Gooday, G. W. (1981). Chemotaxis in the eukaryotic microbes. In *Biology of the Chemotactic Response* (eds. J. M. Lackie and P. C. Wilkinson). Cambridge: Cambridge University Press.

Gross, J. P., Bradbury, J., Kay, R. R., and Peacey, M. J. (1983). Intracellular pH and the control of cell differentiation in *Dictyostelium discoideum*. *Nature*, **303**, 244–245.

Hazelbauer, G. L. (1981). The molecular biology of bacterial chemotaxis. In *Biology of the Chemotactic Response* (eds. J. M. Lackie and P. C. Wilkinson). Cambridge: Cambridge University Press.

Horn, E. G. (1971). Food competition among the cellular slime moulds. *Ecology*, **52**, 475–484.

Kaiser, D., Manoil, C., and Dworkin, M. (1979). Myxobacteria: cell interactions, genetics, and development. *Annual Reviews of Microbiology*, **33**, 595–639.

Kakabeeke, P. I. J., De Wit, R. J. W., Kohtz, S. P., and Konijn, T. M. (1979). Negative chemotaxis in *Dictyostelium* and *Polysphondylium*. *Experimental Cell Research*, **124**, 429–433.

Keating, M. T. and Bonner, J. T. (1977). Negative chemotaxis in cellular slime moulds. *Journal of Bacteriology*, **130**, 144–147.

MacWilliams, H. K. and Bonner, J. T. (1979). The prestalk-prespore pattern in cellular slime moulds. *Differentiation*, **14**, 1–22.

Meinhardt, H. (1983). A model for the prestalk/prespore paterning in the slug of the slime mould *Dictyostelium discoideum*. *Differentiation*, **24**, 191–202.

Morrissey, J. H. (1982). Cell proportioning and pattern formation. In *The Development of Dictyostelium discoideum* (ed. W. F. Loomis). New York: Academic Press.

Morrissey, J. H. (1983). Two signals to shape a slime mould. *Nature*, **303**, 203–204.

Newell, P. C. (1981). Chemotaxis in the cellular slime moulds. In *Biology of the Chemotactic Response* (eds. J. M. Lackie and P. C. Wilkinson). Cambridge: Cambridge University Press.

Olive, L. S. (1975). *The Mycetozoans*. New York: Academic Press.

Olive, L. S. (1978). Sorocarp development by a newly discovered ciliate. *Science*, **202**, 530–532.

Pan, P., Hall, E. M., and Bonner, J. T. (1972). Folic acid as a second chemotactic substance in the cellular slime moulds. *Nature New Biology*, **237**, 181–182.

Pan, P., Hall, E. M., and Bonner, J. T. (1975). Determination of the active portion of the folic acid molecule in cellular slime mould chemotaxis. *Journal of Bacteriology*, **122**, 185–191.

Raper, K. B. and Thom, C. (1941). Interspecific mixtures in the *Dictyosteliaceae*. *American Journal of Botany*, **28**, 69–78.

Raper, K. B. (1984). *The Dictyostelids*. Princeton University Press, Princeton.

Shimomura, O., Suthers, H. L. B., and Bonner, J. T. (1982). Chemical identity of the acrasin of the cellular slime mould *Polysphondylium violaceum*. *Proceedings of the National Academy of Sciences, U.S.A.*, **79**, 7376–7379.

Spemann, H. (1938). *Embryonic Development and Induction*. New Haven: Yale University Press.

Sternfeld, J. (1979). Evidence for differential cellular adhesion as the mechanism of sorting-out of various cellular slime mould species. *Journal of Embryology and Experimental Morphology*, **53**, 163–178.

Thaxter, R. (1892). On the Myxobacteriaceae, a new order of Schizomycetes. *Botanical Gazette*, **17**, 389–406.

Van Haastert, P. J. M., De Wit, R. J. W., Gripjpma, Y., and Konijn, T. M. (1982). Identification of a pterin as the acrasin of the cellular slime mould *Dictyostelium lacteum*. Proceedings of the National Academy of Sciences, U.S.A., **79**, 6270–6274.

Evolutionary Origins of Sex

LYNN MARGULIS AND DORION SAGAN

Introduction

Sex (sexuality) is defined as the process which forms individual organisms that contain genes from more than a single source. Sex, first as DNA recombination, probably arose in bacteria. Sex, as meiosis and fertilization, then evolved in protists, the eukaryotic successors of bacteria. Both kinds of sex emerged as responses to the contingencies of life-threatening dangers. In bacteria direct threats to DNA by ultraviolet radiation were a continuous problem until the ozone layer in the upper atmosphere filtered out most of the radiation. Meiotic sex arose in haploid protists after the evolution of chromatin and mitotic cell division. Starvation led to diploidy when it forced protists into the first quasi-copulatory cannibalistic relations. Failure of cytokinesis led to dikaryosis, the subsequent fusion of nuclei in the dikaryon also resulted in diploidy. From the extent of its variations in protists we infer that meiosis evolved polyphyletically in several protist lineages. The evolution of meiosis in the lineages involved diploidization, delay in kinetochore replication (leading to chromosome rather than chromatid segregation) and the regularization of mechanisms of chromosome pairing (synaptonemal complexes). DNA recognition and repair mechanisms, preexisting in bacteria, were put to use in the origin of crossing over in protists. Two billion years later, much more has happened in the sexual realm. Yet all that has followed has depended on the strong conservatism of the basic rules: fertilization is diploidization and must be followed by its relief (meiosis). In many cases threatening environments brought mates so close together that they shared their genes in the production of new nuclei (karyogamy), new cells (syngamy) and new multicellular organisms (gamontogamy or copulation). Sexuality is not required for reproduction in most members of four out of the five living kingdoms. Indeed sexuality, a facultative process, is dispensable in nearly all taxa and has been lost in many phyletic lineages. It probably has been retained in most animals because of its intimate relationship with cell differentiation, development and reproduction.

AUTOPOIESY, SEX AND REPRODUCTION

Sex, in contrast to reproduction, is the process that forms individual organisms containing genes from more than a single source (or parent). From an evolutionary point of view reproduction is absolutely required – obligate – whereas sex (or sexuality) is facultative, a partial and occasional, rather than imperative phenomenon. For clarity's sake reproduction, the formation of new cells and organisms, should be distinguished from replication, which is the copying process of nucleic acid molecules. Autopoiesis, from the Greek for 'self-making', designates entities able to maintain and perpetuate their identity despite constant perturbations (Varela *et al.* 1974). Carbon compound metabolism, utilizing light or chemical energy, is the mechanism by which cells and organisms are autopoietic. Both replication and autopoiesy are prerequisites to sexuality but sex is not intrinsically required for replication, autopoiesy or reproduction. Physiologically, genetically and evolutionarily sex is entirely distinguishable from reproduction. That the perpetuation of many vertebrate animals, including human beings, is inextricably connected with sex emerges as a peculiarity of the evolutionary history of these animals. Our own requirement for copulatory sex has naturally prejudiced us to believe that sexuality involving the fusion of male sperm with female eggs, is obligate for the reproduction of individuals and hence the perpetuation of most species.

The fact that mammalian sexuality is correlated with so many aspects of existence has strengthened the supposition, articulated especially in the 19th century by Sigmund Freud, that preoccupation with sexuality plays a predominant, if often hidden, role in the formation of human consciousness. As a consequence of the peculiarities of the mammalian sexual-reproductive correlation entire fields of science are explicitly or implicitly concerned with sexuality. The development of differentiated tissue including sex organs (embryology: Markert and Ursprung 1971); the cyclical production of steroid hormones (physiology: Witzmann 1981); the sustenance of offspring (ethology and sociobiology: Wilson 1975) – all these are related to animal sexuality. And the animal-oriented focus of human biology has proved a firm foundation for speculations in other fields. Indeed, as shown brilliantly in a recent work on Freud and the mind (Sulloway 1983), biological concepts have profoundly influenced judgements and actions far beyond the confines of the science of biology. The underpinnings of psychoanalysis depended crucially on Freud's use of theories that reflect 'the faulty logic of outmoded nineteenth century biological assumptions, particularly those of a psychophysiologist, Lamarckian, and biogenetic nature'. (Sulloway 1983 p. 497–98). (Biogenetic here refers to the concept of Ernst Haeckel that 'ontogeny recapitulates phylogeny'). If scholars from a diversity of starting points are to derive their assumptions from the 'established facts' of biological science, biologists must make sure their science is as well-founded and clearly communicated as possible.

Studies of the essence of sexuality far transcend medicine, mammalian physiology and even all of zoology. As we attempt to show here, the vertebrate, and especially the mammalian, form of meiotic sex which weighs so heavily on the human psyche is a relative rarity in the living world. Because of the peculiarities of mammalian evolutionary history many peripheral, only remotely related aspects of sexuality have become confused. Our goal here is to untangle the biological knot of notions related to sexuality. Only when notions such as reproduction and gender

determination are distinguished from the essential sexuality which tran-
spires at the cellular level may the proper scientific problems be posed.
First of all, the evolutionary origin of sex must be distinguished from its
maintenance.

All five kingdoms of organisms have multicellular members.[1] All five
also contain species which lack sexuality throughout their entire life cycle.
Although multicellular individuals of course do engage in sexuality
(gamontogamy) we suggest here that sexuality began in single-celled
microbes and is still fundamentally a cellular phenomenon. Chromonemal
sex of bacteria (DNA recombination) is not directly ancestral to
chromosomal (meiotic) sex of eukaryotes. Modern meiotic sex which
provides the cellular basis for sexuality in animals, plants and fungi,
evolved relatively recently in populations of mitotic protists. Bacterial sex
is an Archean phenomenon (3500 to 2500 million years ago) whereas
meiotic sex appeared in the Proterozoic Aeon (2500 to 580 million years
ago).

Bacterial sex is distinct from the meiotic sex of larger organisms. That
bacterial sex antedates meiosis by such a long time can be weakly inferred
from the fact that bacteria precede eukaryotes in the fossil record by more
than a thousand million years (Knoll and Barghoorn 1977; Knoll and Vidal
1983; Margulis 1982a.) Bacterial sexuality, in which no fixed number of
parental genes enters into the recombinants, probably evolved from
chemical defences. The enzymatic ability to splice and recombine DNA,
which had evolved in bacteria, preadapted eukaryotes for chromosomal-
level recombination (crossing-over.) The form of sexuality involving
meiosis and syngamy, in which approximately 50 per cent of the genes are
contributed to the offspring by each of the parents, evolved independently
and much later than bacterial recombination. A central theme of this paper
is our belief that protistan sex probably arose during extended episodes of
local starvation and desiccation (Margulis and Sagan 1984). DNA
recombination (which involves breakages and repair of nucleic acid
molecules) is fundamentally different from meiotic reduction and syngamy
(which involves union of entire DNA molecules within a common nuclear
membrane but not necessarily breakage of DNA). DNA recombination is
related to repair of ultraviolet light-induced damage in bacteria. Since
chromonemal sex of bacteria has had a different and more ancient history
than meiotic sex, we recognize that the origin of sex, *per se*, is a misnomer.
We are discussing the origins of sex, a complex set of events that is far
more than a single problem with a unique solution. Many things fall into
place if we separate the various elements that have formerly been joined
under the single heading of sex. If, for instance, we accept that meiosis and
syngamy are of separate origin from crossing-over it immediately becomes
apparent why crossing-over does not always accompany meiotic prophase.

It has been assumed in the literature of sexuality that 'The machinery of
sexual reproduction in higher animals and plants is unmistakably an

---

[1] For a listing of the five kingdoms see Table 1, for details of the kingdoms and their phyla
see Margulis and Schwartz 1982.

Table 1

Kingdom	Estimated No. living phyla	Multicellularity	Sexuality
Monera	2–20 prokaryotes all bacteria	+, −	chromonemal merozygotic via plasmids and viruses no mitosis or meiosis
Protoctists	27–60 algae, water moulds protozoa slime nets slime moulds	+, −	amphimixis zygotic meiosis gametic meiosis haplodiplomeiosis plasmids viruses
Fungi	3–5 zygomycotes ascomycotes lichens	+, −	amphimixis zygotic meiosis amixis viruses plasmids
Animalia	28–32 porifera metazoa	+	gametic meiosis amphimixis apomixis amixis, plasmids viruses
Plantae	3–7 bryophytes tracheophytes	+	amphimixis haplodiplomeiosis apomixis, amixis plasmids, viruses

+ present in all genera; +, − present in some genera

adaptation. It is complex, remarkably uniform, and clearly directed at the goal of producing, with the genes of two parental individuals, offspring of diverse geneotypes' by Williams (1966) and many others (see Bell 1982). We challenge the assumption that morphological, chemical and behavioural manifestations of sexuality are adaptations directed at this or any other goal. We argue that biparental meiotic sex is an imperative relic, retained because of its intimate relationship with cell function, embryological development and differentiation. In animals generally the abandonment of sex would be nearly always lethal.

It follows from our argument that the widely touted paradox, 'If asexual organisms can have, on the average, twice as many offspring as sexual ones, why are there not far more asexual organisms?' is not a paradox at all when sexuality is considered in its broad biological context instead of a narrowly animal one. Asexuality is rampant and sex is not necessary for the reproduction of any microbial species. The major reason that animals and many plants have retained sex is historical: sexual fusion has generally been required for their kind of reproduction which involves embryonic development. Asexual reproduction which requires the loss of oogametic sex is secondary in all animals and plants. This loss potentially threatens the loss of reproductive capacity itself. Discussions of the origin and maintenance of sex have tended to assume that adaptive value can be assigned to sexuality independent of its role in reproduction. But sexuality, which originally was independent of reproduction, happens to have become coupled to reproduction in animals and plants because of the peculiar history of animal and plant cell differentiation and embryogenesis. In all organisms other than animals and plants that do not, by definition, form embryos, asexuality is overwhelmingly prevalent. Thus in cases in which sexuality and reproduction are truly independent variables the paradox evaporates. Indeed, we explain here our suggestion that sexuality itself has probably never been selected for or against directly.

The meiotic sexual system of eukaryotes always requires certain organelles of these cells: chromatin and the microtubule system. We present an argument here for an evolutionary connection between the origin of meiosis and the behaviour of the microtubule systems of early eukaryotes. The microtubule system includes cell organelles such as cilia, axopods, dendrites and the mitotic spindle which are composed of 250 Ångström diameter microtubules made of tubulin proteins. The mitotic reproductive system of single eukaryotic cells requires the formation and growth of the spindle, itself composed of bundles of microtubules. The function of all such microtubule-based structures depends on replicating entities called microtubule-organizing centres or MTOCs (Pickett-Heaps 1974). The functioning of MTOCs is intrinsic to embryonic differentiation. During embryonic development certain cells use MTOCs for morphogenesis and simultaneously relinquish their capacity for mitotic cell division. Mitotic cell division is retained in the cell lineage that gives rise to meiotic cell products required for sexuality. Thus meiotic sexuality and fertilization was from the beginning an inseparable correlate of embryogeny, differentiation and reproduction of plant and animal individuals. The fundamental process of differentiation of cells into somatic and germinal tissues in animals originally required the retention of meiotic sexuality. In organisms that develop from embryos, mutations leading to the loss of sexuality were developmentally lethal in most cases. In those organisms in which such mutations were not lethal sexuality was eventually bypassed (apomixis) and even lost (amixis). Each time sexuality was lost in any lineage (by parthenogenesis, e.g., thelytoky, arrhenotoky, heterogony, tychoparthenogenesis; see Table 2) many developmental, physiological and behavioural adjustments had to be made. These were idiosyncratic for the lineage in question.

Table 2
Terminology: Sexual processes, Organisms and Cells

Name of Process	Description
Recombination	Breakage and reunion of DNA molecules
Syngamy	Contact or fusion of gametes (cells)
Conjugation	Contact or fusion of gametes or gamonts (cells or organisms)
Gametogamy	Fusion of gametes (cells or nuclei)
Gamontogamy	Fusion of gamonts (organisms)
Karyogamy	Fusion of gamete nuclei
Crossing over	Breakage and reunion of homologous chromosomes
Amphimixis	Meiosis and fertilization to form individual with two different parents
Amixis	Absence of meiosis and fertilization at any stage in the life cycle
Apomixis	Aborted meiosis or fertilization such that sexual reproduction is bypassed
Automixis	Syngamy or karyogamy of nuclei or cells deriving from the same parent (selfing)
Parthenogenesis	Development of eggs or macrogametes in the absence of amphimixis
Thelytoky	Parthenogenesis in which diploidy is stimulated by karyogamy of the egg with its own female pronucleus
Heterogony	Parthenogenesis is the absence of karyogamy but stimulated by sperm of a second species
Arrhenotoky	Parthenogenetically produced haploid males and amphimictically produced diploid females
Tychoparthogenesis	Occasional parthenogenesis
Gametic meiosis	Meiosis immediately precedes gametogenesis
Zygotic meiosis	Meiosis immediately follows zygote formation
Haplodiplomeiosis	Meiosis precedes an extensive haploid life cycle in organisms which also have extensive diploid life cycle phases
Organelles	Cells/organisms
Prokaryotes	
genophore	DNA, seen as electron dense area, or nucleoid genes of the bacterial genome
chromoneme	DNA, not complexed with protein, which makes up the genophore

Eukaryotes

chromatin	histone-complexed DNA that comprises chromosomes
chromosome	chromatin gene-bearing structure of eukaryotes, at least two per cell
gamete	haploid cell or nucleus requiring fertilization for further development
oogamete	large gamete, egg or macrogamete, if motile called an ookinete
microgamete	small gamete, sperm
zygote	cell or nucleus that is the product of syngamy or karyogamy
kinetochore	spindle fiber attachment or centromere, that portion of the chromosome that connects two chromatids and contacts the spindle or the nuclear membrane
synaptonemal complex	protein matrix that binds homologous chromosomes
dikaryon	binucleate cell (if it is known that the two nuclei are from different parents then the dikaryon is a heterokaryon
gamont	organism or cell capable of forming gametes
agamont	reproducing organism or cell incapable of forming gametes

Both prokaryotes and eukaryotes

genome	the total genetic material of an organism
organelles	morphologically distinguishable substructure of a cell

---

In both the Kingdoms Animalia and Plantae sex began as an imperative process. Certain plant species bypassed syngamy and meiosis, since their developmental systems, which were far less determined than those of animals, could tolerate the evasion of embryogenesis. Indeed, it has been estimated that thousands of species of angiosperms have abandoned sexuality (amphimixis) entirely (Primack 1983; Bawa 1983). In the other three kingdoms sex is far more facultative. Bacteria, protoctists and fungi can all dispense with their sexuality without any loss of viability. These organisms can and have lost sex many times, whereas animals tend to be cytologically, physiologically or behaviourally incapable of such a loss. Thus an unrecognized assumption underlies the 'paradox of sex'. It is that the advantage of sexuality is itself what maintains sexuality in nature. This indeed may never have been true at all.

An excellent and voluminous summary of work on the origin and evolution of sexuality has recently become available (Bell 1982). No plausible detailed concept of the origin of either bacterial or meiotic sex is proferred. In fact most of the review is concerned with the maintenance of sex in animal populations. After collecting and evaluating masses of data

Bell concludes that no single comprehensive explanation for the retention of sexuality (as amphiximis) is acceptable. In fact the most commonly held view, that temporal heterogeneity in the environment explains the maintenance of sex, is resoundingly rejected. There is no evidence that sex is adaptive in animals or plants living in environments that change unpredictably over time. For example, in cases where they can be validly compared, parthogenesis is more prevalent than amphimixis in the rapidly changing environments of fresh water lakes relative to the predictable environment of the sea. It is in the sea where the sexual species of fish and invertebrates abound. Again, in extreme and unpredictably varying high altitude environments sexual reproduction (amphimixis) is less frequent than asexual reproduction (parthenogenesis) in groups of taxa that can appropriately be compared.

Some observations suggest that spatial heterogeneity at any given time can maintain sex. At least when competing parthenogenetic and sexual populations are reproductively isolated sexually reproducing animals may be selected relative to their parthenogenic close relatives. Bell argues that genetically different members of a sexually diversified brood may have different ecological requirements such that strong selection pressures permit the survival of certain genotypes – genotypes that just do not appear at all in asexually reproducing populations. Yet standing variation and rates of change of variation may be high as well as low in natural asexual populations. Thus the generally quoted concept of many evolutionists and population geneticists that meiotic sexuality is maintained because of the rate at which it can produce new well-adapted phenotypes (Maynard Smith 1971) is not really substantiated by data (Bell 1982).

We do not presume to explain why sex is retained in some closely related animal species and lost in others. We suspect, however, that any realistic explanation will require a thorough knowledge of the biology of the organisms in question. No amount of calculation and speculation has provided a satisfactory and universal explanation. Perhaps a more thorough understanding of the origins of sex will provide insight into its maintenance, evolutionary variations and losses.

Broadly speaking, sexuality is any process that coalesces DNA into a single cell from sources that were previously separate. The details of the sexual encounter may differ immensely; hence in general sex is poly-phyletic. Sexuality may be accomplished by many means, for example by genetic engineering in the laboratory (culturally mediated enzyme reactions), through the fusion of two *Chlamydomonas* whole cells behaving as gametes (syngamy), through the exchange of only gamete nuclei by conjugating *Paramecium tetraaurelia* (karyogamy) or even in the spread of infection by the recombination of DNA from resistant and sensitive cells subjected to the selection pressure of antibiotics (bacterial conjugation or plasmid transfer). Sexual encounters are amazingly varied. They may precede, follow, or be directly associated with reproduction. In time any organism, whether formed by an asexual or sexual process, must always reproduce, since it is reproduction, rather than sexuality, that is intrinsically associated with autopoiesy.

Reproduction itself is fundamentally an asexual process. Asexual reproduction involves the formation of offspring from only a single parent. It is far more ancient and still more prevalent than sexual reproduction. Organisms that reproduce sexually always grow by asexual cell reproduction. No organisms are known that require sexual processes for each cell reproduction in their life cycle.

We assume that asexually produced bacterial cells were the first life forms on the planet. Evidence for the first reproducing cells, bacterial microspheres, stretches back to the very beginnings of the fossil record, some three and a half billion years ago (Barghoorn and Knoll 1977). These spherical impressions are seen in thin sections of cherts, siliceous rocks composed of microcrystalline quartz. They are interpreted to be the remains of microbes which once reproduced by direct bacterial cell division (Fig. 1). Since even the most simple sexual system is quite complex, the very earliest life is assumed to have been strictly asexual.

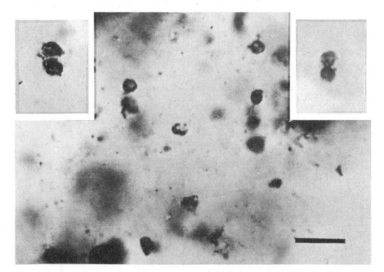

Fig. 1. Swaziland spheres interpreted to be fossils of bacteria (including some in division, insets). Thin sections through chert, a siliceous rock, about 3400 million years old. (See Knoll and Barghoorn 1977 for details).

Although they have never depended on sexuality to reproduce, bacteria, in conjunction with various kinds of smaller, nonautopoietic genetic entities (such as virus particles or plasmids) have evolved ways to donate and receive genes. In any given bacterial sexual encounter genes are transferred efficiently but in only one direction (Fig. 2). The parent bacterium may die as the result of its unilateral genetic donation. On the other hand, the donor, retaining a copy of the donated genes, may survive. The bacterial cells do not fuse, as is the case with most, but not all, meiotically produced sex cells. Nor need the bacteria, which are products of sexuality, have only two parents. The DNA of several viruses may enter

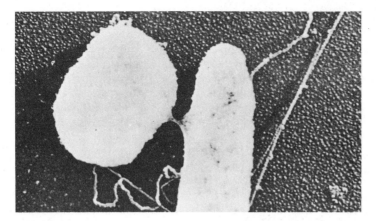

Fig. 2. Conjugating colon bacteria: the rounded cell is the donor.

within the walls of a single bacterium. Furthermore, virus-like particles, such as the F+ factor of *E. coli*, may spread through a bacterial population, converting recipient bacteria into donor bacteria. Some bacteria, such as cyanobacteria (blue green algae), never indulge in sex at all. All others, such as enterobacteria generally, participate in sexuality only under certain conditions. *E. coli*, for example, can only donate genes if the F+ factor is present (either as a virus-like, independently replicating piece of DNA or as that piece of DNA integrated into the bacterial 'chromosome'[2] the genophore).

In well-fed enterobacteria sexuality may be rare, or at least difficult to detect. In general bacterial sexuality is a low frequency process. When it has been studied it has been found that perhaps one in 10,000 to 100,000 cells indulge in sex in a given generation. Threatening conditions, however, such as starvation or exposure to toxins, have traditionally been thought to select for sporadic sexual tendencies, because genetically recombined offspring often survive harsh environments better than their nonrecombinant relatives. If, for instance, there exists a population of enterobacteria, some of which are able to synthesize the amino acid trytophan and others of which contain a gene resisting cyanide, only sexual recombinants, able both to produce their own tryptophan and to resist cyanide, will survive if they are simultaneously exposed to cyanide and stripped of tryptophan in their environment. Because of the great numbers of bacteria, and because genes in bacteria may be traded between organisms belonging to different species and even genera, bacterial sexuality has played and continues to play a key role in the evolutionary process – primarily as the means by which useful genetic information becomes accessibly rapidly on a worldwide scale (Sonea and Panisett 1983, Sagan and Margulis 1985).

[2] Because chromatin made of histone nucleosomes and packaged into chromosomes is unknown in prokaryotes we follow Ris (1961) and use the term 'genophore' for the genetic structure of prokaryotes.

FIRST SEX: VIRUSES AND PLASMIDS

Bacterial sex may have originated as a response to devastating damage inflicted by ultraviolet (uv) radiation and powerful chemical mutagens. During the Archean Aeon, prior to the transition to an oxygen-rich atmosphere, there was no ozone layer as there is today to block out nearly all of the incoming uv radiation (Cloud 1983; Margulis *et al.* 1978). Bacteria were bombarded and damaged by the sun's uv radiation on a daily basis.

Today's bacteria have several sorts of mechanisms to repair uv-induced damage. If one complementary strand of the double-stranded DNA molecule is destroyed it can be repaired by remaking a copy of itself from its complement. Yet if in both strands the genetic information at the same site is damaged there is no way in which the bacterium can recover the loss. Scorched bacteria which suffered breaks at overlapping or the same sites in both strands of their DNA had no available strand from which to copy and replace specific missing DNA. Missing genes, and unable to repair damage, many bacteria died.

Obviously some threatened bacteria must have recovered to produce offspring which eventually led to the diversity of life we see today. We infer from the ability of extant bacteria to repair uv-induced damage through enzymes that some of the bacteria which survived genetic damage from solar ultraviolet radiation did so by recombination: by using neighbouring healthy DNA as a template for replication they survived. This is, in effect, bacterial chromonemal sex. It has been observed many times that bacterial mutants unable to repair uv-induced damage to their DNA are simultaneously unable to indulge in any sexuality (DNA recombination). Certain enzymes required for the repair of uv damage are identical to those required for the splicing of DNA that occurs in bacterial sexuality (Witkin 1969). Furthermore, bacteria can restore their threatened DNA with DNA received from external sources (Anker 1971 and other papers in the Ledoux book). By incorporating bits of relevant DNA capable of replacing their lost sequences bacteria with this sexual aptitude presumably survived during the Archean Aeon as they still do today. Bacteria are known to excrete naked DNA into the surrounding media. DNA excreted by one bacterium may be taken in and genetically incorporated into the genome of a second bacterium (Anker *et al.* 1971). In many bacteria uv light itself induces the release of DNA into the surrounding medium. Generally DNA precipitated by uv light is wrapped in protein coats. Because protein-wrapped DNA has a greater density than the surrounding medium, such DNA, released in response to uv irradiation, may have sunk in the Archean muds and waters, thereby escaping surface sunlight. The selection pressure must have been fierce: any genetically wounded bacterium which took in DNA with enough homology to be recognized repaired its own DNA and was rescued. Today some of the simplest protein-coated particles of DNA are known as viruses (Fig. 3); naked bits of DNA not coated with protein, on the other hand, are called plasmids (Fig. 4).

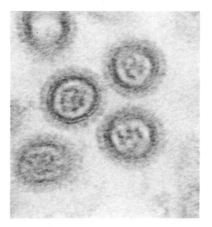

Fig. 3. Influenza virus (Courtesy of Edwin Boatman, University of Washington, Seattle.)

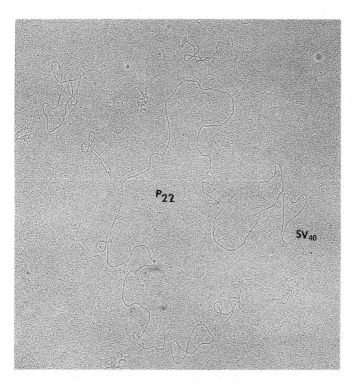

Fig. 4. DNA of phage p22 (a phage of *Salmonella typhimurium*) and of Simian virus 40, a primate virus. (Courtesy of Jonathon King and Massachusetts Institute of Technology.)

Viruses and plasmids are frequently involved in bacterial DNA recombination. Unable to maintain themselves by metabolism they are unable as well to reproduce by themselves. Viruses and plasmids are not autopoietic entities, rather they are genetic 'rules' which can, only when introduced into the proper host cells, make more of themselves. Though they are far smaller than bacteria, containing only several instead of several thousand genes, viruses and plasmids probably evolved after bacteria, since they depend on bacterial or other cellular autopoiesy for their own replication. They may have originally appeared as a result of the activities of DNA-damaging chemicals and radiation upon the biosphere. In an ozoneless Archean world lit up by ultraviolet light viruses and plasmids may have been an early and stabilizing factor in the story of life on Earth. Since threats to bacterial integrity never disappeared even after ultraviolet levels had drastically declined, viruses and plasmids, an aspect of bacterial sexuality, were perpetuated by bacterial autopoiesis and natural selection (Sonea and Panisett 1983).

Recent examples of virus- or plasmid-mediated bacterial DNA recombination continue to the present day. In the human colon, for example, plasmids have transferred the genes for resistance against antibiotics from harmless to pathogenic bacteria. Plasmids carrying genes for penicillin resistance from *E. coli* are known to transfer information to gonococcus bacteria. The plasmid is genetically integrated into the new host DNA by recombination. A plasmid-carrying venereal disease bacterium, the gonococcus/plasmid recombinant does 100 per cent better than its uninfected counterpart because the original penicillin-sensitive gonococcus cannot reproduce at all in the new, 'threatening' habitat: a human bloodstream full of penicillin. Through the sexual union of two different sources of genetic material – plasmid and bacterial – the infected bacterium, adapted to its environment, has overcome intelligent medical efforts to eradicate it.

Another example of the natural selection of bacterial DNA recombination can be found in settings containing potentially high and toxic concentrations of the metallic element manganese. Genes for the oxidation of this metal permit the bacterium containing them to form harmless insoluble manganese dioxide precipitates around its spores (Rosson and Nealson 1982a, b). Although the nature of the genetic determination of manganese precipitation is not known, the genes for manganese oxidation in a few cases have been shown to be borne on plasmids (Lidstrom *et al.* 1983). The genetic ability to oxidize manganese is transferred from donor to recipient bacterium in bacterial populations living in environments containing high concentrations of manganese (Fig. 5). The plasmids carrying genes for manganese oxidation are retained by the recipient bacteria if they are needed at that moment. The more useful the plasmid is in a given moment the more apt it is to replicate quickly, enter other bacteria, recombine with the rest of their DNA and therefore to be further perpetuated. There is a deep relationship between viral 'infection' and the fundamental nature of sexuality. Infective viruses bring new genes into their host cells – sometimes disruptively from the host point of view.

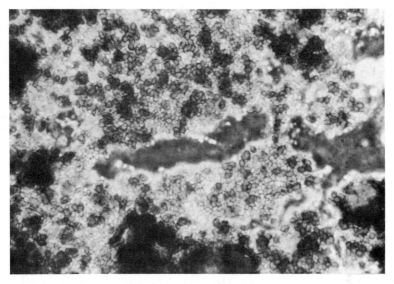

Fig. 5. Spores (of unidentified bacteria) coated with manganese dioxide isolated from a microbial mat at Baja California, Mexico.

Indeed, each time a virus or plasmid comes into a cell it brings with it new genes. The new cell thus contains genes from more than one 'parent'. In this way plasmids and viruses embody the very principle of sexuality; they are sexual 'vectors'.

MATING BACTERIA

In still another bacterial sexual process, conjugation, a bacterium receives a new set of genes directly from a bacterial donor (Fig. 2). The conjugating bacterium may receive from one to several hundred or more genes. In this process two more or less equal bacterial parents attach to each other but do not fuse. The contribution of each of the partners to the recombinant in this sort of sexual encounter is far from equal. The mating consists of a donor bacterium who squirts 'his' genes into the recipient. The recipient may receive all, most, a few, or nearly none of 'her' genes from the donor. There are no universally regular rules governing how many genes will be transferred in conjugating bacteria. Unlike mating animals and plants, almost never do half the genes from each conjugating bacterium arrive to form the genetic components of the recombinant. Furthermore, a bacterial donor that donates all of its genes will die. Apparently, however, the donor bacterium may survive by retaining copies of its entire genome for itself. While it is convenient to call donors 'he' and recipients 'she', it is misleading. 'Sex change' is very frequent. A 'male' donor easily can become a 'female' recipient after a single heat or drug treatment, for example, if the fertility factor, F+, is lost.

MEIOTIC SEX

To discuss the origin of an entirely different, nonbacterial sort of sex – the meiotic sex of eukaryotic cells – it is necessary to leap over millions of years of evolutionary time. Meiotic sex, the kind in which each parent makes an approximately equal genetic contribution to each offspring, probably arose in shallow waters about a billion years ago. This date is based on the interpretation of the late Proterozoic fossils as members of the Protoctist Kingdom (Knoll and Vidal 1983) and the well-documented appearance of soft-bodied metazoans in the late Vendian (Ediacaran animal fossils about 680 million years old: Cloud 1983; Kaveski and Margulis 1983). The presence of metazoans is of course *prima facie* evidence for the prior evolution of meiosis.

By the time the first meiotic sex developed in single-celled eukaryotic microbes two fundamental innovations had already occurred. The first was the origin of the eukaryotic cell itself, which probably resulted from the increasingly integrated symbiotic activities of different kinds of bacteria (Margulis 1981). Second was the innovation of mitosis, by which enormous amounts of genetic material, generally about a thousand times more than that in a bacterium, was reliably distributed to offspring cells. In all eukaryotic cells genetic information resides as DNA bounded by nuclear membrane. In nearly all eukaryotes this nuclear DNA is coiled around histone proteins to form eight-part, knob-like structures called nucleosomes. The knobbed string of nucleosomes, making up the material called chromatin, is further coiled into packages called chromosomes. In standard mitosis chromatin condenses into chromosomes in the early stages of mitotic division and then uncoils to form invisible or barely visible strands at the later stages.

In many types of cells, chromosomes, which by weight are mostly protein, are visible with the light microscope only during mitotic cell division (Fig. 6). Yet standard mitotic division involving visible chromosomes is not present in all eukaryotic cells. Even if visible mitosis can not be found in certain protoctists or fungi, the process itself, or some less visible variant of it must be universal in nucleated cells since accurate distribution of at least one copy of each gene is always imperative. Mitotic cell division and its variants are of course asexual processes. The complex mitotic form of cell reproduction which involves chromatin condensation into visible chromosomes must have evolved prior to the equally visible chromosomal condensation that occurs in meiosis. Meiosis in protoctists, fungi, animals and plants is a sort of series of embellishments on a basic mitotic process. Furthermore, all meiotic organisms also have standard mitotic cell divisions whereas organisms made of cells that do not divide by standard mitosis (e.g., trypanosomes, euglenids, amoebae) do not have life cycle stages involving meiosis. Thus it is generally agreed that the evolution of mitosis precede the evolution of meiosis.

In eukaryotes during mitosis, the chromosomes, bounded by the nuclear membrane, contain dot-like structures called kinetochores attached to

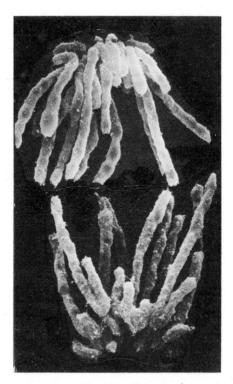

Fig. 6. Anaphase chromosomes. The scanning electron microscope reveals the chromosomes to be complex coiled structures. (Courtesy of Morten Laane, University of Oslo.)

them. The kinetochores, also called spindle fiber attachments or centromeres, are usually located on the chromosomes. Sometimes, however, they may be loose in the nucleoplasm or embedded in the nuclear membrane (Raikov 1981). Kinetochores attach to mitotic spindle microtubules, which in several different ways, depending on species, move the chromosomes. The microtubules of the mitotic spindle are required for the movement of the chromosomes and the segregation of chromosomes to the two poles at either end of a given parent cell. Such a parent cell, containing chromosomes in two discrete groupings at each end of itself, elongates dividing into two offspring cells. The end result of mitosis is the production of two new cells from one, each just like its parent. Protoctists, of which over 60,000 species have been estimated to exist (Corliss 1983), show remarkable variation on the mitotic theme. The variations range from the total absence (e.g., *Pelomyxa palustris*) of mitosis to very strange mitotic patterns involving huge extranuclear cylindrical spindles. For example in some diatoms the chromosomes attach to an amorphous material and move along the surface of an established huge cylinder of microtubules. No direct connection between the chromosomes and the spindle are formed (see Pickett-Heaps *et al.* 1979 and earlier papers in that series). Other protist mitoses also involve large unique associated cell structures, for example the 'attractophores' of hypermastigotes and the centroplast of heliozoans, (see Raikov 1981, for review). It is reasonable then to assume that mitosis arose in protist ancestors to the animals, plants and fungi in the Proterozoic Aeon (earlier than 580 million years ago). Prior to half a billion years ago many kinds of animals have already appeared in the fossil record. The mitotic process must have had a circuitous evolution of its own because it differs in many details in different lineages of eukaryotes (water mold protists and fungi, for example, see Heath 1980 a, b; or for ciliates, see Raikov 1981). No matter how different the details of the process from species to species, mitosis permits large amounts of parent DNA to be distributed equally to offspring cells. The evolution of protists from bacteria, and of multicellular protists (protoctists), fungi, plants and animals from protists fundamentally depended upon the innovations of mitosis. Large amounts of genetic material could be routinely handled in mitosis relative to what was needed for the reproduction of bacterial cells. This ability to replicate and deploy large quantities of nucleoprotein, in the form of chromatin, was a crucial precursor to the sophisticated forms of recombination known as meiotic sex.

MEIOSIS FROM MITOSIS IN PROTISTS

The main bases for the assumption that meiosis evolved from the asexual cell divisions of mitosis are twofold: (a) the wider distribution of mitosis and (b) the identification of the steps required in the conversion of a mitotic cell division to a meiotic one. Vastly different eukaryotes as varied as chlorophyte algae, mushrooms, banana trees and whales always grow by mitosis. In every example fertilization in these different species is either followed by or preceded by mitotic cell divisions. Embryos, spores or any sexual-organism-to-be grows into and maintains its form by mitotic division of somatic cells. The fact that no protoctist, plant, animal or fungus has more than an extreme minority of cells which undergo meiosis at any time argues for the prior evolutionary development of mitosis.

Fertilization, by definition, is the process that restores the chromosome number from the halved value that meiosis produces. Meiosis may be gametic, as it is in most animals. Meiosis may also be zygotic – as it is in many protoctists and most fungi. For example in chlorophytes such as *Spirogyra* (Fig. 7) and *Chlamydomonas*, or in the parasitic apicomplexans, fertilization is followed immediately by meiosis. During most of the life cycle of these organisms cells are haploid. In all the cases of organisms that undergo meiotic reduction of the number of chromosomes and restoration of that number by fertilization, the body of the organism itself, whether haploid or diploid, grows by mitosis.

It is possible to envisage the steps by which meiosis could have evolved from mitosis in protists. Even today these organisms display unique

Spirogyra, a green alga

Mating of haploids

Male on left,
on right
diploid zygotes

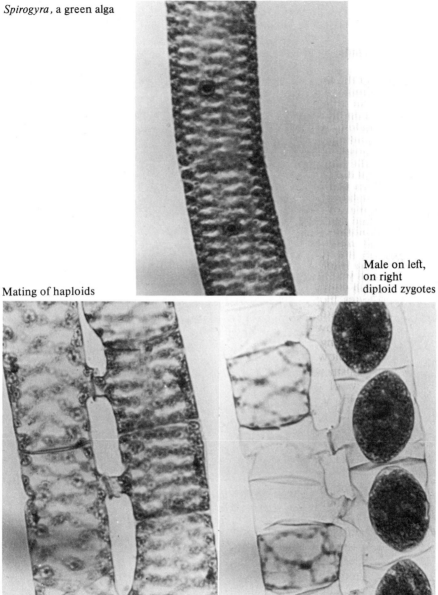

Fig. 7. Conjugating protoctist: *Spirogyra*, a chlorophyte.

variations on the meiotic life cycle, as if they were still experimenting with meiotic options that have been precluded in animals and plants which develop from diploid embryos. L. R. Cleveland (1947) was probably correct in claiming that meiotic sex evolved first in protists.

Ciliates belong to the protist phylum Ciliophora, which includes about eight thousand microbial species. Ciliates undergo meiosis reducing by half their chromosome numbers and then, like animals and plants, they reestablish the number of their chromosomes by fertilization. Yet in none of the several dozen species that have been studied does any sperm fertilize any egg. Two mature ciliates come together and mate. Each mate has at least two nuclei. These nuclei, products of meiosis, contain only half the normal number of chromosomes, and thus only half the quantity of DNA of the original cells. Each ciliate partner has at least one nucleus which it keeps and another which it passes on to its mate. Ciliates thus have sex by the unusual *modus operandi* of trading nuclei. Separate ciliate cells normally do not fuse at all; in many species the mating partners look identical. The trade is an example of organized meiotic sex, of a variation on a common theme. Karyogamy produces in each partner at least one new nucleus which contains half old and half new genetic material.

Chlorophytes like *Clamydomonas* and *Dunaliella* live out their entire lives as sorts of independent 'sperm' or 'egg'. Haploid, they reproduce by mitosis. They show willingness to mate only after external conditions become threatening, for example when the ammonium or light levels in the medium drop below a certain level. Sexual fusion leads to encystment: the doubled organism walls itself off, surviving the drought or famine. These are just a few of many examples of meiotic sex in single cells of the microbial world.

FIRST FERTILIZATION BY CANNIBALISM

The essence of meiotic sexuality if the halving of DNA quantity (chromosome number per cell) and the subsequent reestablishment of normal DNA quantity by the fusion of two cells of separate parentage. Therefore a major step in the evolution of meiotic sex from mitotic ancestors involves the formation of two sets of chromosomes, that is the doubling of the number of chromosomes in a cell. There are at least two known methods by which early protists could have doubled their chromosomes. The first is by cannibalism and the second is normal reproduction of the chromosomes followed by retardation of cytokinesis (Fig. 8).

When hungry organisms live together in crowded quarters circumstances often confront them with the 'choice' of starvation or cannibalism. Eating of conspecifics not only occurs among shipwrecked sailors and alpinists but it has also been observed in populations of protists which have exhausted their food supply. Under severe enough conditions only those microbes which are cannibalistic survive.

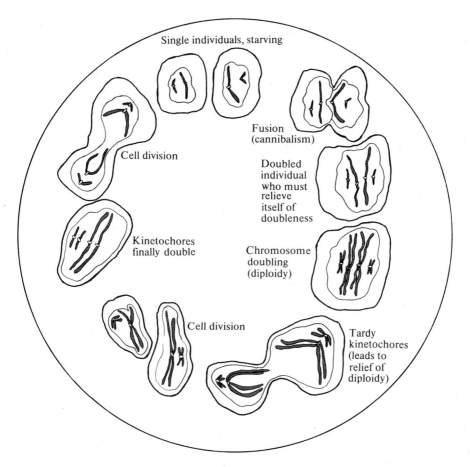

Fig. 8. Premeiosis: the early protist 'cannibalism and relief of diploidy' cycle.

Cannibalistic fusion is not uncommon. *Acanthamoebae* and ciliates including *Stentor* have been observed ingesting their neighbours under threats of starvation. Cannibalism may cause the formation of a fused pair in which cell membranes fuse. The product of fusion is a doubled but still single-celled organism containing two sets of chromosomes, mitochondria and other organelles. This sort of double cell may be considered a first step on the path to the origin of meiotic sex.

Microbes, like all organisms except most vertebrates, lack immunological responses. They tend to accept grafts and fuse easily, at least temporarily. It seems that in the waters of the Proterozoic Aeon protists cannibalistically devoured each other in their quest for food. A minority failed to digest the live food within them. In some cases ingestion without digestion led to a non-destructive co-existence. Perhaps after ingestion of the conspecific, better sources of food for both were found. The combined, cannibalized microbe may have developed an adaptive advantage over its haploid neighbours. Larger size or greater quantity of chromatin may have confered selected advantages. If the nuclei and membranes of the doubled organism were rearranged, a new diploid microbe with twice as many chromosomes would have appeared long before reproduction was coupled in any way to sexuality. The cellular state of this hypothetical ineffective cannibal would then be responsible for the first appearance of a doubled chromosome state, known as diploidy.[3]

The primordial fertilization act apparently emerged from the haphazardly cannibalistic behaviour of hungry haploid protists. This kind of accidental 'fertilization' has been observed in normally haploid microbes. Called 'diploidization', it was documented in the 1940s and 1950s by Cleveland (1935, 1957, 1963). He observed 'hairymen', hypermastigote protists which live in the intestines of wood-eating cockroaches and termites. Occasionally these protists became cannibalistic, ate each other and fused their nuclei (Fig. 9). The partners sometimes lived for a while afterwards but most fusions led to the death of both fused partners. From these studies Cleveland noted that for meiosis to begin as an evolutionary phenomenon it must have been followed by any process which brings the doubled number of chromosomes in the fused or 'fertilized' nucleus back to its original haploid state. Meiosis, Cleveland said, must first have evolved for the 'relief' of diploidy (Cleveland 1947).

Fig. 9. Hypermastigote mating: fertilization cone protrudes from the fertilization ring in the female (the anterior partner). Drawing based on 16 mm film by L. R. Cleveland.

[3] Because most plant and animal cells are normally diploid, we may tend to overestimate the biological importance of diploidy. By way of contrast cells of 'adult' mosses, red algae, apicomplexa and nearly all fungi are not diploid; most of their lives are spent as haploid individuals. Protoctists may be haploid (such as volvocalean green algae), diploid (such as diatoms), polyenergid i.e., with many full sets of chromosomes joined in a single structure (such as radiolarians), polyploid with changing levels of ploidy (such as *Colpoda* and other ciliates), multinucleate haploid or diploid (such as acellular slime moulds) or not even mitotic at all (such as pelobiontid amoebae). They may be enormously polyploid (with multiple sets of chromosomes, such as the spirotrichous ciliates) or polytene, that is, containing the normal number of chromosomes each one with many more than the usual one copy of a double DNA strand (such as the hypotrichous ciliate *Stylonichia* after conjugation). Only in tracheophyte plants and most animals, on the other hand, are diploid cells in the vast majority.

For meiotic sex to evolve and become a regular happening in the life cycle of a species cannibalism is itself insufficient: the fused partners must regularly reduce their doubled set of chromosome back to a single set. A recursive process in which the cannibalistic doubling (fusion) is followed each time by reduction in the number of chromosomes (meiosis) must begin before meiotic sex could have evolved as a mechanism of genetic interchange. In other words, fertilization must be followed, in each and every generation, by some sort of reduction of chromosome number. But, as Cleveland (1947) also pointed out, the relief of early eukaryotes from the burden of diploidy is not too difficult to envisage either.

The major necessary step involves a certain cellular tardiness. In general, the kinetochores, the points of attachment for the movement of the chromosomes, reproduce each time the chromosomal DNA itself reproduces. In mitosis the ratio of kinetochore to DNA replication is one to one. But meiosis involves a delay in kinetochoric reproduction. For, if the chromosomes divide on time, or prematurely, and the kinetochores are tardy in their own reproduction, each kinetochore will be attached to and will pull two chromatids (half chromosomes) to a pole instead of one (Fig. 8). The relief of diploidy was achieved, in the origin of meiosis, when kinetochoric reproduction was delayed and chromatids, instead of segregating from each other, went together to the offspring cell.

It has been suggested elsewhere that kinetochores and mitotic apparatus generally are descendants of an ancient spirochetal apparatus symbiotically co-opted for chromosomal motion (Margulis 1982a). If this analysis of the fundamentally reproductive behaviour of kinetochores is correct, the probability is high that delayed or accelerated replication of kinetochores occurred many times independently of the chromosomes to which they were attached (Margulis 1982b).

Being of independent origin, delayed kinetochores which were slow to divide, provided the mechanism needed for the 'relief of diploidy'. When they fail to reproduce prior to cytokinesis tardy kinetochores permit the reduction division that is the cornerstone of meiotic sex. But tardy kinetochores alone could not ensure the origin of meiosis. Take, for example, a protist cell with delayed kinetochores and only two different chromosomes, such a cell might divide becoming two offspring cells lacking the normal complement of chromosomes. In the first case, the protist might become two protists with two still-doubled chromosomes in one offspring and none in the other. Secondly, it might become two protists one of which has three chromosomes and the other just one. Thirdly it might become two protists one of which has the correct two distinct chromosomes and the other also an appropriate combination of two. All of these protist offspring, except those with one copy each of the chromosome, would die. Only the equal distribution of complete sets of chromosomes to offspring holds any potential either for immediate survival or for the origin of meiotic sex. Selection always must have been very vigorous in maintaining offspring with at least one complete set of chromosomes.

Small events accumulated to trigger the beginnings of meiotic sex. Two complete haploid sets of chromosomes were led into separate cells by the tardy kinetochores attached to spindle microtubules. The original doubled parent probably had been formed by cannibalism. However, a doubled parent also could have been produced by reproduction of the nucleus followed by a failure of the rest of the cell to divide. Such a delay in cytokinesis would lead to dikaryosis, two nuclei in the same cell. In some cases these nuclei must have fused. The dikaryosis and fusion led to autogamy – the fusion of nuclei derived from the same parent. Examples of autogamy are well known. It regularly follows meiosis in some foraminifera, some ciliates and the heliozoan *Actinophrys sol*. In any case diploid cells could have been formed from haploid predecessors either by cannibalism or failure of cytokinesis. Whatever the mistake leading to doubleness was it is doubtful it occurred continually. Diploid, tetraploid and octaploid microbes probably were rare and fatally encumbered. In populations in which haploid protists with single sets of chromosomes were better adapted to growth by mitosis than were diploids, tetraploids and higher ploidy cells, mechanisms for relieving diploidy would have been strongly selected. Eventually the haphazard would become ritualized.

From these inauspicious beginnings animal, plant and fungal meiotic sex emerged. Meiotic processes are not perfect, even as cell biologists know them today they are subject to occasional errors. As long as haploid protists were optimally suited to prevailing conditions, they thrived, reproducing mitotically. Hardships led to coupling, the pooling of cellular resources. Eventually a regular rhythm of nuclear fusion (karyogamy, fertilization) and relief of diploidy (meiosis) emerged. The origin of meiosis is in the 'errors' of the feeding, digesting and mitotic division process. Errors were seen for example by Cleveland, in 1956, who filmed matings of *Leptospironympha* (a hypermastigote). One mating involved an attempted fusion by three instead of two partners. Most likely it, as other fusions by three, led to the lethal state of triploidy. Another kind of evolutionary important error is made by kinetochores. Cleveland observed (1926) and even induced (1956) cells in which kinetochores failed to divide and grow and therefore produced nuclei without chromosomes which of course eventually died. It appears that the microbial cannibalism which still takes place usually results in regurgitation, or death as cells attempt to regurgitate. But in the late Proterozoic Aeon selection presumably honed the products of fusion and relief of diploidy. The prerequisites for the evolution of sexual flower parts, mating birds, and human sweethearts had already appeared a billion years ago or so in protists struggling to survive.

It seems likely that protists, mitotic cells that became diploids, had small chromosome numbers at first. A protist, prior to the evolution of regularized meiosis, with a diploid number of two or four has a far greater chance of returning to haploidy than a cell with a diploid number of twenty or forty. In protists such as certain hypermastigotes that have a few, very large chromosomes, even by chance alone a diploid with a tendency toward lagging kinetochoric divisions will produce a haploid offspring along with a string of aneuploids (cells with incomplete sets of chromosomes or extra chromosomes) doomed to death. In cells doubled by mistake the selection pressure for healthy haploids with single, complete sets of chromosomes rather than unbalanced aneuploids must have been relentless (Margulis 1982).

CROSSING OVER AND SYNAPTONEMAL COMPLEXES

We have seen that meiosis and fertilization could have evolved in protists in a process that involved fusions of whole cells, but not necessarily the recombination of DNA molecules. Crossing over is an exchange of DNA between homologous chromosomes. Many organisms experience meiosis without crossing over, and all organisms may complete meiosis without it. This breakage and reunion of chromosomes themselves is not intrinsic to the mitotic process. DNA breakage and reunion, the excision and insertion of pieces of genetic material was probably first perfected by entities which evolved in the Archean: bacterial viruses and plasmids. Crossing-over presumably used the fundamental DNA recombination process which dates back to the repair of damaged bacterial and virus DNA, but crossing-over involves far more. Genophoric DNA recombination was augmented by the synaptonemal complex and other specifically chromosomal features.

When crossing over occurs during the meiotic cell divisions the special structure formed is called the synaptonemal complex (Fig. 10). This complex protein network ties together lengthwise members of the pairs of chromosomes (homologues). Just before the moment of chromosome separation prior to cell division the synaptonemal complex dissolves. This permits one member of the pair to go to one offspring cell and the other member of the pair to go to the other. The synaptonemal complex is an insurance policy against aneuploidy. The synaptonemal complex ensures an even distribution of already doubled chromosomes. The paired

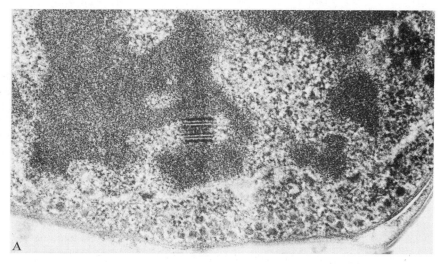

Fig. 10.A . Synaptonemal complex from a marine parasitic protoctist, transmission electron micrograph. (Courtesy of Isabelle Desportes, Paris.)

B

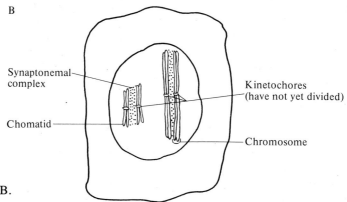

Synaptonemal complex

Kinetochores
(have not yet divided)

Chomatid

Chromosome

Fig. 10.B.

homologous chromosomes, held together by a reproductively tardy kinetochore, are aligned next to each other by the synthesis of the synaptonemal complex. The synaptonemal complex permits meiosis to proceed normally in organisms with large chromosome numbers. In terms of the origin of sex, the elegant flourish of 'crossing-over', the swapping of stretches of chromatin by paired chromosomes locked in place by the synaptonemal complex is a clever but not really essential refinement of the meiotic masterpiece. It may have evolved under selection pressures for the distribution of increasing quantities of chromatin.

REGULARIZATION OF SEX

Synaptonemal complexes ensuring accurate meiosis, fertilization and embryogeny are prerequisites to the existence of animals and plants. These indispensables have the fortuitous property of forcing sexuality each generation in most animal and plant species. As a consequence of the requirement to mix and match half their genes to form embryos in each generation, sexually reproducing beings are secondarily apt to generate low frequency unique genotypes that survive unpredictable situations (Bell 1982).

Sex takes different forms in plants (which are not always barred, as animals are, from having three or more sets of chromosomes), fungi (which fuse their cytoplasms but not their nuclei; Day 1978), protoctists (whose sexual variations are amazingly diverse) and animals with large eggs and tiny sperm. Therefore meiotic sex very likely evolved from mitosis in protoctist ancestors to animals, fungi and plants more than once. Probably it evolved many times. There is a very important difference in the nature of the problem of the maintenance of sexuality in protoctists, in which meiotic sex developed as an option, and in animals and plants in whose ancestors it became inevitably conjoined to reproduction of the individual.

The maintenance of meiotic sex has both great advantages and great 'costs' (Maynard Smith 1971). Whereas sexual reproducing organisms never have to attract mates, the sexually reproducing organism must attract its mate to an astounding extent. Sexual animal partner's must eventually develop a relationship of enough intimacy to assure the fusion of their bodies (gamontogamy), their single cells (syngamy) and ultimately their nuclei (karyogamy) for the purpose of mingling and even recombining their DNA. Asexually reproducing organisms are usually capable of producing far more offspring at a given moment than sexually reproducing animals and plants. Sexually reproducing populations – when they can escape from the bondage sexuality imposes on them – secondarily revert to asexuality by different routes. This secondary acquisition of asexuality has occurred in nearly every animal taxon (Bell 1982; Buss 1983).

At first, when meiotic sex arose, the eukaryotic partners were nearly identical in appearance as many sexually fusion protists still are today. Eventually mating types or genders evolved. The only rule of mating type or gender is definitional: no organism ever mates successfully and has living offspring with others of the same mating type. Although 'female' is an example of one mating type and 'male' of another, mating types tend in general not to be that fixed. For example, certain protists such as the ciliate *Paramecium multimicronucleatum* have several different mating types. Mating types can change or be lost according to the time of day (Barnett 1967). During the day one clone will be of mating type '1' and will mate only with mating type '2'. At dusk members of the clone will not mate with anyone at all. By nightfall the mating type '1s' will have changed into '2s' and thus will refuse to mate with other mating types '2s'. By changing the lighting conditions, making 'dawn' and 'dusk' come at different times the formation of different sexes or mating types can be controlled in these paramecia. Mating type, it seems, is determined by the presence of proteins on the surface of the cilia. These proteins are such strong attractants that the cilia from organisms of compatible mating types will 'mate' all by themselves. That is, even when sheared from the rest of the protist the cilia will stick to those of the 'opposite sex', as if the rest of the protist cell were in fact still there (Watanabe 1977).

As protists and animals became increasingly long-lived and multicellular the tendency toward sexual dimorphism, for mating partners to diverge into two different forms became increasingly more marked. Sexual dimorphism has evolved millions of times – from the mating type 'plus' in *Chlamydomonas*, to the booming prairie chicken, the bull seal and the malodorous female ginkgo tree. Phenotypically distinct sexual types result from only small genetic differences. At the minimum they involve only the difference of expression of a single gene at a single locus, which determines two opposite mating types (I and II in the group A stocks of *Paramecium aurelia*). In addition, differences in gender, sexual dimorphism, represent intraspecies specializations which are analogous to the selective advantages established by societies which diversify their economies. Since members of the same species generally only mate successfully with each other, each time a new species of animal or plant appeared a new change in gender also evolved. Thus the extent of polyphyly of sex determination is as astounding as it is obvious. It follows that changes in 'gender' occurred at least as many times as sexual species newly evolved. In some cases at least these changes

are modifications in the chemistry of secondary compounds and concomitant modifications in reproductive physiology (Swain 1984). What has
been treated in the literature as a single problem comprises literally
millions of problems with as many solutions.

Many single eukaryotic organisms whose component cells divide
asexually by mitosis can produce two or more kinds of gamates capable,
later, of fusion with each other. This is the phenomenon of heterothallism
so common in many fungi. With time, in many lineages of organisms single
individuals could only make one kind – either male or female. The cost of
this specialization, like the diminishment of progeny numbers in sexual
organisms, was balanced by specific advantages connected with the
complexification of large meiotic organisms. Male sex cells, so designated
because of their propensity to move on their own, became smaller, more
motile and more numerous. Female cells became increasingly large and
stationary. The trend from isogamy or sex cells which are equal in
appearance to anisogamy, sex cells that are different in appearance,
occurred in protoctists, plants and fungi many separate times. Genera of
green algae, ciliates, apicomplexa, and even rhodophytes (red algae,
organisms in which the smaller 'male' cells are not motile by themselves)
have isogamous and anisogamous member species. Indeed the practical
definition of 'male' is simply that organism (gamont) itself or single cell
(male or microgamete) which produces moving gametes, usually in
profusion. A female, by general definition, is usually that gamete which
stands still or that gamont which produces gametes that stand still.
Relieved of the need to seek out cells of a different mating type, gametes
or gamonts in many species were specialized to devote their time to making
fewer products thereby retaining more nutrient and expending less energy
in motility.

DIFFERENTIATION AND ANIMAL SEXUALITY

All members of the Kingdom Animalia develop from a blastula and hence
are intrinsically multicellular. All of the genetic material of at least one
mitotic product of the developing zygote must be reserved to insure the
continuity of the individual to the next generation. The irreversible use of
mitotic microtubule organizing systems and microtubules in cells for
physiological purposes accompanies embryological differentiation. In the
phyletic history of animals the cells of the germ plasm became those in
which the mitotic apparatus remained uncommitted to purposes other than
accurate mitotic reproduction. In body cells greater cell specialization
followed leading to a progressively greater loss in individual cell reproductive capacity. Cell and tissue differentiation precluded totipotency in all
cells but those of the germ line. This has led to an obligatory relationship
between sex and differentiation. Organisms such as vertebrates, which
relegated somatic cells irreversibly to differentiation, were forced to
reserve an undifferentiated germ lineage for reproduction of the individual.
Asexual reproduction of individuals, such as budding of hydroids,'

production of strobili in medusoids or gemma in poriferans is characteristic of animal phyla which show relatively little determinant growth. In animals that have highly differentiated somatic cells asexual reproduction of individuals is a secondary phenomenon. For example, the major mechanism of asexual reproduction in vertebrates is parthenogenesis which, since it involves meiosis and fusion of meiotically produced nuclei, was originally a sexual process. Since sexuality is obligately correlated with differentiation its loss in these animals tends to be lethal. The fact that loss of meiotic sexuality is precluded in animals, especially vertebrates, by the developmental system has not been properly addressed by those modelling the maintenance of sexuality in animal populations.

LOSS OF SEXUALITY

Sexuality, which humans have come to associate not only with reproduction but with the emotions of jealousy and hate, ecstasy and anxiety is never such an ultimate priority as are autopoiesy and reproduction. Autopoiesy and reproduction are imperatives whereas in many species sex never appeared at all or became completely gratuitous: it disappeared. In general it is very difficult to observe the process of loss of sexuality. Since the ancestors of many plants, fungi and animals engaged in well known sexual practices, it is inferred that many species have secondarily lost their sexuality. This is also the case of the ciliate protist *Stentor coeruleus*, a common pond water organism. *Stentor*, which has been under continuous scrutiny since Ehrenberg's pioneer work (c. 1870), seems to be in the process of losing its sexuality.

Each individual *Stentor coeruleus* is capable of a wide range of physiological and behavioural responses. No mutants, altered forms that breed true asexually, have ever been reported. All isolates can 'regulate', that is form a whole repertoire of normal stentors (Tartar 1961). Stentors will occasionally indulge in meiotic sex ... or try to (Fig. 11). But both the mating partners die within about four days of starting the act of conjugation. Since *Stentor* sex always ends in double demise we assume that sex, in this species, is on its way to being lost. Once useful, the orderly process of meiosis followed by nucleus-swapping and then fertilization, has apparently outlived its purpose in this ciliate.

Such plants as seedless grapes, oranges and bananas can be selected for the loss of sexuality quite easily as long as reproduction is insured by other means, such as farmers. Asexual reproduction works faster and more securely. We human beings provide many such food plants, through agricultural grafting and growing from cuttings, with environments in which they can reproduce asexually.

In certain organisms sexuality is reserved for only some members of the species. Many social insects have sacrificed the ability to reproduce independently via sex. Most individual termites no longer are able to propagate themselves. Instead they depend on special reproductives. The workers forage, feed and protect the 'queens' which mate with the male

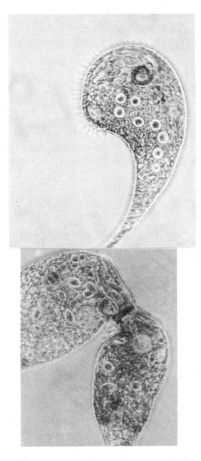

Fig. 11. Mating *Stentor*. The outcome four days later is lethal for both partners.

'kings'. Together they bring more sterile soldiers and workers into the world. Obviously in these societies the individual is selected for only as part of the collective. Sterile casts demonstrate how easily asexuality can be selected for secondarily, when reproduction is usurped by other means such as that of the family unit. Likewise, futurology suggests the possibility of human societies which are asexual through a technological procedure of cloning. *Brave New World* (Huxley 1946), a novel based on the projection of the totalitarian biology of social insects onto human affairs, puts the reproduction of the individual under complete control of the state.

From the broad biological viewpoint of the reproductive imperative, meiotic sexuality is merely an epiphenomenon. It is intimately tied to embryology, tissue and organ differentiation and development in general. The phenomenon itself is the mixing and matching of DNA from different sources in the biosphere to create new 'recombinant' organisms. Sexuality, the production of any given recombinant from a variety of sources, is an absolute precursor to reproduction only in certain animals and plants. Sexuality involves complex, originally separate phenomenon. Recombining bacterial DNA, cannibalistic protists with tardy kinetochores, embryological patterns and development became hooked up in different species in different ways at different times. Reproductive sex has no single origin. It is a set of ancient, embedded accidents endured to accommodate the autopoiesy of organisms whose lives could not be dissociated from sex as easily as a factor is added to an equation. Meiotic sex and fertilization, because they became tied to embryogeny, cell and tissue differentiation and reproduction in animals and plants were difficult to lose. Many lineages secondarily dispensed with sexuality nevertheless.

Sex seems to be a legacy of bacterial DNA patching and protist cannibalism. Meiotic sex depends on cell and nuclear fusion and on the intrinsic property of kinetochores to replicate a bit out of synchrony relative to the chromatin. These are the common denominators of molecular and cellular sexuality. Aside from these conserved products of history there is a multitude of variations on the theme of meiotic sexuality. Bacterial sexuality is fundamentally different and was probably far more important evolutionarily as a generator of genetic novelty than meiotic sex. As one studies living organisms, it becomes clear that the term 'sex' represents separate phenomena (i.e., bacterial and meiotic sex) with distinct evolutionary origins and extraordinary diversity.

Acknowledgements

The authors are grateful to Pamela Hall and Betsey Dexter Dyer for helpful suggestions. We acknowledge the support of this work by the Boston University Graduate School and NASA Life Services Division (NGR-004-025 to L.M.).

References

Anker, P., Stroun, M., Gahan, P., Rossier, A., Greppin,. H. (1971). Natural release of bacterial nucleic acids in plant cells and crown gall induction. In *Informative Molecules in Biological Systems*, (ed. L. G. H. Ledoux) North-Holland, Amsterdam.

Barnett, A. (1966). A circadian rhythm of mating type reversals in *Paramecium multimicronucleatum. J. Cell Physiol.* **67**: 239–270.

Bell, G. (1982). *The Masterpiece of Nature*: The Evolution and Genetics of Sexuality, University of California Press, Berkeley and Los Angeles.

Bradbury, E. M., Maclean, N., Mathews, H. R. (1981). *DNA, Chromatin and Chromosomes*, John Wiley & Sons N.Y.

Bawa, K. (1983). (in press).

Buss, L. (1983). Evolution, development and the units of selection. *Proc. Natl. Acad. Sci.* **80**, 1387–1391.

Cleveland, L. R., (1935). The cell and its role in mitosis as seen in living cells. *Science* **81**, 597–600.

Cleveland, L. R., (1947). The origin and evolution of meiosis. *Science* **105**, 287–288.

Cleveland, L. R., (1956). Cell division without chromatin in *Trichonympha and Barbulanympha*. *J. Protozoology* **3**, 78–83.

Cleveland, L. R., (1957). Types and life cycles of centrioles of flagellates, *J. Protozoology* **4**, 230–240.

Cleveland, L. R., (1963). Function of flagellate and other centrioles in cell replication. In *The Cell in Mitosis*, (ed. L. Levin), Academic Press, N.Y.

Cloud, P. E. Jr. (1983). The Biosphere. Scientific American **249**, 176–189.

Corliss, J. O. (1979). *The Ciliated Protozoa* 2nd ed. Pergamon Press, N.Y. & London.

Corliss, J. O. (1983). *Composition of the Kingdom Protista* (ms in preparation).

Day, P. R. (1974). *The Genetics of Host-Parasite Interaction*, W. H. Freeman, San Francisco.

Heath, I. B. (1980a). Variant mitosis in lower eukaryotes: indication of the evolution of mitosis? *International Reviews of Cytology* **64**, 1–80.

Heath, I. B. (1980). Mechanisms of nuclear division in fungi. In *The Fungal Nucleus*, (eds. K. Gull and S. Oliver), Cambridge University Press, Cambridge, England.

Huxley, A. L. (1946). *Brave New World*, Harper and Brothers, N.Y.

Kaveski, S., and Margulis, L. (1983). The 'sudden explosion' of animals about 600 million years ago: Why? *Amer. Biol. Teacher* **45**, 76–82.

Knoll, A. and Vidal, G. (1983). Proterozoic evolution. *Bull. Geol. Soc. Amer.* (in press).

Knoll, A. and Barghoorn, E. S. (1977). Archean microfossils showing cell division from the Swaziland System of South Africa, *Scienc* **198**, 396–398.

Lidstrom, M. E., Engebrecht, J. & Nealson, K. H. (1983). Plasmid-mediated manganese oxidation by a marine bacterium, *Fed. European Microbiol. Soc. Letters* (in press).

Margulis, L., (1982a). *Symbiosis in Cell Evolution*, W. H. Freeman and Co., San Francisco.

Margulis, L., (1982). Microtubules in microorganisms and the origins of sex. In *Microtubules in Microorganisms*, (eds P. Cappucinelli and R. Morris) p. 341–350.

Margulis, L. and Sagan, D. (1985). *The Origins of Sex*   Yale University Press, New Haven, CT. (in press).

Margulis, L. and Schwartz, K. V. (1982). *Five Kingdoms*, W. H. Freeman and Co., San Francisco.

Margulis, L., Walker, L., J. C. G. and Rambler, M. B. (1976). A reassessment of the roles of oxygen and ultraviolet light in Precambrian evolution Nature **264**: 620–624.

Markert, C. L. and Ursprung, H. (1971). *Developmental Genetics*. Prentice-Hall, Englewood Cliffs, NJ.

Maynard Smith, J. (1978). *The Evolution of Sex*. Cambridge University Press, Cambridge, England.

Pickett-Heaps, J. D. (1974). Evolution of mitosis and the eukaryote condition. *BioSystems* **6**, 37–48.

Pickett-Heaps, J. D., Tippett, D. H. and Andreozzi, J. A. (1978). Cell division in the pennate diatom *Pinnularia* V. Observations on live cells. *Biologie Cellulaire* **35** 295–304.

Primack, R. (1983) (in press).

Ris, H., (1961). Ultrastructure and molecular organization of genetic systems. *Canadian Journal of Genetics and Cytology* **3**, 95–120.

Raikov, I. B. (1981). *The Protozoan nucleus*. Springer-Verlag, Heidelberg and New York.

Rosson, R. and Nealson, K. H. (1982a). Manganese bacteria and the Marine Manganese Cycle in *The Environment of the Deep Sea*. (eds. J. G. Morin and W. G. Ernst). Prentice-Hall, Englewood Cliffs, N.J. p. 201–216.

Rosson, R. and Nealson, K. H. (1982b) Manganese binding and oxidation by spores of a marine bacillus *J. Bacteriol.* **151**, 1037–1044.

Sagan, D. and Margulis, L. (1985). *The Expanding Microcosm*. Summit Books, NY., (in press).

Sonea, S. and Panisett, P. (1983). *The New Bacteriology*. Jones and Bartlett Publishing Co. Boston, MA.

Sulloway, F. J. (1983). *Freud, Biologist of the Mind*. Basic Books, Inc., Publishers, New York.

Swain, T. (1984). *Biochemical Evolution*. Jones and Bartlett (in press).

Tartar, V. (1961). *The Biology of* Stentor. Pergamon Press, Oxford and New York.

Varela, F. and Maturana, H. R. (1974). Autopoiesis: the organization of living systems, its characterization and a model, *Biosystems* **5**, 187–196.

Watanabe, T. (1977). Chemical properties of mating substances in *Paramecium caudatum*: Effect of various agents on mating reactivity of detached cilia, *Cell Structure and Function* **2**, 241–247.

Wilson, E. O. (1975). *Sociobiology: The New Synthesis*. Harvard University Press, Cambridge, MA.

Williams, G. C. (1966). *Adaptation and Natural Selection*. Princeton University Press, Princeton, NJ.

Witzmann, R. F. (1981). *Steroids: Keys to Life*. Van Nostrand Reinhold Company, New York.

Witkin, E. M. (1969). Ultraviolet-light induced mutation and DNA repair, *Annual Rev. of Microbiol.* **23**, 487–514.

On Deception, A Way of All Flesh, and Firefly Signalling and Systematics

JAMES E. LLOYD

'Lies ain't no worse than tellin' the truth, and truth is the Devil's disguise'.
(Author unknown)

Truth has been the quarry of philosophers since Plato and before, and is one of the Great Ideas of Encyclopaedia Britannica's *Great Books* collection. In nature, in matters that count, truth is but one alternative, used when expedient and adaptive – 'Pieces of information are allowed to reach the enemy in such a way as to convince him that he has discovered them by accident . . . real and dummy aircraft, tanks, guns . . . calculated indiscretions . . .' (Cruickshank 1979). Deception is not a Great Idea, but it is an accomplishment, to be achieved in the teeth of increasing resistance – 'Animals have a mandate to penetrate each other's disguise.' (Goodwin 1982). Organisms may be passively truthful when there is nothing at stake, but deception requires effort, and because of its ubiquity and inevitability certainly makes telling 'intended' truth more expensive (e.g. see Dawkins and Krebs 1978; Weldon and Burghardt in press).

In consideration of truth, philosophers have recognized two concepts (Hutchins 1952). To speak truth, speech must conform to thought; and, what is stated must be correct with respect to physical reality. Man can be untruthful in either or both respects. He may wilfully misplace his ontological predicates, as in philosopher Josiah Royce's definition of a liar, and state something that is contrary to what he thinks or believes, or, what he believes and says may not be factual. Analogues of both of these concepts are relevant for fireflies and frogs. For example, the roach in Fig. 1 that has, to play upon a phrase, displaced its phylogenetic predicates and taken the appearance of a firefly is a liar of sorts; and the gauge for a deception is the template (IRM) or engram (i.e. the 'belief') within the perceptual mechanisms of the deceived organism, and not reality itself. Thus, an organism deceives another when it misrepresents something, and, on the other hand, a deceived organism may not 'know' reality, not being perfectly tuned, and be unable to distinguish bogus information from the real thing. Conscious thought permits human beings the luxury or burden of contemplating whether factual truth can be known at all, but the distinction or difference may be quickly resolved in nature, for it can be tough on functional nihilists when the proof of the tiger is in the eating.

Deception, to be more precise, is when an actor (operator) causes another organism, the dupe, to err in its adjudication (perception, evaluation, computation) of objects and circumstances, to the ultimate reproductive benefit of the actor. That is, both participants are organisms, and the actor induces erroneous judgement in a dupe by providing (for)

Fig. 1. This cockroach, *Schultesia lampyridiformis*, collected from abandon oriole nests in a flooded Brazilian forest, is an apparent mimic of firefly beetles as its name implies (Roth 1973). (Specimen provided by D. Alsop). © *James E. Lloyd.*

stimuli that are mistakenly interpreted as belonging to another (model) category or circumstance. In deception there has been a convergence by the deceiver upon a model, in certain monitored features, and continued erring by dupes who persist, though usually with rising sophistication, to confuse the two (Otte 1974; Anderson 1980). It is at the least a concept-sharpening exercise to examine so-called deceptions for the presence of these defining elements. Consider the case of 'indirect social mimicry'. In social mimicry members of different bird species are said to converge on each other in coloration and visual signal patterns because these 'promote the formation and maintain the cohesion of mixed flocks' – that is, because each individual is better able to gain and coordinate a protective cover of other selfish birds around him. In indirect social mimicry two allopatric species are said to converge because they independently flock with a third species (Moynihan 1968). The two species in question are not true mimics of each other any more than flying squirrels and flying phalangers, having evolved on separate continents in response to similar selective pressures, are mimics of each other. Though a geometry is involved, that of a selfish herd, two species that mimic the same species do not *ipso facto* mimic each other.

Likewise, consider 'automimics' in monarch butterflies – this term is used for those individuals that are not distasteful because they grew up on plants that lacked the poisons they would have sequestered for defence (Brower 1969). Though a potential predator that sees them may incorrectly infer that they are not edible, this circumstance is conceptually distinct from one in which tasteful monarchs had converged in appearance upon distasteful ones. The latter, for example, would occur if by eating plants without the poisons their development had been knocked out of its proper channel and only through a corrective selection had the butterflies been able to maintain their protective (monarch) appearance. Monarch automimics are not legitimate mimics either.

A tropical firefly provides an illustration of corrective selection. Fireflies are often foul-tasting, even poisonous (Lloyd 1973; Meinwald *et al.* 1979). Their elongate, dark form, sometimes with stripes and often with red or orange marks at the anterior end, makes them easily recognizable, and members of a sort of familial Mullerian mimicry complex (see also McDermott 1961). *Aspisoma* fireflies of the neotropics are broadly oval with explanate margins that make them look like tortoise beetles. Their fender-skirts are used against ants (Figs. 2 & 3). The oval form of *Aspisoma* that results from an adaptation against ants would prevent them

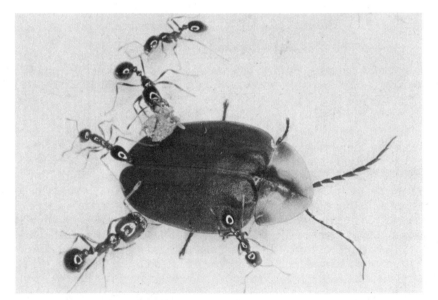

Fig. 2. One function of the broad margins of the elytra of certain fireflies, such as this *Tenaspis angulata*, is to fend against ants. Note the worker with the crumb of soil. See Fig. 3. © *James E. Lloyd.*

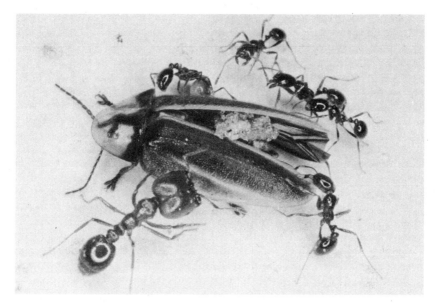

Fig. 3. Ants have penetrated the protective shield of this *Aspisoma* and a crumb has been placed under one elytron (from J. Lloyd and A. Bhatkar, unpublished, at Cardenaz, Mexico). © *James E. Lloyd.*

Fig. 4. *Aspisoma aegrotum* from Colombia, S.A., showing the typical firefly on its back. © *James E. Lloyd.*

from being recognized as fireflies and subject them to attack by other predators. In some *Aspisoma* selection has maintained a typical firefly appearance by making their skirts pale and translucent, and even added fake legs at the side (Fig. 4). Unlike the mynah bird in the Gainesville pet shop that said it was a starling, which to all but ornithologists would be a lie because of limited factual knowledge, *Aspisoma* seems to have reduced the chances of shopper error by telling a small lie in favour of a larger truth, and tailored its aposomatic signal to the conceptual limitations of its important receivers.

The apparent bending of a stick at the surface of a pool of water is not a deception, though perceptual illusions of various sorts sometimes provide loopholes for deceptions (Gregory and Gombrich 1973); nor are 'spell-binding' inputs that manipulate receivers like electrodes in the brain of a laboratory cat (Dawkins and Krebs 1978). Accidental or fortuitous similarities that result in judgemental errors are not deceptions, but happenstances are presumably the evolutionary origins of many deceptions. Mechanisms by which deceptions are achieved, both on the deceiver and dupe side, and the sensory channels that are involved, are not important to the definition, and there is a variety observed and exploited. In exceptional extremes, the seeds of *Camelina sativa*, a weed of flax fields, have so converged in size and weight that winnowing machines, extensions of human sensors (and under the control of their CNS analyzers!), no longer separate them from flax seeds (Wickler 1968); and the edible Japanese crab *Dorippe japonica* has the face of a Sumurai on its carapace (Fig. 5), improved through selection over the centuries by humans throwing back better mimics and eating poorer ones (Huxley 1957). The concept of 'intent', important to psychologists, is replaced (although see Dennett 1983) for organisms other than human ones and for many human features as well, by that of natural selection.

Before Darwin, deception, as we are finding it today, might have been an anathema for some naturalists, those who were natural theologians and 'found it necessary to invoke the creator, his thought, and his activity in every detail of the life of every individual of every kind of organism' (Mayr 1982). In recent years, examples and varieties of deception have been found, invoked, and tabulated at an alarming rate, and not necessarily because biologists have become cynics and expect perfidy anywhere. It is partly because we are refocusing on individuals, and seeing them as genetically competitive, selfish egoists. The revolution in the way adaptation was viewed, the shift from a population to an individual perspective that happened in the 1960s (due to the inspired work of W. D. Hamilton and G. C. Williams), was a watershed, and led to a review of practically everything, even the way classic examples of deception were interpreted (Alexander 1980). Today only rarely does one hear the assertion that within-species deception is unexpected (see Otte 1974, 1975), or that the adaptive significance of so-called Mullerian mimicry (Mullerian convergence, Wiens 1978) is that each species needs sacrifice only a few of its members. But it does seem paradoxical that although deception, and in particular that connected with defence,

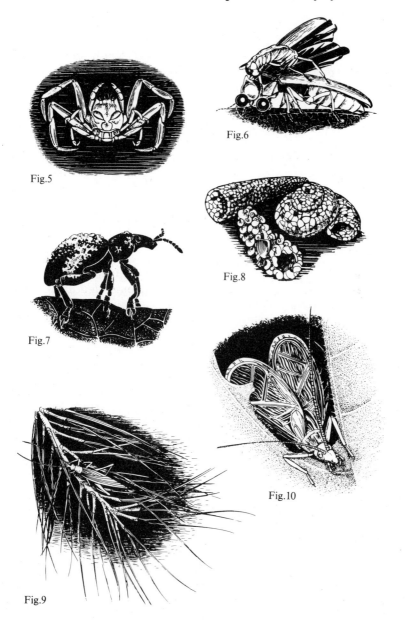

Fig. 5. The Sumurai crab. The Chinese call this 'the crab with the human face' (Schmitt 1965)! Could Huxley have been myth-taken? (See text; redrawn from various sources) Fig. 6. Male Thai firefly *Pteroptyx valida* atop a female, bending his abdomen left around to her face (both facing left, with left eye of each visible; his wings and elytra project up to right). Males of this species did not flash during this display as in *P. tener*, but instead opened an apical pocket presumably presenting a chemical message (J. Lloyd, S. Wing, and T. Hontrakul, unpublished).

Fig. 7. Cryptogamic plants, oribatid mites, rotifers, nematodes and micro-organisms live on the backs of beetles, especially weevils in montane New Guinea. (*Gymnopholus* (?) drawn from photos and specimens, see Gressitt 1969.) Fig. 8. Caddisfly larvae are aquatic, build and hide in cases. These three cases, representing different genera, are made of sand (*Micrasema*), snail shells (*Oecetis*), and sand assembled in the form of a snail shell (*Helicopsyche*). (Drawn from specimens loaned and identified by L. Berner.) Fig. 9. Female pine tree cricket *Oecanthus pini* on a pine twig amidst needles which her colours match. The antennae will next be laid along the body, parallel with the needles. (Drawn from specimens and photos by T. J. Walker.) Fig. 10. Male fast calling tree cricket, *Oecanthus celerinictus*, uses leaf as an acoustic baffle to prevent interference of out-of-phase sound leaving front and back surfaces of wing. (Drawn from specimens and photos by T. Forrest.) © *James E. Lloyd.*

provides the most graphic and best understood examples of adaptation and natural selection, general biology texts often teach mimicry only for mimicry's sake, invoking the uninformative and misleading Batesian-Mullerian 'dichotomy' (pigeon-holes, Huheey 1976; see Wickler 1965), and do not use it extensively to teach the principles of 'natural selection thinking'. 'Mimicry presents us with an unusually clear account of the dynamics of adaptation in that the nature of the selective forces, the genetical outcome, and the theory which links them are exceptionally well understood' (Turner 1977).

A long paradigm ago, well before Bates' (1862) benchmark publication, Kirby and Spence used the words mimicry, deceive, imitation, simulate, and alarm (i.e. intimidate by bluff) in their *Entomology* (Letter XXI, 'Means by which insects defend themselves', 6th edition, 1846, pp. 439–465). They discussed the use of colour, form, texture and behaviour, and the mimicry of soil, pebbles, twigs, fruit, flowers, a miniature quadruped, dead and decomposing leaves, and the perching of mottled moths on the north, lichen-covered sides of trees. They told how tortoise beetle larvae cover themselves with – 'yet as I am bound to confess the faults of insects as well as to extol their virtues, I must not conceal from you this opprobrium' – excrement umbrellas – a 'stercorarious parasol'. And, they gave examples, and a rather clear explanation only one step removed from modernity, which I will take the liberty of adding, of what came to be called aggressive mimicry: 'A beautiful instance of the wisdom of Providence in adapting means to their end' is the mimicry of syrphid flies whose larvae live in the nests of humble-bees. 'Many of the species . . . strikingly resemble those bees in shape, clothing, and colour . . . that they may enter their nests and deposit their eggs undiscovered. Did these intruders venture themselves amongst the humble-bees in a less kindred form, their lives would probably pay the forfeit of their presumption' [as did so many of their ancestors' less-well-costumed species-mates in the gradual evolution of this adaptation]. 'In like manner . . . [do] the larvae of those tropical [bee flies] which have such a bee-like form live on the larvae of the bees they so strikingly represent . . . and . . . [also] probably the object of nature in giving such an ant-like form to [a certain spider] is to deceive the ants on which they prey.' Kirby and Spence also gave an example that apparently involves the mimicry of an intraspecific, acoustical signal, 'the death's head moth . . . when menaced by the stings of ten thousand bees enraged at her depredations upon their property, possesses the secret to disarm them of their fury . . . a sharp, shrill, mournful cry . . . affects and disarms the bees, so as to enable her to proceed in her spoilations with impunity'.

CLASSIFYING DECEPTION

How can I deceive thee, can I count the ways? Rothschild (1967; see Remington 1963) observed that 'Several thousand papers have been published that are directly or indirectly concerned with mimicry . . . and when mimicry is looked at carefully, almost every case – even if it can be squeezed into one of the well-known categories – presents a fascinating 'special situation' that requires clarification'. To this it can be added that when deceptions and related phenomena are looked at closely they are seen to flow one into another like braided channels in an ancient valley. This is especially obvious from an evening's study of Cott's *Adaptive Coloration in Animals* (1940), in which he left practically no stone or 'transition' between them unturned.

As a guide for appreciating the diversity of deception as well as for analytical dissection, a number of distinctions can be kept in mind, including the same ones that have been used for straight and innocent communication (see Sebeok 1968, 1977). For example, the standard physical channels – light, sound, chemical, tactile, etc. – provide an obvious distinction, and they can be further divided, light into movement, bioluminescence, reflected-light, etc. Although 'proximate', there are important 'ultimate' consequences because each channel, like other proximate factors, imposes its own peculiar constraints and provides certain advantages to deceivers or their dupes. Some deceptions are vegetative, and others involve neural activity of a high order; some are fixed, some facultative; they seek different dupe action (attraction, hesitation, deflection, Wiens 1978; Dawkins 1982); misrepresent different informational transactions ('mutual' signals, clues, cues, Lloyd 1983); have different costs (part or all of reproduction, a scarce resource, a few minutes, or life, Otte 1975); are used between individuals with different degrees of interest mutuality and conflict (Otte 1974); and come in different sizes (restrained embellishment, unrestrained embellishment, total deception – and total truth, Alexander 1980, ms., see Otte 1975); are used in different positions in interaction chains (*conceal*-run-*bluff*-fight, Crane 1952); involve different asymmetries (life-dinner, resident-intruder, male-female, Dawkins 1976); connect different relationships among the three key elements (dupe, operator, and model, Vane-Wright 1976); are used in different contexts (nutrition, protection, reproduction, and distribution, Wiens 1978; defence, offence, competition and seduction, Lloyd 1983); involve behaviour, morphology, physiology and biochemistry; and some substitute, some exaggerate, and some conceal identity, quantity, future action. . . . In the next section I will illustrate several of these distinctions as well as interesting if not always logical, and sometimes irritating transitions, extensions, and sidelights, in a montage of camouflage.

VARIATIONS ON A HIDING THEME

Geronimo Cardano, Neapolitan, friend of Leonardo da Vinci, author of 130 books and more than 100 unpublished manuscripts on astronomy, dreams, morals, wine, wisdom, and syphilis, among other things, invented the grille cipher – letters of a message are distributed through an innocent text and identified at deciphering because they peek through holes of a grille placed over the text. In 1645 a supporter of Charles I awaiting execution in Colchester Castle escaped from the chapel at vespers as *per* instructions received in a sophisticated Cardano cipher concealed in a personal letter. Cardano believed that 'the only really unbreakable cipher is one that is unrecognizable as a cipher so that nobody will have any reason to try to break it' (Haldane 1976). In nature what schemes there are to hide from the *oeil de maître*! One can in general (Impressionism) or in detail (Realism) simulate background, cover up with material from the background, manufacture a background, get behind the background, or get lost in time, or space as but one more member of a useless crowd that is the background, or though in plain sight, be voided, cancelled out in a mental background.

The grasshopper *Bootettix argentatus* blends with the shiny foliage of creosote bushes on which it lives exclusively (Otte 1981), and the pine tree cricket is pine-green and thin with a tan anterior: it stands on its head amongst needles, becoming a needle with a tan fascicle (Fig. 9; T. J. Walker, pers. comm.). Noctuid and geometrid moths perch on the correct background (Sargent 1968). Males of the meadow katydid *Neoconocephalis triops* are either green or brown, depending upon the time of year they are born into, and hence the colour of grass upon which they live (Whitesell 1974), and the adults of several psyllids change colour from bright green to dark red-brown during sexual maturation, to match the colour of the part of hawthorn they are on (Sutton 1983). Orchid spiders '. . . with their colours and patterns so exact that they might have been fashioned in the same petal shop . . .' hide in flowers: some eat away at the heart of the blossom, substitute their legs for stamens and palps for pistils, and with the unharmed nectary still emitting an attractant, await bees (Beebe 1925). Various Lepidoptera pupae simulate parasitism, with parasite emergence holes or as many as 40 little silken 'wasp' cocoons of the moths' manufacture attached on their cuticle (Hinton 1973). The pupa of the nymphalid butterfly *Limnitis populi* appears to have been broken open, partly eaten and rejected. It simulates pieces of cuticle 'floating in the expelled yellow liquid', and, with proper reference to gravity, presents the illusion that 'some of the liquid has flowed forwards over the fore part of the pupa, which is highly polished and appears to be covered by a liquid film' (I. Portischinsky, in Hinton 1973). Are such pupae hiding as something useless to be ignored; are they invoking unpleasant memories that will turn predators disgustingly away; or are they Mullerian proxies for unpupated, untasted siblings?

'Coarse briar' seeds on beaches in the Philippines mimic pebbles in 'shape, size, lustre, texture, and stratification' and there is polymorphism that duplicates the variation in the beach pebbles (W. Sherzer, in Wiens 1978) – at a distance they are lost against background, up close each mimics one of an inedible multitude. The tube-cases of caddis fly larvae illustrate a transition from background blending to useless-object mimicry with a flare: larvae of several genera build cases of tiny pebbles, but those of *Helicopsyche* coil theirs, and they were first described as the work of snails (Fig. 8; Lea 1834). But predaceous horse fly larvae merely lie under mud and hook and pull on the bottoms of toads that sit on them (Jackman *et al.* 1983): the undisturbed mud is the concealing agent, and so the medium is not the message, the behaviour is. Female digger wasps hide their nest entrances by closing the holes and removing the excavated dirt – some dig decoy burrows into which parasites mistakenly throw their eggs (Evans 1966).

Weevils of the moss-forests of New Guinea have cuticular structures that provide a foothold for algae, fungi, liverworts, and mosses that grow on their elytra: the beetles move under leaves in sunny weather, and when it is foggy climb to the tops of trees and bushes to water their gardens (Fig. 7; Gressitt 1969). Lacewing larvae put the skins of aphid prey on their backs, a technique used by various human hunters, to escape attacks from the aphids' ant-shepherds (Eisner *et al.* 1978) – 'Macbeth shall never vanquisht be, until great Birnam wood to high Dunsinane hill shall come against him'. In World War II the Japanese used wire and cable to tie the tops of palm trees in place, cut off and removed the trunks, and built an airfield underneath (Reit 1978).

Certain glass- and hylid-frogs (Centrolenidae, Phyllomedusinae) reflect near-infrared so they do not appear as heat sinks to bird and pit-viper predators (Schwalm *et al.* 1977). Marine decapod crustaceans, cephalopods, and fish have ventrally directed, tunable light-organs which let them match their background, when viewed from below, and eliminate their silhouette (Herring 1977), but the floating eggs of the mosquito *Culex pipiens* blend with the shimmery surface because of a reflective film of air that is held across a fine meshwork of walls within a cup, or if fallen on their sides, by an open network of struts (Hinton 1968). Because the seedlings of the arboreal but ground-germinating tropical vine *Monstera gigantea* grow toward potential host trees by tracking the darkest sector of their horizon (Strong and Ray 1975), some tropical trees surely have evolved paler, more reflective bark. Epicuticular blooms and reddish colours may help leaves hide from colour-discriminating, chlorophyll-seeking insect herbivores (Prokopy *et al.* 1983). Because plants compete with neighbours for light and other limited essentials, some plants perhaps deceive rivals about the real origin of the shadow they cast, and through dissected or perforated leaves simulate shadows from unassailable and unbeatable interceptors overhead.

In a tactile, vegetative deception, the antennae and bristles around the trapdoor into the bladder of the carnivorous, aquatic plant *Utricularis vulgaris*, resemble filamentous algae: prey such as chydorid cladocera travel and feed along these structures as they would on algae, and are guided to the bladderwort's door, touch the trigger and get sucked in, literally this time (Meyers and Strickler 1979).

Bark-inhabiting bugs track the colour of their background as it changes from being wetted, by becoming wetted themselves (Silberglied and Aiello 1980). Since tortoise beetles can easily change from light to dark by water manipulation (Mason 1929), if female lady beetles choose mates on the basis of colour in a frequency dependent manner (O'Donald and Muggleton 1979; Majerus *et al.* 1982), why should male beetles not use facultative colour change and beat the odds, until truth catches up with them?

The limpet *Notoacmea paleacea* lives in surfgrass (*Phyllospadix*) in the lower, rocky, intertidal zone of the Pacific coast of North America, with its predator the seastar *Leptasterias hexactis*. Comparatively few of this limpet are captured by the seastar because the mollusc incorporates into its shell a flavenoid it obtains from feeding on the surfgrass. When touched by the seastar the limpet withdraws its soft body-parts and clamps its shell down firmly against the plant, smelling or tasting like surfgrass, in a chemical crypsis (Fishlyn and Phillips 1980). After a thorough analysis of crypticity, Endler (1978) suggests that all visual patterns be regarded as cryptic until proven otherwise.

Flying noctuids that hear ultrasonic calls of distant hunting bats, turn away, perhaps reducing their reflective surface to one per cent and less, and 'hide, acoustically speaking' (Roeder 1967). Flying, glowing females of the New Guinea firefly *Luciola obsoleta* turn off their glows to lose ardent unwanted pursuers, disappearing into the background of darkness (Lloyd 1972). The infant cheetah, resembling the mean ratel (and perhaps the aardwolf, because it looks like a hyaena) may sometimes cause animals with which they would have problems to turn away while still at some distance (Gingerich 1975; Eaton 1976). Territorial males of Anna's hummingbird hide the richness of their territory from intruding males: for a few minutes after they have fed and available nectar is reduced, they mimic the defence of poor-quality territories (Ewald 1979). Arctiid moths emit bat-like sounds that apparently give their attackers a confusing echo (Fullard and Fenton 1979). The scarab *Myrmecaphodius excavaticollis* lives in ant nests, obtains food from workers by tropholaxis and it eats ant larvae and booty. It is a parasite that the ants should throw out, but, through contact with its various hosts, it passively acquires their specific hydrocarbon medleys (Van der Meer and Wojcik 1982). The rove beetle *Trichopsenius frosti* is chemically more sophisticated though seemingly ecologically more limited. It synthesizes its deceiving cuticular hydrocarbons, in apparent and fairly close mimicry of its termite host *Reticulitermes flavipes* (Howard and McDaniel 1982).

At a point between the chemical virtuosity of *Trichopsenius* and the simple act of turning off a light has the definitional border of deception been crossed? Or, is hiding in the dark, inasmuch as misrepresenting circumstances has been the context of selection, a deceptive act? What, then, if the operator tampers with the organs of detection, and manipulates the 'dupes' sensory threshold to make such hiding easier? The firefly *Pteroptyx tener* gathers in broad-leaved trees in the tidal swamps of Malaysia, and perched, flashing males attract females. When a male mounts a female he bends his tail forward and puts his light-organ in her face while continuing to flash (Fig. 6). Perhaps this blinds her dark-adapted eyes to the flashes of neaby rivals that she would otherwise continue to treat as potential mates (Case 1980). Male armyworm moths emit a pheromone that inhibits the responses of rivals to available females (Hirai *et al.* 1978). Entomologists evaporate artificial sex pheromones into crop-field atmospheres and disrupt the sexual communication of pest insects (Bartell 1982), and have invented repellants that adapt ('habituate') or shut off the sensors of mosquitoes (Wright 1975).

These are without the natural finesse of a New Guinea katydid's tactic: calling males of *Hexacentrus munda* sing a two-part song consisting of a long buzz followed by many, short, horn-like quanks. At the beginning of each quank is an individually-distinctive 'signature'. A neighbour will attempt to synchronize a 'tart' (a flatulent sounding chirp) with the beginning of each quank. It has been argued whether rivals should waste potential advertisement time covering up one-another's song (Alexander 1975; Otte 1977), but these contests are probably not symmetrical. Perhaps established males prevent new males from signing in with resident females (Lloyd 1979a, 1981a). A next logical step from *Hexacentrus*' coverup is suggested by competing bumblebees: *Bombus fervidus* males gather at nest holes where gynes (virgin queens) emerge for mating, and stand at favoured stations at the hole's lip or perch on overhanging vegetation fanning their wings. Perhaps they waft chemical signatures down the shaft to monitoring gynes whose subsequent choices of mates can be influenced by individual signatures received. If this is true, and at present it is merely conjecture, then the dive-bombing attacks that males make upon males standing at the prime lip positions could be to smear their own signatures on rivals, that until groomed will cause smearees to pimp for the bombers (Lloyd 1981a). Would this qualify as a deception; or because it has become part of mate rivalry and integrated into a species-usual beau assessment program, is it no longer?

Behaviour is usually a critical element of attention-avoiding tactics. Reef fish that are ambushers freeze, and are cryptically coloured, and stalkers drift very, very, slowly, sneaking past the movement detectors of their adversaries (Hobson 1975). The 'pet' gar in my garden frog-pond lies in vegetation, stick-like, and allows me to pick it up and top-minnows to 'kiss' it, but it also drifts imperceptibly toward minnows and has, like the barracuda, the tubular body of the stalker. But behaviour that would seem to make some tender animal conspicuous, may actually mimic a common, fairly specific, trivial distraction that is 'intentionally' disregarded (gated) by dupe perception mechanisms. Walkingsticks and mantids that oscillate like twigs and leaves caught on strands of spider silk responding to unique airfoil and pendulum dynamics, and nearly-transparent glass-shrimp that seem projected across a pond bottom fully exposed in broad-daylight like the shadow of a ripple at the surface, may be tuned to such predator mental blocks. Zone-tailed hawks look like turkey vultures and may closely approach prey that has habituated, grown a mental block, to the very common vulture (Willis 1963). In the Red Sea, sling-jaw wrasse (*Epibulus*) join schools of the algae-feeding sailfin tang, *Zebrasoma veliferum*, changing colour to match, and accompany them to algae patches where they pounce on the crustacea and small fish that overlooked them. The serranid fish *Diploprion drachi* is a riding predator, and sometimes presses close against a grouper or surgeonfish where it is easily mistaken for a fin, and from this concealment attacks smaller fish and crustaceans (Ormond 1981).

Individuals can improve their chances of being missed by disappearing into their selfish herd (Williams 1964; Hamilton 1971). Because herd animals that reveal idiosyncracies become targets of predators from hyaenas to stickleback fish (Kruuk 1972; Malinski and Lowenstein 1980), injured, weak, or sick individuals must fake health and vigour if at all possible, to remain members of their monotonous crowd. This is why predators make feints at herds and perhaps why females of some species, such as certain katydids, demand such marathon, hard-driving perform-ances from their suitors. A number of phenomena associated with schooling and herding animals, including the collective confusion of a shimmery mêlée and the super-organismic, 'coordinated' form an aggre-gation sometimes takes, may actually provide some benefit to individuals but this is logically viewed as an effect and epiphenomenon. There is an extensive literature on this subject, beginning with Williams (1964), and including synchronously flashing fireflies (Lloyd 1983).

Organisms hide in time as well as space. In WW II when a submarine stalked a tanker the 'lens of the attack scope was never exposed for more than three or four seconds, nor more than inches above the surface. . . .' (O'Kane 1977). If a male of the firefly *Photinus collustrans* reaches a female after another male has mounted and is copulating with her, the pair remains coupled until after the end of the species' flight activity. The copulating male will release his genital hold on the female only after she has re-entered her burrow (the rival sometimes then digs her out; S. Wing, submitted). However, if the late-comer withdraws, then checks the pair periodically but briefly, the copulating male will fly away in about a minute to search for another female. The deceptive male can then mate with the female. Organisms that appear or reproduce at long, or irregular intervals (e.g. certain seeds, periodical cicadas, Janzen 1976; M. Lloyd and Dybas 1966), thus avoiding a build-up of predators, seem in some misleading sense comparable, and are using a 'deception' reminiscent of protean displays in which the fleeing animal incalculably jerks thither and yon (Humphries and Driver 1970) – this is in turn comparable to certain of the bizarre exoskeletons of treehoppers that may fit no part, or mash parts of a predator search image (Robinson 1969; Schall and Pianca 1980).

The cost of being taken in by a deceiver, hence the intensity of selection against being duped, varies in subtle ways. A worker ant that blunders into a sticky, silk strand of a spider's trap 'typically' has but a tiny bit of inclusive fitness to lose, but a real individual loses much more, approaching one. But, if the ant is a dominant worker that sneaks in selfish reproduction by laying male-producing eggs, the cost of a mistake is far more in terms of her inclusive fitness – less in kin fitness and more in individual fitness. It is not surprising then, that dominant workers take fewer risks than their subordinates (Franks and Scovell 1983) – selfish genes 'making the best' of a bad generation. Of course a misjudgement could cost a dupe nothing, and in fact it might even benefit (Otte 1975).

A possible example of a white lie in fireflies is when an unmated *Photinus collustrans* female emits a double flash that a distant male mistakes for a sexual exchange between another male and a female (Fig. 13a). If the female flashed only once, her part of a typical sexual signal exchange, it would be identified as the flash of another searching male and not be attractive. Such a deception would benefit dupe and deceiver (Lloyd 1979b). Is this legitimately called a deception? If the ability to recognize a male-female interaction in progress is presumed to be present in all males, and maintained by strong selection, then there will be no further selection on the genes for that circuitry in the deceptive context described (see Curio 1973). On the other hand, selection would act on females, promoting their double-flash behaviour (deception) at times of low male density. Since the female behaviour stimulates a male programme that has evolved and is maintained in another context, it is technically legitimate to call such female behaviour deceptive. What if strong selection pressure against flying, flashing males, such as from light-seeking, aerial hawkers (Lloyd and Wing 1983), began favouring males that flashed less and sought double-flashes more?

I have stretched the meaning of hiding unabashedly in contrived free-association. Included were nominate categories commonly found in the literature – eucrypsis, special protective resemblance, bizarre forms (Robinson 1969) – and many others which centred on but strayed from a tactic of keeping potential adversaries from detecting or processing information that could be incriminating. Few themes are as rich in examples as hiding, and what is known about it, even in a restricted meaning of the word, would fill an encyclopaedia. Hiding is a first line of defence and offence, but deceptions incorporated into sexual and reproductive activity are at the bottom line, and can result from selection pressures as strong as those in life-costing contexts.

Nowhere is a deception option more clearly illustrated than in mate-seeking behaviour where territorial and sneaky tactics occur in the same species, even the same individual in a conditional strategy. Field crickets (Cade 1979) and green tree frogs (Perrill *et al.* 1978) and many others (Dunbar 1982) remain near calling males and intercept approaching females; bluegill sunfish mimic the appearance of females, enter the nests of territorial males sometimes in the company of a female, and squirt copious sperm (Dominey 1980). Sexual deception takes other forms: nectarless 'female' flowers mimic nectar-rich 'male' flowers and dupe sphinx moths (Bawa 1980); pregnant female langurs display a false estrus when a new male takes over their troop and mate with him to smuggle their unborn Moses past him (Hrdy 1977). Bass croaking frequencies are an advantage in toad rivalry because they mean their emitter is big (Davies and Halliday 1978): Fowler's toads favour sitting in colder water thus lowering their ectothermous voices (Fairchild 1981). Mole crickets sing from tuned burrows (Bennett-Clark 1970) and tree crickets from holes in leaves that then function as sound baffles, which at their first appearance had the deceptive effect of making singers sound louder than their neighbours to choosy females (Fig. 10; Forrest 1982). Male scorpionflies mimic females, seduce other males and receive nuptial gifts that the males had risked their lived to capture, and then give the flies to females to purchase copulation: females evaluate these gifts and reject males whose flies do not measure up (Thornhill 1979) – why shouldn't males add water to prey to increase its heft, and then, later in evolutionary time, an aphrodisiac to help underweight flies pass inspection, or a narcotic to numb the female so a great deal of sperm can be transferred, and then omit flies altogether? (see Borgia 1979). Male greenhouse whiteflies approach ongoing courtships and are sometimes able to slip in between the pair, seize the female's terminalia and insert their own (Las 1980). Male salamanders dupe their rivals into misplacing spermatophores (Arnold 1976).

   This tactic has been carried to an illogical confusion in certain co-habitants of human and bat bedrooms. Bedbugs (Cimicidae) are repro-ductively eccentric. Males inject sperm through the female body wall into the cavity (hemocoel) and there evolutionarily new structures conduct and store sperm (Carayon 1966). Traumatic insemination probably got started because of the competitive advantage it gave to males that were able to put their sperm ahead of that of earlier maters, those that had gone through normal channels (Lloyd 1979a). Males of bat parasites (*Afrocimex*) are transvestites and have external patches on their abdomens that receive the genital jabs of other males, and these ectospermaleges are even more developed than those of females. Competing males probably use their female parts either to steal nutritional ejaculates or sexually to disarm rivals (Lloyd 1979a; Sivinski 1980). During *ménage à trois* competition males can be diddled into losing in both ways. As tactile deceivers the exaggerated details of the male ectospermalege, a technological triumph that has completely altered the truth of 'the deed of kind', provides clues to what it is that heterosexually-oriented males are feeling for when they reach back there. To function this way, the patches must be found easily but not feel conspicuously wrong, and perhaps even super-right before and after penetration. How super can super-normal stimuli be, and still survive without a countermeasure getting off to a running start? Darryl Gwynne observed several jewel beetles, with genitalia extruded, each sitting on top of a stubby, shiny bottle that shone like a female jewel beetle, his little mind unprepared for the distortions at large in the modern world (personal comm.; photo in Thornhill and Alcock 1983, p. 133). It might be argued that it is better to err on the side of emission, because sperm is cheap (not necessarily so, see Dewsbury 1982). A related bug, *Xylocoris*, shows what might happen next as a countermeasure in the arms race of *Afrocimex*: some of the sperm injected into the prime-positioned male finds its deceptive way into his sperm ducts and then into the female (Carayon 1966).

In spider beetles (Ptinidae), the stimuli used to persuade males to expend sperm futilely are enigmas. *Ptinus mobilis* is parthenogenic but females must mate with males of *P. clavipes* before they can lay 'fertile' eggs (Woodroffe 1958). Ptinids have been observed extensively, and mating is seldom seen. 'Against this background the mating response of *clavipes* males to *mobilis* females was remarkably vigorous . . . inspection of a standard culture at any time invariably revealed several pairs in copulo. . . .' To seduce males female *mobilis* stood on their heads, slowly extruded and withdrew their abdomens, and emitted fluid at the tip. Since this behaviour was never observed in *clavipes* females it is more than mere exaggeration, more like a true aphrodisiac. Why have males not evolved resistance to this temptation? Female *mobilis* must be under intense selection pressure to deceive males, far more than that on males to detect or escape it. This is suggested by the fact that a female must mate with a male for her eggs to be triggered to develop. Parthenogenesis without a trigger should be easy to evolve, and the fact that it has not suggests that without the nongenetic contributions of males, female reproduction may not be significantly above nil.

Argiope tells the truth in the stabilimentum that the spider puts in its web to warn birds, reducing the number of repairs and replacements needed (Eisner and Nowicki 1983). Spiders hide behind this truth just as deceptions hide behind 'truths' in the perceptual mechanisms of dupes. I have used the terms mimicry and deception nearly interchangeably, perhaps raising eyebrows because mimicry would seem to be a subset of deception – in mimicry we always can see a model, but in some deceptions none are apparent. However, both depend upon an engram or IRM within the dupe, upon how the dupe sees things. The monarch may be *our* model for the viceroy mimic, but it is the bluejay's engram that is of consequence for the participants (Wickler 1965; Hinton 1977). The extent to which the viceroy and monarch are alike to us, one might say, for sake of argument, is the extent to which we think like jays.

A new deception that exaggerates a parameter such as size in an agonistic confrontation or value in mate choice, eventually becomes the usual – so truth gets bigger and depends upon contemporary standards of the community (Wallace 1973; Borgia 1979). Like taxonomic subspecies of a generation ago, some truths may need a 75 per cent rule. (The subspecies rule is forgot.) If deceptions evolutionarily arise from fortuitous accidents that are then improved upon; and some truths are known to grow out of deceptions, might students of the phylogeny of animal signals profitably 'treat signals generally as having passed through an original mimetic stage'? (Wickler 1965).

These few illustrations of the use of deception in sexual conflict were selected to show a variety of form and tactic, and to restate points made previously. In the next section I will note some ways that deception seems to have played an important part in the evolution of firefly communication, and indicate the importance such knowledge has for understanding some basic problems in firefly systematics.

SIGNALS, DECEPTION AND FIREFLY SYSTEMATICS

Eastern and Western fireflies are as *Yang* and *Yin*. The best-known Asian species are those that aggregate in sparkling and in some cases synchronously-flashing swarms of thousands of individuals. These tree-based choruses have been known to cast with their collective beacon, a mind-numbing spell over those who had but visited them. Such firefly behaviour is unknown in America where females of the genus *Photuris*, of which the Old World has no known counterpart, are aggressive predators that use the males' own sexual signals against them. The females aim aerial attacks at flying males, guided by their luminescence, as well as mimic the signals of their preys' own females. These predators would eat up the swarms in Asia, and it may have been such easy eating in early America that gave *Photuris* the taste for fireflies in the first place (Lloyd 1981c, 1983; Lloyd and Wing 1983).

Photuris females are of special interest with respect to the vigour of the selection they bring to bear and the dimensions of their hunting finesse. Male animals often show extremism in sexually-selected characters, and this is explained on the basis of high male variance in reproductive success (see Thornhill and Alcock 1983). There may be equivalent high variance among *Photuris* females. Each female is probably capable of producing a limited number of eggs on the nutrition she stored as a larva, but successful predations, which continue for two weeks or more, may allow some greatly to increase their egg production. Though not as extreme as the successes of harem bulls, this may be greater than reproduction by even the greatest of the scrambling males in her species, and, with appropriate scaling, in the prey species that 'she' is arms-racing. What then happens to the predictions of a life-dinner asymmetry (Dawkins 1982)? These considerations might suggest that no *Photuris* will be a species specialist, and that prey will commonly lose arms races, escaping eradication only because of the availability of alternative temporarily more abundant prey. However observed capture rates of males are low (Lloyd 1975, 1979b). For example, in a study in which 199 male *Photinus collustrans* were followed for a total of about 11 measured miles, 11 predators and two *collustrans* females answered the males' flashes. No predator made the capture, whereas both *collustrans* were mated: in one study site more than 50 females (of an as yet unnamed species 'C') simultaneously attempted to attract *Photinus macdermotti* males in an area of less than 100 square metres, but because of mutual interference and coy males only one capture was observed in over a week of observation (Fig. 11; Lloyd and Forrest unpub.). Nevertheless, the shock waves that the evolution of light-aimed attack and aggressive mimicry sent throughout the fireflies of the Western domain were powerful, and are still rumbling.

Fig. 11. Aggressive mimic *Photuris* 'C' female attracted this male *P. macdermotti* by mimicking female *macdermotti* response flashes. © *James E. Lloyd*.

Predation by aggressive mimicry and the deceptions used in counter-measure to it, are of interest to the naturalist who tries to understand firefly species and their evolution, and especially to the taxonomist who tries to catalogue them. With the Modern Synthesis and the development of the biological species concept, attention was focused on gene flow, and the means and mechanisms of reproductive isolation. Understanding communication was recognized as essential for modern taxonomic studies on many kinds of organisms, including the fireflies (Barber 1951; Mayr 1963; Lloyd 1966, 1969a, see 1979a). It is of considerable theoretical interest to understand which has a greater impact on the communication and lives of American fireflies, reproductive isolation or 'digestive isolation'? It can be argued that reproductive isolation is easy, and not apt to require much complexity in signals because there is selection, though assuredly asymmetrical, on both species to diverge. In contrast, there is an evolutionary chase that results from the predation of *Photuris*, from both hawking and signal mimicry interactions. It is reasonable to expect that countermeasures in the form of physical avoidance and tricks should have been incorporated into the mating signals of species that confront *Photuris*.

Experimental testing of potential reproductive isolating mechanisms in the patterns of the much simpler *Photinus* fireflies was straightforward and positive, and revealed that male flash duration and rate, and female flash delay were discriminated and could isolate species (Lloyd 1966). But, any inference that these discriminations had evolved in the context of reproductive isolation would surely have been misplaced. For 20 years I looked for character displacement relating to reproductive isolation and found none (see also Otte 1974). I suspect now that the reason is that the dominating pressures on American firefly signals come from predator-prey interactions and not mismatings. The species that would have shown or keyed 'patric' differences are those whose behaviour was too complex and confusing, and taxonomy too muddled, and I had been forced to ignore them. These are the *Photuris* species themselves and the recipe for the biosystematic confusion that they present is this: add to the basic signalling adaptations they have for coping with the environment in general, and the occurrences of sibling species, poor taxonomic characters, and 'meaningless' morphological variation within populations (Barber 1951; McDermott 1967; Lloyd 1969a and in progress); deceptive countermeasures to avoid predation; prey mimicry by males to locate their own hunting females as an alternative mate-seeking tactic (Lloyd 1980); behavioural variation in time and space; and 'quantum' evolutionary origins of new species-specific or 'sub-species'-specific flash patterns from what were formerly prey species mating signals. As a result, the 'species problem' in *Photuris* looks like a bad road on a dark night – and indeed it is, for that is the laboratory – but the problem is of considerable theoretical interest. For instance, it would seem that mating signals could be the *first* character to diverge between subpopulations, and this be the speciation event itself (Lloyd in prog.).

This last section will list the contexts in which deception might be used as a tactic in firefly mating behaviour, and give example illustrations of how deception and countermeasure in a 'consumer avoidance' context seem to have been largely responsible for making American firefly signals and systematics what they are.

The adaptations that adult fireflies have for meeting their environment may be put into seven categories. Deceptive tactics are of no value in two, those that involve the physical environment (ambient light, temperature, wind), and elements of the biological environment that are irrelevant for fireflies, with nothing to be exploited or which have no interests in conflict. The remaining five are interactions in which deception has been found or can be expected: (1) mate competition, (2) mate choice, (3) the manipulation of cooperators, (4) sexual parasites, and (5) consumers (predators and parasites).

If these contexts are ordered according to their relative importance in the historical adaptation-budget of a firefly lineage, I suspect that the orders for an Asian swarming species and an American *Photinus* would contrast as follows: *Pteroptyx*: 1 2 3 4 5; *Photinus*: 5 1 3 2 4. Used as guides for finding deception, these arrangements suggest where to look for the fastest and dirtiest results, and perhaps reveal which contexts will present the more important and complex deceptions, and those that have biosystematic significance. For example, a model for the origin of the species-specific, 2-4 modulation flashes of six (of nine) species of synchronizing *Pteroptyx* (both sides of this diphyletic genus; L. Ballantyne, ms.) is that in originally single-flashing populations, lone males that mimicked pairs or groups of males attracted more comparison-shopper females to land near them.

Consumers and countermeasures

The predation of *Photuris* (Photurinae?) adults apparently is unique for fireflies. Other species, so far as known, feed on plant fluids, if at all. *Photuris* females hawk fireflies in the dark, aiming at their luminescence, and some use this tactic with aggressive signal mimicry in which they attract prey males by mimicking the sexual signals of the males' own females. Hawking may be near the original form of *Photuris* firefly predation, and insectivory itself may have evolved through a 'typical' route from feeding on plant exudates, to 'aphid' exudates, then on to 'aphids' and other insects. This is suggested by a Mexican *Photuris* that captures flies and beetles on grassheads where it also feeds on the sticky seed coating (Fig. 12; Lloyd 1981c). Aimed attacks at the light of fireflies aposomatically twinkling at feeding sites, or at flashing courtship displays in mating congregations would then have given *Photuris* a rich, largely uncontested source of nutrition and defensive compounds (see Eisner 1982). In summer in Florida three unnamed *Photuris* species ('C', 'D', and 'E'), relatives of the larger *Photuris lucicrescens* from farther north, are avid hawkers and, varying among the species: strike out of darkness; emit false signals while approching prey in the air; wait in ambush near prey-species females; emit false mating signals and attack attracted dupes; and move darkly through the vegetation after unlit males that have landed (Wing 1982; Lloyd and Wing 1983; Lloyd 1983; Lloyd and Forrest unpublished). These triple-threat species appear during the midsummer low of *Photuris versicolor*, which is the largest of the aggressive mimics and probably an important

Fig. 12. Mexican *Photuris* female on grass head eating a crane fly. Female also ate leaf beetles like the one shown here. © *James E. Lloyd.*

danger to the others. *P. versicolor* seldom hawks approaching males but will do so on bright moonlight nights. *Photuris* incorporate subtle refinements in their hunting: they begin answering from vegetation-tops and move down stems into the tangle when prey approaches, dim their flashes as prey draws near, and skip answering, perhaps to manipulate males by mimicking a lost signal situation. When a target passes them by, females of *Photuris* 'A' and 'C' fly up ahead, land and try answering again as he flies over. From this it is apparent that *Photuris* is an inconstant fly whose point of attack varies greatly among species, sites, seasons, and geographic locales, and perhaps also facultatively, depending upon the *Photuris* species with which they are 'partitioning' prey at a locality and at the time. How can a male know who a respondent is, what he is up against, and which tricks to use to manipulate one predator against another, or to deceive and beat a rival to a conspecific female?

The following are recommendations for safe mate-searching flight within the time and space of *Photuris*. Do not emit continuous glows, especially bright ones as species-specific mating signals. Such mating signals are rare in American species, and with one exception in the US relate to male signal convergence (see below). Do not leak light from the light organ unless you fly fast, but shut the light completely off when making an approach to an answering light. Some *Pyractomena* species characteristically glow dimly, but they drop to the ground when answered and wait several seconds before flashing again. Members of this genus seem to be ancient prey of *Photuris* for many species are the season's earliest in their area, beating all *Photuris*, and the species are the rarest of American flashing fireflies, though many have very broad distributions. The flicker of *P. angulata* is mimicked by males of several *Photuris* that geographically occur with it in various parts of its range, and flickers and flashes of other *Pyractomena* are matched by sympatric, synchronic *Photuris*. (In fact the signal of a rare, as yet unstudied species of the *Pyractomena dispersa* complex can be predicted to be a 4.2 Hertz (16°C) flicker on the basis of a *Photuris* that occurs in its range and season.) – Do not fly against bright skylight, come out later, fly under a canopy or overhanging boughs, or become tiny or pale and translucent. *Photinus macdermotti* males begin activity later in the evening during the season and in sites of the superlative hawker *Photuris* 'D' (Wing 1982). Some populations of the American *Photinus marginellus* were once distinguished as a separate species (*castus*) because of their pale colour. – Give a quick pattern then hide in the dark, and after receiving an answer prolong your normal inter-pattern interval (see below). Flash then move quickly, sidestep, fly erratically, and unpredictably (*Photinus leucopyge* of Jamaica is so erratic as to make recording of its flashes in flight practically impossible). Fly fast while flashing then turn and look back from the cover of darkness to see an answer. *Photinus collustrans* and *tanytoxus* of Florida, for instance, often glow dimly between their flashes, but fast flight and quick turns perhaps relax pressure on absolute light-organ control. – When approaching an answering light, land in the bush opposite the light and approach through the bush. This technique is used by males of *Photuris* 'D' in most observed populations. – In areas of intense hawking pressure do not fly, but instead flash from a perch and search with your eyes, then fly rapidly to the next signalling station. *Photuris* 'D' near Ocala, Florida behaves this way. – Hide in a seasonally compacted crowd, but this will change your sex life (*Photuris congener*, Florida). – Use a flash pattern with an optical illusion uniquely tuned for the predator's eye and attack problems . . .

Consider the unusual signal of *Photuris* 'D' males. The male flash pattern is a crescendo with a superimposed flicker of about 40 Hertz (Fig. 13b). This is more than four times the rate of other North American *Photuris* flickers, and the relatives of *Photuris* 'D' ('C', 'E', and *lucicrescens*) emit unmodulated crescendoes. This species is active during the season of intense hawker pressure and its females are those used exclusively in a major part of the original study on hawking (Lloyd and Wing 1983). The flickering crescendo of 'D' could lever attacker perception mechanisms in two ways. First, a moving, aerial attacker of moving targets in the dark gets little information except that which is emitted by the prey: attackers could be misled into making spatial misjudgements because of the 'slow'-rising ON-transient. Second, the rapid flicker of the flash, combining with the flicker characteristics inherent in the insect compound eye might distort information required for attack. A deception explanation is also possible for the function of the flicker as an antipredator mechanism: the rapid flicker is approximately the same as the wing-beat frequency of fireflies – perhaps the wing-beat oscillator was coupled into the light organ? The flicker thus mimics the appearance of a steady flash seen through beating wings and thereby may distort information an attacker gets about her angle of attack. If an attacker charges through vibrating wings, it and prey can be knocked apart – luminescing fireflies that brush against wiregrass are sometimes seen to be thrown centimetres. Aerial attackers may approch prey at an angle to avoid their flapping wings, and a flickering flash could delay attack for an instant, as predators try to get a better position, allowing the 0.5 second flash to end and 'D' males to escape into darkness.

This has significance for the bio-systematist because in western peninsular Florida what seems to be this same species has lost part of its flicker (Figs. 13c, d). As noted, in Ocala there is intense hawking pressure and flying is greatly reduced. Hawking may be less frequent 80 miles to the NW, allowing the flicker to erode. Flicker-sampling between and beyond these extreme localities is necessary to resolve the taxonomic problems. As an aside, such geographic change also confuses taxonomic judgement in the classic and distinctive flash-dark-glow '*pennsylvanica*' pattern (Fig. 13e) that has held a special place in *Photuris* behavioural-taxonomy since Barber's (1951) pioneering study. This pattern deteriorates in some populations in northeastern US and may become the 'slow blue' long flash that Barber used to distinguish a new species (*Photuris caerolucens*) west of Lake Michigan (Figs 13f–h).

The several species of the *Photinus consanguineus* group illustrate other ways in which aerial predation could have greatly influenced attributes that are of special taxonomic significance. As noted above, a species that is out

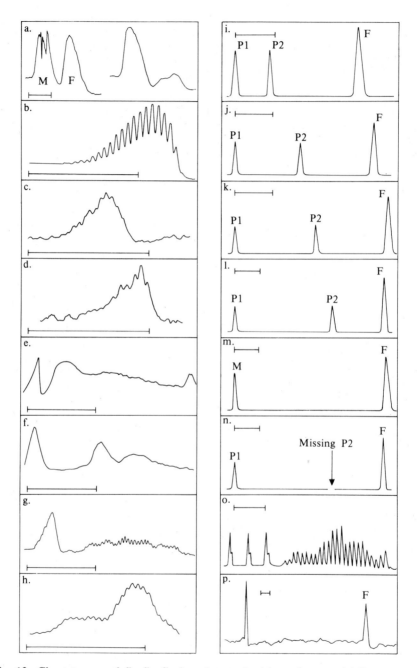

Fig. 13. Chart traces of firefly flashes detected with a photo-multiplier system. Horizontal axis = time, bars are 0.5 sec; vertical axis = relative intensity. Abbreviations: M, male; F, female; P1 and P2, the two flashes of the *Photinus consanguineus*-group flash patterns. (a) *Photinus collustrans*: at left, male flash

(ragged top indicates overload of recorder) and female answer; at right, double flash of an isolated, unmated female. (b) Rapidly-modulated, crescendo flash of male *Photuris* 'D'. (c,d) Poorly modulated crescendo flashes of 'D' males from western peninsular Florida. (e,f,g,h) Classic flash-off-glow pattern of *P. pennsylvanice* and variations and 'degenerations' of it observed in certain populations. Modulations in g and h are caused by wing shuttering. (i–m) Male double-flash patterns and female responses of several species in the *Photinus consanguineus* group. (i) *P. consanguineus*. (j) Barber's *Photinus*. (k) *P. greeni*. (l) *P. macdermotti* (m) *P. ignitus*, showing long female delay. (n) Missing P2 in experimental pattern and resulting long delay of a *P. macdermotti* female, compare with Fig. 13m, see text. (o) Flash pattern of male *Photinus ceratus*, composed of a combination of single flashes and a flicker. (p) Response of aggressive mimic *Photuris* 'A female to a single flash. Compare with Fig. 14a.

of the range of *Photuris* congregates (Cicero 1984), completely unlike other American species, including those in its species group with which it could be morphologically confused. Another species in the group, *P. indictus*, has abandoned nocturnal sexual activity and luminosity, and uses pheromones during daytime. For decades this species was placed in the wrong genus. Five of the species, those of the *macdermotti* complex, may demonstrate another taxonomically important alteration of behaviour as a consequence of aerial predation.

The flash codes of four of the species are: male, 2-flashes – female: 1-second delay, short flash. The timing of the male patterns differs among the species (Figs. 13i–l) and females of each species will answer only appropriately-timed pairs. In the fifth, *P. ignitus*, the male pattern is a single flash and the female waits several seconds before emitting a single flash (Fig. 13m). *Photuris* hawkers could have caused the observed differences in the 2-flash patterns. If a predator began orientation and approach with the first (P1) flash of a pair, a long interval would allow time for it to reach the target airspace and strike at the second flash (P2). The rapid couplet of *P. consanguineus* (0.5 sec) could have been derived from a longer one like that of Barber's photinus.

The code of *P. ignitus* probably evolved from a code similar to that of *P. macdermotti* by the omission of P2 and coupling of the female interval timer with the delay timer. I tested females of *P. macdermotti* to see if they could be made to flash answers to single flashes at a long delay. They were given series of species-typical, 2-flash patterns and then an experimental single flash, a situation that might often occur in nature because of occluding vegetation. The response was unexpectedly strong, in what would appear to have been the recreation of an evolutionary event that took place in *ignitus*' history thousands of years ago (Compare Figs. 13m and 13n; Lloyd 1984). The pressure on pre-*ignitus* males to omit the second flash could have been the same as suggested for *P. consanguineus*, to escape a P2 strike. That this pressure is real is suggested by the signalling of both *P. consanguineus* and its relative *P. greeni* in a Florida habitat where the intensive hawker *Photuris* 'E' occurs. When males are given an artificial female response, they do not signal again for two to five times the inter-pattern interval observed at sites without hawkers. It is also

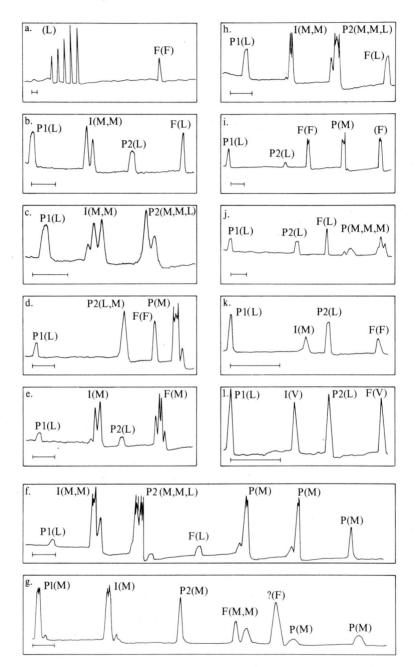

Fig. 14. Chart traces of firefly flashes as in Fig. 13. Abbreviations as in Fig. 13, and in addition: I, injected flash; P, post flash; letters in parentheses indicate whether male (M), female (F), predator (V), or artificial light (L) emitted the flash. (a) Response of 'A' female to train of single flashes is timed from the last flash. (b)

Previous simulations of *macdermotti* flash exchanges (see Fig. 131) caused two caged males to inject flashes into this one. This and other exchanges in which more than one male emits similar or identical responses following the same antecedent conditions, indicate that specific male programmes are stimulated. (c) Two *macdermotti* males inject and then synchronize with P2. (d) A *macdermotti* male synchronizes with P2 and also flashes after the female's response. (e) A *macdermotti* male injects, and also emits transvestite flash. (f) Two *macdermotti* males inject, try to synchronize with P2, and one or the other flashes three times after the female simulation. (g) Maryland *macdermotti* male emits pattern, another injects, others emit transvestite and post flashes, and the female emits her flash at an unusually long delay, perhaps actually answering the 2-flash pattern made up of the (I) and first 'transvestite' flash. This interaction suggests a deceptive evolutionary origin for the (I) tactic – an (I) would make the female flash appear to be a male P2 flash, confusing rivals. Carlson and Copeland (1983) have suggested an evolutionary scheme based on Long Island *macdermotti*. (h) Two males inject and synchronize with P2, again showing the identity of responses. (i) Male emits a post flash and the female flashes again, perhaps a coded countersign (j) Two or three *macdermotti* males simultaneously flare at *P. greeni* intervals after a simulated *macdermotti* male-female interaction. (k,l) Comparison of a *macdermotti* male-female interaction with a rival male injecting (k), with the rival-plus-female mimicry of *Photuris versicolor* (l).

interesting that it is in this same area and season that a '*macdermotti*' with a too-short interval occurs.

There is a second context, not necessarily alternative, that could have brought about the code of *P. ignitus*, and this leads into a discussion of deceptive countermeasures to *Photuris*' aggressive signal mimicry. Such countermeasures may make use of the generically different physiological mechanisms of the flash-control circuitry, play one prey code off against another and confuse the predator, or even mimic another predator. In the *ignitus* example, males might have omitted the P2 flash on close aapproach and after several normal exchanges, as a test. Because a *Photuris* has different mechanisms for achieving a workable mimicry of a *Photinus macdermotti* female, the predator might not answer at all, or confuse the single flash with that of another prey species and answer inappropriately. Experiments on hunting *versicolor* reveal that both 'retrodictions' are reasonable – when given single flashes after preliminary 2-flash patterns, they do not answer or they answer improperly.

In Florida *Photuris versicolor* hunts three members of the *P. macdermotti* complex, and has a single neural circuit to handle these three species. It properly mimics females of three species but taxonomically lumps them. Unlike the *Photinus* females, which only answer the narrow P1P2 interval-range of their own species, *versicolor* females answer any pair of flashes within a range between about 0.4 and 2.5 seconds (21°C). Thus a testing male of any of the prey species could find a female and begin his approach using the interval characteristic of his own species, then emit nonsense pairs or those timed like one of the other species. His own female would reject them but the predator would respond. It can be seen then, that the species-specific P1P2 intervals that 'function' in reproductive isolation could have evolved and first served in the context of 'digestive isolation'.

Note again that in different parts of the range of a prey species, with different predator species, IRMs, tactics and signals may change: the reason that I have not formally named Barber's photinus is that until populations are sampled at several points between southeastern US and the central Atlantic states, I cannot decide whether (1) it is but a clinal form of *P. consanguineus* or (2) it is specifically distinct from *consanguineus*, speciation having already occurred.

Other deceptions to trip up signal mimics, which would have significance to a systematist trying to understand phylogenies, probably include (1) patterns that combine elements from the patterns of other species and cause predators to misidentify and incorrectly answer their targets, and (2) those that confuse the timing circuits of the predators. For examples: (1) some Jamaican *Photinus* males have flash patterns composed of two parts, several discrete flashes followed by a flicker (Fig. 13o). This may cause *Photuris jamaicensis* females to answer inappropriately because the preliminary flashes resemble those of another prey species. (2) The delay of the female answer to a male is important to the species-specific codes of a number of *Photinus*. This puts the burden of species recognition on the shoulders of the male, an unusual situation for animals in which the female makes the greater energetic investment in progeny, and it also requires that male and female agree upon the 'mark' point to key their timers. If they use the OFF transient of a male flash, but a predator always uses the ON because all of its other important prey do, then the male can cause the predator to vary its delay by varying his flash length, while its own females have a constant one, with respect to the OFF. Or, if the code is to mark at the fourth flash of a three to nine flash pattern, but the predator always times from the last flash, as the females of *Photuris* 'A' do (compare Figs. 13p and 14a) the predator can be tricked. Some species that use a long female-delay coding device may have been able gradually to sneak away from their predators in evolutionary time because of the nutritional inertia that other and short-delay prey provided.

There is another way that a prey might sneak away from a signal-tracking predator. There are limits to quantitative changes that can be detected by perceptual systems. A small change against a low baseline will be detected but a change of identical magnitude against a high baseline will not. Cohen (in press) has pointed out that this could have important consequences in mate choice, and limit runaway selection. So also for perceptual mechanisms and deception: a signal might be modified significantly in the prey species with a change that was imperceptible to the predator, at least for some evolutionary time.

Relaxation of *Photuris* predation was probably the key factor in the evolution of an aggregative mating system in *Photinus knulli* in New Mexico, and paradoxically, it is the aggressive mimicry of *Photuris versicolor* that has led to a situation like it in *Photinus macdermotti*. When male *macdermotti* approach an answering light they usually land several centimetres away and approach slowly. Because of the slow approach other searching males arrive and receive answers, and sometimes several will gather in a shrub or thatch of grass near a responding light. Exactly what goes on in these groups is not known, and it will take simultaneous photo-cell recording, and visual monitoring and video-recording through an image intensifier to understand it. (Clearly demonstrated during filming of this behaviour by John Paling, for TV presentation.) But, the following can be said: males mimic female flashes and inject flashes into the patterns of other males, certain of which inhibit female responses; males synchronize flashes with P2s of other males, and flash after female response flashes; and when 'pushed' in experimental situations they use these responses in combination. For example, if a male is shown artificial male patterns and female responses, he will then inject a flash into the male pattern (Fig. 14b). If immediately presented with another pattern he will often flash after the imitation female flash (post flash; Fig. 14d). Occasional females flash after a post flash (Fig. 14i). If artificial flash patterns continue to be shown to the male, perhaps foreign to natural encounters, he combines responses, putting an injection with a P2 synchrony (Figs. 14c, f, h), or a 'transvestite' flash with an injection (Fig. 14e). During such treatment males also emit bright flares, pairs of flashes timed like those of related species, and modulated flashes that closely resemble flashes that *P. versicolor* predators emit when hunting (e.g. Fig. 14j). One interesting match-up between the flashes of rivals and predators is that hunting females of *P. versicolor* and others not only mimic the female response flashes of *macdermotti*, but also the injected flashes of competing males (Fig. 14k, l). This seems to be a mimicry of a mimicry (Lloyd 1981b).

When a Florida *macdermotti* male lands in the vicinity of a responding female or a group of competing males, and these are the only ways a male is able to obtain a mate, the circumstances he faces are difficult. His respondent may be a potential mate or one or more hunting females of up to four different species. After he lands other males will attempt to deceive him with transvestite or predator-mimicking flashes, and the flash groups he sees may be but fragments of complete patterns because of poor visibility, or manipulative fragments mimicking poor visibility. Different predator species use different tactics. For example, though *versicolor* females remain perched and seldom approach their prey, females of *Photuris* 'C' apparently scurry around in the vegetation after a male has landed, trying to find him by touch. In habitats with this hunter *P. macdermotti* does not form congregations and emit the variety of flashes (e.g. injections, post flashes) observed in *macdermotti* in *versicolor*'s time and place. The point is, with different pressures on males, and presuming there is some limitation on how much an individual male can be programmed to carry out, can sustained pressure from different *Photuris* cause rapid divergence of local populations of *macdermotti* and wholesale incipient species? Would females through mate choice reinforce such divergence? It is interesting to note that *versicolor* in northeastern US differs from Florida *versicolor* in a number of ways, and the 'form' of *macdermotti* there is very different from Florida *macdermotti*. Not only is the flash pattern it uses for searching different (Lloyd 1969b), but so is the behaviour of congregating males around an answering female. For example, when a Maryland male in a group emits a flash pattern, rivals immediately emit post flashes, injections, and transvestite flashes (Fig. 14g). Further north on Long Island, NY, injections are apparently seldom used (Carlson & Copeland 1983). This suggests that the techniques of *versicolor* and other resident *Photuris* are different from those encountered by Florida *macdermotti*. The study of predator and prey behaviour in this system can not only provide clues to the fine-tuning of prey and predator adversarial systems, and do this along geographic transects, but also, because northeastern *macdermotti* is a strikingly-different variation on a 2-flash theme, on evolution products and processes within the *Photinus* species complex.

The *pièce de résistance* of deceptions influencing firefly systematics, from identification to phylogenetics, is the mimicry by *Photuris* males of the signals of the males of sympatric, synchronic species. There can be little question that this is primarily a mate-seeking tactic because it occurs during the species' mate-seeking prime-time, when reproductive competition is keen. Males emit mimicked *Photinus* (or other prey species) signals as they fly and search through their habitat, and there is nothing to indicate by their actions that these signals are not 'their own'. Males of some species conspicuously switch back and forth between their own and mimicked patterns, but to reveal changes in other species it is necessary to mark them (paint dots) and compare patterns and marks of recaptures (Lloyd 1983). Males of several species switch from mimicry patterns to 'their own' as they hover and land near responding flashes, the apparent moment of truth being when a male attempts to seduce and change the female's mind. It is especially noteworthy that though males of Florida *versicolor* mimic only one other species – a not-so-common *Pyractomena* – roving *versicolor* males fly down from their tree-top paths and repeatedly emit their own species-diagnostic pattern as they hover within inches of *macdermotti*-timed flash exchanges. Just as some hawkers remain near *macdermotti* females to attack males they attract, male *versicolor* approach conspicuous flash interactions that may involve one of their hunting females in mute counterpart to the prey-mimicking tactic of other *Photuris*. It should be noted that in the northeast males of *P. versicolor* emit a variety of patterns that have not been matched with habitat associates (see below).

The special problems that male mimicry has caused for the systematist that uses flashing behaviour taxonomically are most easily appreciated by brooding on three not impossible worst cases: (1) Local populations of a species may behave differently because of interspersed populations of different prey species, and appear to be sibling species. This may be the reason for the interdeme variations that troubled Barber (1951) when he confronted the problem of how formally to treat *Photuris lucicrescens*. (2) Two sibling *Photuris* species may mimic the same prey species, thus a series of behaviour voucher specimens collected while behaving identically at the same time and place, and presumably the ultimate in taxonomic material, could appear by all hard-won, and current methodologically sound evidence and criteria, to be a single species. (3) Finally, as the worst of conceivable taxonomic nightmares, consider a bucolic meadow of two

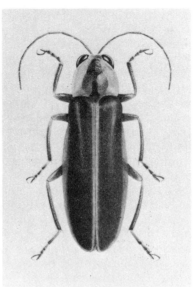

Fig. 15. *Photuris versicolor*, male. © *James E. Lloyd.*

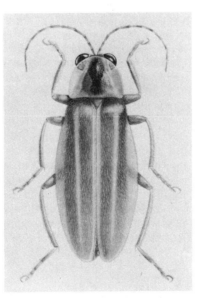

Fig. 16. *Photuris* 'C' male. © *James E. Lloyd.*

Photuris species with polyphenism combined with polymorphism and sexual parasitism by a parthenogenic sibling species, with the usual seasonal, geographic, and ecological variations, with the species preying upon each other by aggressive mimicry, and with mate cannibalism, and an overlay of female mate-choice. However, it should not be concluded that all *Photuris* or that *Photuris* in general present such problems. Apparently most are morphologically and behaviourally distinct (Figs. 15, 16; Lloyd 1983). The worst cases are focused on because they seemingly have more to offer. Considerations of the problems of reproductive isolation and its mechanisms seem to have taken a very back seat, but that is because only now are we working our way back to try to put them properly into the overall scheme of things.

After recognizing the occurrence of male mimicry, and the probable role that it plays in reproductive behaviour, there yet remains a question about the generality of the model. Males of some species use 'supernumerary' flash patterns that apparently do not match the patterns of their habitat associates. Is male mimicry a subset of a more general behaviour pattern? I do not believe so. Possibly *Photuris* females hunt 'creatively' and invent *ad hoc* answers and experiment, and so any number of male patterns will work, or the deviant patterns fit into poorly-tuned IRMs. This question sharply focuses attention on *Photuris* species that contrast in this respect. *Photuris cinctipennis* males match their patterns to those of other species with some precision: in Tennessee *Photuris* TN males emit flash pairs that are different from the sympatric, synchronic *Photinus*. From experiments on *versicolor* in Florida can it be concluded that TN's pair of flashes is good enough, and a mimicry, though it does not look like one to us because we expect too much? Supporting this is the observation that the timing of TN's pair is more variable than that observed in two-flash *Photinus*.

When I completed an extensive behavioural-systematic study of *Photinus* in 1966, and reflected upon how their signals had become the way they are I concluded: 'In this discussion the origin and evolution of the signals of *Photinus* groups have been considered on a single time transect. We can only guess at the firefly species that must have interacted through the ages, at the multiplicity of environments that may have helped to shape their behaviour, and at complexities and constraints of the neurological mechanisms that directed that behaviour. The simple signals we read today are products of an infinitely complicated and kaleidoscopic history.' I never should have guessed that the coloured glass and mirrors in the kaleidoscope were prismatic and elastic!

Acknowledgements

A 'review' of even a corner of mimicry/deception is practically impossible. One cannot even cite the essential literature and give significant contributors their due, to say nothing of reading, comprehending and synthesizing the facts and ideas that are the body of the subject. What an opportunity for all sorts of academic illusion and deception! I apologize to those whom

I have knowingly slighted, such as Lincoln Brower, Jack Hailman, James Huheey and Wolfgang Wickler, and to those I have so treated unknowingly. I thank them and others, such as John Alcock, Dick Alexander, Richard Dawkins, Bill Hamilton, Dan Otte, Randy Thornhill, Tom Walker, and George Williams from whom I have learned so much on the subject. I wish I had an encyclopaedia on deception with these contributors, many others whose work I have cited, and many who here remain anonymous though they are here in intellectual spirit.

I thank Richard Dawkins for inviting me to contribute this paper, Ngo Dong for technical assistance during its preparation, Laura Reep for making the illustrations, and Barbara Hollien for her patience in typing the score and more drafts. Florida Agric. Exp. Sta. J. Series No. 5307.

References

Alexander, R. D. (1975). Natural selection and specialized chorusing behavior in acoustical insects. *Insects, Science and Society*, D. Pimentel, ed. New York: Academic Press. pp. 35–77.

—— (1979). *Darwanism and Human Affairs*. Seattle and London: University of Washington Press. 317 pp.

—— (1980). The study of animal communication: a new era. (Paper given at Animal Behaviour Society; revised in 1981).

Andersson, M. (1980)   Why are there so many threat displays? *Journal of Theoretical Biology* **86**: 773–781.

Arnold, S. J. (1976). Sexual behaviour, sexual interference and sexual defense in the salamanders *Ambystoma maculatum, Ambystoma tigrinum* and *Pletbodon jordani. Zeitschrift fuer Psychologie* **42**: 247–300.

Barber, H. S. (1951). North American fireflies of the genus *Photuris. Smithsonian Miscellaneous Collections* **117(1)**: 1–58.

Bartell, R. J. (1982). Mechanisms of communication disruption by pheromone in the control of Lepidoptera: a review. *Physiological Entomology* **7**: 353–364.

Bates, W. H. (1862). Contributions to an insect fauna of the Amazon Valley Lepidoptera: Heliconidae. *Transactions of the Linnean Society, Zoology* **23**: 495–566.

Bawa, K. S. (1980). Mimicry of male by female flowers and intrasexual competition for pollinators in *Jacaratia dolichaula* (D. Smith) Woodson (Caricaceae). *Evolution* **34(3)**: 467–474.

Beebe, W. (1925). *Jungle Days*. New York: G. P. Putnam's sons. 201 pp.

Bennet-Clark, H. C. (1970). The mechanism and efficiency of sound production in mole crickets. *Journal of Experimental Biology* **52**: 619–652.

Borgia, G. (1979). Sexual selection and the evolution of mating systems. *Sexual selection and Reproductive Competition in Insects*, M. S. Blum and N. A. Blum, eds. New York: Academic Press. pp. 19–121.

Brower, L. P. (1969). Ecological chemistry. *Scientific American* **220(2)**: 22–29.

Cade, W. (1979). The evolution of alternative male reproductive strategies in field crickets. *Sexual Selection and Reproductive Competition in Insects*, M. S. Blum and N. A. Blum, eds. New York: Academic Press, pp. 343–379.

Carayon, J. (1966). Traumatic insemination and the paragenital system. *Monograph of Cimicidae*, Vol 7. College Park, Maryland: Thomas Say Foundation Entomological Society of America. pp. 81–166.

Carlson, A. D. and Copeland, J. (1983). Male-male interactions and female response in the firefly *Photinus macdermotti* (abstract). *American Zoologist*, **23**: 929.

Case, J. F. (1980). Courting behaviour in a synchronously flashing, aggregative firefly, *Pteroptyx tener*. *Biological Bulletin* **159**: 613–625.

Cicero, M. (1984). Lek assembly and flash synchrony in *Photinus knulli* Green. *Coleopterists' Bulletin* (in press).

Cohen, J. A. (1984). Sexual selection and the psychophysics of female choice. *Zeitchrift fuer Tierpsychologie*, **64**: 1–8.

Cott, H. B. (1940). *Adaptive Coloration in Animals*. London: Methuen and Co. Ltd. Strand. 508 pp.

Crane, J. (1952). A comparative study of innate defensive behaviour in Trinidad mantids (Orthoptera, Mantoidea). *Zoologica* **37**: 222–293.

Cruickshank, C. (1979). *Deception in World War II*. Oxford: Oxford University Press. 248 pp.

Curio, E. (1973). Towards a methodology of teleonomy. *Experentia* **29**: 1045–1180.

Davies, N. B., and Halliday, T. R. (1978). Deep croaks and fighting assessment in toads *Bufo bufo*. *Nature* **274**: 683–685.

Dawkins, R. (1976). *The Selfish Gene*, New York and Oxford: Oxford University Press. 224 pp.

—— (1982). *The Extended Phenotype. The Gene as the Unit of Selection*. Oxford and San Francisco: W. H. Freeman and Co. 307 pp.

Dawkins, R., and Krebs, J. R. (1978). Animal signals: information or manipulation? *Behavioural Ecology an Evolutionary Approach*. Sunderland, Massachusetts: Sinauer Associates, Inc. Publ. Chapter 10, pp. 282–309.

Dennett, D. (1983). Intentional systems *Behavioural and Brain Sciences*, 6, 343–390.

Dewsbury, D. A. (1982). Ejaculate cost and male choice. *The American Naturalist* **119(5)**: 601–610.

Dominey, W. J. (1980). Female mimicry in male bluegill sunfish – a genetic polymorphism? *Nature* **284**: 546–548.

Dunbar, R. (1982). Intraspecific variations in mating strategy. *Perspectives in Ethology*, P. Bateson and P. Klopfer, eds. New York: Plenum Press, 385 pp.

Eaton, R. L. (1976). A possible case of mimicry in larger mammals. *Evolution* **30**: 853–856.

Edmunds, M. (1978). On the association between *Myrmarachne* sp. (Salticidae) and ants. *Bulletin of the British Arachnological Society* **4**: 149–160.

Edmund, M. (1978). On the association between *Myrmarachne* sp. (Salticidae) and ants. *Bulletin of the British Arachnological Society* **4**: 149–160.

Eisner, T. (1982). For love of nature: exploration and discovery at biological field stations. *Bioscience* **32(5)**: 321–326.

Eisner, T., Hicks, K., Eisner, M., and Robson, D. S. (1978). 'Wolf-in-sheep's clothing' strategy of a predaceous insect larva. *Science* **199**: 790–794.

Eisner, T., and Nowicki, S. (1983). Spider web protection through visual advertisement: role of the stabilimentum. *Science* **219**: 185–187.

Endler, J. A. (1978). A predator's view of animal color patterns. *Evolutionary Biology* **11**: 319–364.

Evans, H. E. (1966). The accessory burrows of digger wasps. *Science* **152**: 465–471.

Ewald, P. W. (1979). The hummingbird and the calorie. *Natural History* **88**: 93–98.

Fairchild, L. (1981). Mate selection and behavioural thermoregulation in Fowler's toads. *Science* **212**: 950–951.

Fishlyn, D. A., and Phillips, D. W. (1980). Chemical camouflaging and behavioural defenses against a predatory seastar by three species of gastropods from the surfgrass *Phyllospadix* community. *Biological Bulletin* **158**: 34–48.

Forrest, T. G. (1982). Acoustic communication and baffling behaviours of crickets. *Florida Entomologist* **65**: 33–44.

—— (1983). Calling songs and mate choice in mole crickets. *Orthopteran Mating Systems: Sexual Competition in a Diverse Group of Insects*, D. T. Gwynne and G. K. Morris, eds. Boulder, Colorado: Westview Press. pp. 185–204.

Franks, N. R., and Scovell, E. (1983). Dominance and reproductive success among slave-making worker ants. *Nature* **304**: 724–725.

Fullard, J. H., and Fenton, M. B. (1979). Jamming bat echolocation: the clicks of arctiid moths. *Canadian Journal of Zoology* **57**: 647–649.

Gingerich, P. D. (1975). Is the aardwolf a mimic of the hyaena? *Nature* **253**: 191–192.

Goodwin, N. (1982). *Animal Imposters*. (NOVA PBS TV film) Cambridge, Massachusetts: Peach River Films.

Gregory, R. L., and Gombrich, E. H. (1973). *Illusion in Nature and Art*. New York: Charles Scribner's Sons. 288 pp.

Gressitt, J. L. (1969). Epizoic symbiosis. *Entomological News* **80(1)**: 1–5.

Haldane, R. A. (1976). *The Hidden World*. New York: St. Martin's Press. 207 pp.

Hamilton, W. D. (1971). Geometry for the selfish herd. *Journal of Theoretical Biology* **31**: 295–311.

Herring, P. J. (1977). Bioluminescence of marine organisms. *Nature* **267**: 788–793.

Hinton, H. E. (1968). Structure and protective devices of the egg of the mosquito *Culex pipiens*. *Journal of Insect Physiology* **14**: 145–161.

—— (1973). Natural deception. *Illusion in Nature and Art*, R. L. Gregory and E. H. Gombrich, eds. New York: Charles Scribner's Sons. pp. 96–159.

—— (1977). Mimicry provides information about the perceptual capacities of predators. *Folia Entomologica Mexicana* **37**: 19–29.

Hirai, K., Shorey, H. H., and Gaston, L. K. (1978). Competition among courting male moths: male-to-male inhibitory pheromone. *Science* **202**: 644–645.

Hobson, E. S. (1975). Feeding patterns among tropical reef fishes. *American Scientist* **63**: 382–392.

Howard, R. W., and McDaniel, C. A. (1980). Chemical mimicry as an integrating mechanism: cuticular hydrocarbons of a termitophile and its host. *Science* **210**: 431–432.

Hrdy, S. B. (1977). *The Langurs of Abu*. Cambridge, Massachusetts: Harvard University Press. 361 pp.

Huheey, J. E. (1976). Studies in warning coloration and mimicry. VII. Evolutionary consequences of a Batesian-Mullerian spectrum: a model for Mullerian mimicry. *Evolution* **30(1)**: 86–93.

Humphries, D. A., and Drivers, P. M. (1970). Protean defence by prey animals. *Oecologia* **5**: 285–302.

Hutchins, R. M., (ed.-in-chief). (1952). Truth. *The Great Ideas*, Vol. 2. *Great Books of the Western World*. Chicago, Illinois: Encyclopedia Britanica, Inc. Chapter 94, pp. 915–938.

Huxley, J. (1957). *New Bottles for New Wine. Essays*. London: Chatto and Windus. 318 pp.

Jackman, R., Nowicki, S., Aneshansley, D. J., and Eisner, T. (1983). Predatory capture of toads by fly larvae. *Science* **222**: 515–516.

Janzen, D. H. (1976). Why bamboos wait so long to flower. *Annual Review of Ecology and Systematics* **7**: 347–391.

Kirby, W., and Spence, W. (1846). *An Introduction to Entomology* 6th edition. Philadelphia, Pennsylvania: Lea and Blanchard. 600 pp.

Kruuk, H. (1972). *The Spotted Hyaena; A Study of Predation and Social Behavior*. Chicago, Illinois: University of Chicago Press. 335 pp.

Las, A. (1980). Male courtship persistence in the greenhouse whitefly, *Trialeurodes vaporariorum* Westwood (Homoptera: Aleyrodidae). *Behaviour* **72(1–2)**: 107–126.

Lea, I. (1834). Observations on the Naiades and descriptions of new species of that and other families. *Transactions of the American Philosophy Society New Series* **4**: 63–121.

Lloyd, J. E. (1966). Studies on the flash communication system in *Photinus* fireflies. *Miscellaneous Publications* No. 130. Ann Arbor, Michigan: Museum of Zoology, University of Michigan. pp. 1–95.

—— (1969a). Flashes of *Photuris* fireflies: their value and use in recognizing species. *Florida Entomologist* **52(1)**: 29–35.

—— (1969b). Flashes, behaviour, and additional species of nearctic *Photinus* fireflies (Coleoptera: Lampyridae). *Coleopterists' Bulletin* **23**: 29–40.

—— (1972). Mating behaviour of a New Guinea firefly: a new communicative protocol. *Coleopterists' Bulletin* **26(4)**: 155–163.

—— (1973). Firefly parasites and predators. *Coleopterists' Bulletin* **27(2)**: 91–106.

—— (1975). Aggressive mimicry in *Photuris* fireflies: signal repertoires in femmes fatales. *Science* **187(4175)**: 452–453.

—— (1979a). Mating behaviour and natural selection. *Florida Entomologist* **62(1)**: 17–34.

—— (1979b). Sexual selection in luminescent beetles. *Sexual Selection and Reproductive Competition in insects*, M. S. Blum and N. A. Blum, eds. New York: Academic Press, 463 pp.

—— (1980). Male *Photuris* fireflies mimic sexual signals of their females' prey. *Science* **210(4470)**: 669–671.

—— (1981a). Sexual selection: individuality, identification and recognition in a bumble bee and other insects. *Florida Entomologist* **64(1)**: 89–117.

—— (1981b). Firefly mate rivals mimic their predators and vice versa. *Nature* **290**: 498–500.

—— (1981c). Aggressive mimicry in fireflies. *Anima* **105**: 16–21. (in Japanese)

—— (1983). Bioluminescence and communication in insects. *Annual Review of Entomology* **28**: 131–160.

—— (1984). Evolution of the firefly flash code. *Florida Entomologist* **67(2)**: 228–239.

Lloyd, J. E., and Wing, S. R., (1983). Nocturnal aerial predation of fireflies by light-seeking fireflies. *Science* **222**: 634–635.

Lloyd, M., and Dybas, H. S. (1966). The periodical cicada problem. I. Population ecology. *Evolution* **20(2)**: 133–149.

Majerus, M., O'Donald, P., and Weir, J. (1982). Evidence for preferential mating in *Adalia bipunctata*. *Heredity* **49(1)**: 37–49.

Mason, C. W. (1929). Transient color changes in the tortoise beetles (Coleoptera: Chrysomelidae). *Entomological News* **40**: 52–56.

Mayr, E. (1963). *Animal Species and Evolution*. Cambridge, Massachusetts: The Belknap Press of Harvard University Press. 797 pp.

—— (1982). *The Growth of Biological Thought*. Cambridge, Massachusetts: Harvard University Press. 974 pp.

McDermott, F. A. (1962). 'Mimetism' in Lampyridae. *Coleopterists' Bulletin*. **15(4)**: 116.

—— (1967). The North American fireflies of the genus *Photuris Dejean*. A modification of Barber's key (Coleoptera: Lampyridae). *Coleopterists' Bulletin* **21**:106–116.

Meinwald, J., Wiemer, D. F., Eisner, T. (1979). Lucibufagins 2. esters of 12-oxo-2β, 5β, 11α – trihydroxy bufalin, the major defensive steroids of the firefly *Photinus pyralis* (Coleoptera: Lampyridae). *Journal of the American Chemical Society* **101**: 3055–3060.

Meyers, D. G., and Strickler, J. R. (1979). Capture enhancement in a carnivorous aquatic plant: function of antennae and bristles in *Utricularia vulgaris*. *Science* **203**: 1022–1025.

Milinsky, M., and Lowenstein, C. (1980). On predator selection against abnormalities of movement, a test of an hypothesis. *Zeitchrift für Tierpsychologie* **53**: 325–340.

Moynihan, M. (1968). Social mimicry, character convergence versus character displacement. *Evolution* **22**: 315–331.

O'Donald, P., Muggleton, J. (1979). Melanic polymorphism in ladybirds maintained by sexual selection. *Heredity* **43(1)**: 143–148.

O'Kane, R. H. (1977). *Clear the Bridge! The War Patrols of the U.S.S. Tang.* Chicago, Illinois: Rand McNally and Co. 480 pp.

Ormond, R. (1981). Deceptions on the coral reef. *New Scientist* **89(1245)**: 730–733.

Otte, D. (1974). Effects and functions in the evolution of signalling systems. *Annual Review of Ecology and Systematics* **5**: 385–417.

—— (1975). Letters to the editors on the role of intraspecific deception. *The American Naturalist* **109**: 239–242.

—— (1977). Communication in Orthoptera. *How Animals Communicate*, T. A. Sebeok, ed. Bloomington, Indiana: Indiana University Press, pp. 334–402.

—— (1981). *The North American Grasshopper. Vol. 1: Acrididae: Gomphocerinae and Acrininae*. Cambridge, Massachusetts: Harvard University Press. 275 pp.

Pasteur, G. (1982). A classificatory review of mimicry systems. *Annual Review of Ecology and Systematics* **13**: 169–200.

Perrill, S. A., Gerhardt, H. C., and Daniel, R. (1978). Sexual parasitism in the green tree frog (*Hyla cinerea*). *Science* **200**: 1179–1180.

Propopky, R. J., Collier, R. H., and Finch, S. (1983). Leaf color used by cabbage root flies to distinguish among hosts. *Science* **221**: 190–192.

Reit, S. (1978). *Masquerade: The Amazing Camouflage Deceptions of World War II*. New York: Hawthorn Books, Inc. pp. 255.

Remington, C. L. (1963). Historical background of mimicry. *16th International Congress of Zoology Proceedings* **4**: 145–149.

Rettenmeyer, C. W. (1970). Insect mimicry. *Annual Review of Entomology* **15**: 43–74.

Robinson, M. H. (1969). Defenses against visually hunting predators. *Evolutionary Biology* **3**: 225–259.

Roeder, K. D. (1967). *Nerve Cells and Insect Behavior*. Cambridge, Massachusetts: Harvard University Press. 238 pp.

Roth, L. M. (1973). Brazilian cockroaches found in birds' nests, with descriptions of new genera and species. *Proceedings of the Entomological Society of Washington* **75**, 1–27.

Rothschild, M. (1967). Mimicry: the deceptive way of life. *Natural History* **76**: 44–51.

Sargent, T. D. (1968). Cryptic moths: Effects on background selections of painting the circumocular scales. *Science* **159**: 100–101.

Schwalm, P. A., Starret, P. H., and McDiarmid, R. W. (1977). Infrared reflectance in leaf-sitting neotropical frogs. *Science* **196**: 1225–1227.

Schall, J. J., and Pianka, E. R. (1980). Evolution of escape behaviour diversity. *The American Naturalist* **115(4)**: 551–566.

Schmitt, W. (1965). *Crustaceans*. Ann Arbor, Michigan: University of Michigan Press, 204 pp.

Sebeok, T. A. (1968). *Animal Communication. Techniques of Study and Results of Research*. Bloomington, Indiana: Indiana University Press. 686 pp.

—— (1977). *How Animals Communicate*. Bloomington, Indiana: Indiana University Press, 1128 pp.

Silberglied, R., and Aiello, A. (1980). Camouflage by integumentary wetting in bark bugs. *Science* **207**: 773–775.

Sivinski, J. (1980). Sexual selection and insect sperm. *Florida Entomologist* **63**: 99–111.

Strong, D. R., Jr., and Ray, T. S. (1975). Host tree location behaviour of a tropical vine. *Science* **190**: 804–805.

Sutton, R. D. (1983). Seasonal colour changes, sexual maturation and oviposition in *Psylla peregrina* (Homoptera: Psylloidea). *Ecological Entomology* **8**: 195–201.

Thornhill, R. (1979). Male and female sexual selection and the evolution of mating strategies in insects. *Sexual Selection and Reproductive Competition*, M. S. Blum and N. A. Blum, eds. New York: Academic Press. pp. 81–121.

Thornhill, R., and Alcock, J. (1983). *The Evolution of Insect Mating Systems* Cambridge, Massachusetts: Harvard University Press. 547 pp.

Turner, J. R. G. (1977). Butterfly mimicry: the genetical evolution of an adaptation. *Evolutionary Biology* **10**: 163–206.

Vander Meer, R. H., and Wojcik, D. P. (1982). Chemical mimicry in the myrmecophilous beetle *Myreme caphodius excavaticollis*. *Science* **218**: 806–808.

Vane-Wright, R. I. (1976). A unified classification of mimetic resemblances. *Biological Journal of the Linnean Society* **8(1)**: 25–56.

Wallace, B. (1973). Misinformation, fitness, and selection. *The American Naturalist* **107(953)**: 1–7.

Weldon, P. J., and Burghardt, G. M. Deception divergence and sexual selection. *Zietchrift für Tierpsychologie*. (in press).

Whitesell, J. J. (1974). *Geographic Variation and Dimorphisms in Song, Development and Color in a Katydid: Field and Laboratory Studies (Tettigoniidae: Orthoptera)*. M.S. Thesis, University of Florida, Gainesville, 74 pp.

Wickler, W. (1965). Mimicry and the evolution of animal communication. *Nature* **5010**: 519–521.

—— (1968). *Mimicry in Plants and Animals*. London: World University Library. 154 pp.

Wiens, D. (1978). Mimicry in plants. *Evolutionary Biology* **11**: 365–403.

Williams, G. C. (1964). Measurement of consociation among fishes and comments on the evolution of schooling. *Publications of the Museum, Michigan State University Biological Series* **2(7)**: 349–384.

Willis, E. O. (1963). Is the zone-tailed hawk a mimic of the turkey vulture? *The Condor* **65**: 313–317.

Wing, S. (1982). *The reproductive Ecologies of Three Species of Fireflies* M.S. Thesis. University of Florida, Gainesville, 68 pp.

Wing, S. (1984). Female monogamy and male competition in *Photinus collustrans* (Coleoptera: Lampyridae). *Psyche* (submitted)

Woodroffe, G. E. (1958). The mode of reproduction of *Ptinus clavipes panzer* from mobilis Moore (= P. latro auct.) (Coleoptera: Ptinidae). *Proceedings of the Royal Entomological Society of London (A)* **33(1–3)**: 25–30.

Wright, R. H. (1975). Why mosquito repellents repel? *Scientific American* **233(1)**: 104–111.

Two ways to be a tropical big moth: Santa Rosa saturniids and sphingids

DANIEL H. JANZEN

The world has two species-rich families of big-bodied moths: Saturniidae and Sphingidae (Figs. 1–4). In the New World they co-occur from Canada to Patagonia, from sea level to the upper limits of vegetation, from extra-tropical deserts to the wettest tropical forests. The species-specific live body weights (e.g., Tables 1–2) occupy about the same ranges (0.1–7.0 g) but saturniids and sphingids represent two quite different ways of being a large moth. Using the saturniid and sphingid faunas of a small mosaic of dry lowland tropical habitats – 10,800 ha Santa Rosa National Park in northwestern Costa Rica – I propose and discuss answers to three conspicuous eco-evolutionary questions about their natural histories. My eventual goal is to understand the selective pressures and ecological processes that have made Santa Rosa saturniids and sphingids what they are. I fully recognize that this understanding will eventually require study of the Santa Rosa species in the other parts of their broad ranges. However, I use and discuss this local fauna because it is the one that I know the best. I use a local fauna because many of the traits discussed must be first understood in their local adaptive sense before they can be viewed in aggregate over a species' range. I restrict myself to only three questions because this is not a book.

1. Why do saturniids go to lights differently than do sphingids?
2. Why do saturniid wings differ strikingly in shape between the sexes and among species, while sphingid wings are monotonously similar in shape?
3. Why do saturniid caterpillars feed on more and different families of plants, but on fewer plant life forms, than do sphingid caterpillars?

Before embarking on the details of these questions, I offer a brief caricature of these taxonomically well-known moths (Ferguson 1972, Hodges 1971, Rothschild and Jordan 1903, Lemaire 1974, 1978, 1980, 1985, Michener 1949, 1952). While long of interest to caterpillar fanciers (e.g., Gardiner 1982, Collins and Weast 1961, Moss 1912, 1920) and often the subjects of physiological and ethological experiments, saturniids and sphingids have generally been neglected by field ecologists and evolutionary biologists (some exceptions are, Saturniidae: Blest 1960, 1963, Brown 1972, Capinera 1980, Capinera *et al.* 1980, Farge 1983, Cryan and Dirig 1977, Hogue *et al.* 1960, 1965, Janzen 1984a, 1984b, 1984c, Wangberg 1983, Marsh 1937, Peigler 1975, 1976b, 1981, 1983, Smith and Turner 1979, Quezada 1973, White 1972, Carolin and Knopf 1968, Lawson *et al.* 1982, Beutelspacher 1978, Vuattoux 1981, Crocomo and Parra 1979, van den Berg 1974a, 1974b, van den Berg and van den Berg 1974, van den Berg *et al.* 1973, Waldbauer and Sternburg 1967, 1973, 1979, 1982a, Waldbauer *et al.* 1984, Sternburg and Waldbauer 1969, 1978, Scarborough *et al.* 1974,

Sternburg *et al.* 1981, Janzen and Waterman 1984, Scriber 1977, 1978, Rivnay 1970, Rivnay and Sobrio 1967; Sphingidae: Bullock and Pescador 1983, Fleming 1970, Gregory 1963, Rivnay and Yathom 1967, Beutelspacher 1978, Young 1972, Janzen and Waterman 1984, Janzen 1984b, Grant 1937, Laroca and Mielke 1975, Casey 1976, Schneider 1973, Stewart 1969, 1975, Thurston and Prachuabmoh 1971, Owen 1969, 1972, Vuattoux 1978, Giles 1968, Haber 1983a, 1983b, Haber and Frankie 1984, Wolda 1980, Dillon *et al.* 1983).

The style of this essay departs from convention in that much of it is based on data from an unpublished study still in progress. Rather than decorate every other sentence with 'Janzen, unpublished' I assume that the reader will recognize the source. Likewise unconventionally, I dwell on the implications of traits evident in the field and what they may mean in big moth biology rather than on documenting their means and variances. I am willing to relax my scrutiny of individual trees in order to keep the forest in view. My generalizations are, however, intended to apply only to the Santa Rosa saturniid and sphingid faunas, and do occasionally deviate from those for these moths in other regions.

The saturniid nomenclature followed here is that used by C. Lemaire, the most recent reviser of the family (Lemaire 1974, 1978, 1980, 1985). I depart from using *Sphingicampa* and *Oiticicia* as was used in my guide to the saturniids of the Park (Janzen 1982), in deference to *Syssphinx* and *Othorene* (Lemaire 1985). Sphingid names are those used by Hodges (1981) and Haber (1983a). All species of saturniids and sphingids mentioned here by name are easily identified at Santa Rosa, and I am deeply indebted to C. Lemaire, J. Cadiou, R. Hodges and W. Haber for confirming my field determinations.

Saturniid caricature

Adult Santa Rosa saturniids (Figs. 1–2) are medium-weight to very heavy moths (Table 1). All but one of the 30 species that breed in the Park (Janzen 1982), *Schausiella santarosensis* (Lemaire 1982), range over many tens of degrees of latitude (C. Lemaire, personal communication); the most widespread is the imperial moth, *Eacles imperialis* (Fig. 1.7–1.8; Canada to Argentina (Lemaire 1985)). The adults fly during at least part of the night and spend the day hanging motionless and cryptic in the vegetation; their diurnal goal is to avoid desiccation and discovery by carnivores. Some make mimetic or aposematic displays after being discovered (e.g., *Citheronia, Arsenura armida, Automeris, Hylesia, Dirphia, Ptiloscola, Periphoba, Molippa*). Saturniid adults have only rudimentary mouthparts and apparently do not feed; they harvest all of their water and nutrient resources while they are caterpillars. Immediately after eclosing from the pupa and leaving the cocoon or underground pupation chamber, the adult hangs from vegetation and expands its wings. Without having flown, the female pheromonally calls males on the night of eclosion (all non-hemileucines and *Periphoba*) or in the night immediately following an afternoon eclosion from the pupa (*Automeris, Dirphia, Hylesia*). She often mates with the first male to arrive (but see Brown 1972) and mates only once. She lays 40 per cent or more of her eggs during the next night (see Rau and Rau 1913, Miller 1978, Miller and Cooper 1977, for extra-tropical examples) and within two to eight more days she lays the remainder of her eggs and dies. She lays her eggs irrespective of whether she has located larval host plants. The male flies shortly after dusk, and then again later in the night when seeking calling females (except for the males of *Dirphia avia* and *Adeloneivaia isara*, whose females call shortly after dusk). He may stay in copula for less than an hour (*Dirphia, Automeris*) or until the afternoon of the following day. He is capable of mating on successive nights and the successively mated females lay fertile eggs. He lives about the same number of nights as does the female (five to 12). Death, in both sexes, is associated with attacks by predators, wing wear, weight loss (e.g., Waldbauer *et al.* 1984), and body-water loss; however, death occurs after five to 12 days irrespective of environmental events. Wild females customarily weigh two to four times as much as do conspecific males at the time of eclosion (Table 2) and usually produce 200–500 large eggs weighing 2 mg (e.g., *Adeloneivaia isara, Automeris rubrescens*) to 11 mg each (e.g., *Eacles imperialis*). For a more familiar reference point, cecropia moth (*Hyalophora cecropia*) eggs weigh 4.7 mg each (Schroeder 1972). The female's initial egg load usually constitutes more than half her initial body weight, but as she oviposits her weight approaches that of the male (Table 1, compare weights of moths at lights with weights at eclosion).

The eggs hatch in six to 15 days and except for *Hylesia lineata* (Janzen 1984a), are not the stage that passes the severe five-month rainless season at Santa Rosa. Larvae feed for four to five weeks (non-hemileucines) or six to 10 weeks (hemileucines). The pupal stage lasts about three weeks or else pupae become dormant during the long dry season. Caterpillars of all species feed on adult (and rarely juvenile) dicot woody plants (Table 3); all feed externally on the leaf blades of mature foliage, and, except for certain hemileucines and *Copaxa moinieri* and *Syssphinx mexicana*, all are found primarily in the crowns of large trees. Over 50 per cent have Leguminosae among their host plants. More than half of the species at Santa Rosa have two or more larval host plants that are in different families (Table 3). While all rest on the foliage, some species also rest in silk leaf-nests (*Hylesia lineata*, Janzen 1984a) or away from the foliage (e.g., *Dirphia avia, Citheronia lobesis*). They occasionally defoliate their host plants (e.g., Janzen 1981, 1984a). Saturniid caterpillars are conspicuously subject to vertebrate and invertebrate predation, parasitoids, diseases, inclement weather, and intra-specific competition (direct during defoliation events, diffuse all the time through sharing carnivores). The larvae vary strongly among species as to whether they are cryptic, aposematic and/or mimetic of urticators; at least 40 per cent urticate, and other 30 per cent are mimics of urticators. Larval colour polymorphism is rare within an instar and usually produced by crowding or shading (e.g. Hintze-Podufal 1977). The last larval instar leaves the host plant to spin a cocoon or burrow into litter or soil to form a pupation chamber. Larval and pupal duration are

Table 1

Live weighs (g) of the Santa Rosa breeding saturniids taken at lights (therefore of mixed ages) and newly eclosed (wild reared only). The newly eclosed weight is that of a representative maximum sized individual.

	Males				Females			
	At lights			New eclose	At lights			New eclose
	X̄	s.d.	n		X̄	s.d.	n	
Arsenurinae								
Arsenura armida	.83	.17	10	1.2	1.28	.46	4	3.7
Caio championi	.91	.26	10	1.5	2.15	.84	10	4.2
Copiopteryx semiramis	.69	.17	10	NA	.55	.20	2	NA
Dysdaemonia boreas	.90	.25	10	1.4	1.61	.51	3	3.0
Titaea tamerlan	.88	.25	10	1.3	2.13	.70	10	4.0
Ceratocampinae								
Adeloneivaia isara	.25	.06	10	.3	.46	.13	10	.6
Citheronia bellavista	.92	.23	10	1.4	.91	.12	2	3.3
Citheronia lobesis	.93	.14	10	1.3	1.19	.52	2	3.3
Eacles imperialis	1.30	.27	10	1.6	2.38	.91	10	7.1
Othorene purpurascens	.80	.15	10	1.0	1.77	.41	6	2.9
Othorene verana	.74	.14	10	.9	1.92	.55	7	3.0
Ptiloscola dargei	.34	.08	10	.4	.52	.19	10	1.3
Schausiella santarosensis	.77	.13	10	1.0	1.64	.57	10	2.8
Syssphinx colla	.85	.19	10	1.1	1.20	.49	4	2.8
Syssphinx mexicana	.63	.16	10	.9	1.15	.41	10	3.4
Syssphinx molina	.80	.33	10	1.3	1.82	.80	10	3.8
Syssphinx quadrilineata	.59	.13	10	.8	.99	.27	9	2.3

Hemileucinae						
Automeris io	.25	.05	10	.3	.82	.19	6	1.9
Automeris metzli	.89	.15	10	1.2	2.01	1.01	3	4.4
Automeris rubrescens	.38	.09	10	.5	.94	.42	10	3.0
Automeris zugana	.30	.06	10	.3	.66	.17	10	1.5
Automeris zurobara	.32	.08	10	.4	NA			2.8
Dirphia avia	.64	.15	10	.9	1.81	.60	10	3.5
Hylesia dalina	.09	.02	10	.1	.18	.10	10	0.4
Hylesia lineata	.10	.01	10	.1	.52	.22	10	0.6
Molippa nibasa	.29	.03	10	.3	.69	.06	4	1.6
Periphoba arcaei	.58	.16	10	.8	1.45	.70	10	3.7
Saturniinae						
Copaxa moinieri	.30	.10	10	.4	.44	.30	4	2.0
Rothschildia erycina	.39	.08	10	.5	.69	.12	5	1.8
Rothschildia lebeau	.49	.12	10	.9	1.53	.37	10	3.1
Range	.09–1.30			.1–1.6		.18–2.38		.6–7.1

Table 2

Live weights (g) of the Santa Rosa sphingids taken at lights. Breeding species unless marked with an asterisk.

	Males			Females		
	$\overline{X}$	s.d	n	$\overline{X}$	s.d.	n
Aellopos clavipes	.25		1			
Aellopos fadus	.62	.08	2			
Aellopos titan	.57	.21	3	.50		
Agrius cingulatus	1.42	.34	10	1.61	.39	7
Aleuron carinata						
Aleuron chloroptera				.81		1
Aleuron iphis	.30		1			
Amplypterus gannascus	.59	.07	10	1.13	.25	9
Amplypterus ypsilon	.85	.13	10	1.36	.25	2
Callionima falcifera	.53	.04	10	.92	.15	10
Cautethia spuria	.17	.02	10	.35	.09	2
Cautethia yucatana	.14	.03	10	.39		1
Cocytius antaeus	3.02	.53	8	4.58	.94	3
Cocytius duponchel	2.35	.27	10	3.21	.83	6
Cocytius lucifer	2.79	.43	7	4.00		1
Dalbogene igualana						
Enyo gorgon				.81		1
Enyo lugubris	1.14	.15	6	1.11	.15	5
Enyo ocypete	.57	.07	10	.69	.15	10
Erinnyis alope	1.56	.30	3	1.29		1
Erinnyis crameri	.81	.21	10	1.36	.22	7
Erinnyis domingonus	.38		1	.54		1
Erinnyis ello	1.23	.35	10	1.33	.27	10
Erinnyis lassauxii	1.10	.25	10	2.04		1
Erinnyis obscura	.39	.09	10	.52	.10	7
Erinnyis oenotrus	.94	.11	10	1.11	.20	10
Erinnyis yucatana	1.12		1			
Eumorpha anchemola	3.28	.32	6	4.41		1
Eumorpha fasciata						
Eumorpha labruscae	2.59	.66	4			
Eumorpha satellitia	1.59	.28	10	2.31	.67	10
Eumorpha triangulum	2.12		1			
Eumorpha vitis ،	1.41	.19	10	1.65	.06	2
Eupyrrhoglossum sagra	.49	.04	10	.66	.26	2
Hemeroplanes triptolemus	.90	.16	10	2.16		1
Hyles lineata	.45		1	1.00		1
Isognathus rimosus	.93	.08	10	1.68	.36	10
Madoryx oiclus	.98	.21	10	1.99	.30	10
Madoryx pluto	1.35	.23	2			
Madoryx bubastus						
Manduca barnesi	1.42	.30	10	2.13	.40	10

Manduca corallina	1.32	.08	10	1.74	.51	10
Manduca dilucida	.65	.07	10	.91	.23	10
Manduca florestan	1.16	.17	10	1.99	.41	10
Manduca lanuginosa	.80	.12	10	1.46	.32	10
Manduca lefeburei	.76	.07	10	1.02	.10	10
Manduca muscosa	1.08	.37	10	1.58	.24	5
Manduca occulta	.99	.12	10	1.48	.39	7
*Manduca ochus	1.55		1			
Manduca rustica	2.74	.53	10	3.31	.85	10
Manduca sexta	1.33	.23	9	1.87	.51	4
*Manduca hannibal						
*Manduca sp.						
Neococytius cluentis						
Nyceryx coffeae	.73	.08	10	.95	.14	6
Nyceryx riscus	.39	.07	10	.64	.17	3
Pachygonia drucei						
Pachylia ficus	2.12	.34	10	2.91	1.23	4
Pachylia syces	2.55	.39	3	2.73		1
Pachylioides resumens	.95	.14	10	1.42	.14	9
Perigonia lusca	.57	.17	10	.68	.13	10
Phryxus caicus	.38		1			
Protambulyx strigilis	.74	.11	10	1.11	.41	10
*Protambulyx xanthus						
Pseudosphinx tetrio	2.30	.37	5			
Sphinx merops	.79	.12	10	1.32	.13	2
*Unzela japyx						
Unzela pronoe						
Xylophanes anubus	.69	.08	10	.80		1
Xylophanes ceratomioides	.79	.12	5	1.19		1
Xylophanes chiron	.69		1			
Xylophanes libya	.45	.08	6	.69		1
Xylophanes maculator	.44	.02	4			
Xylophanes pluto	.42	.06	10	.64	.19	7
Xylophanes porcus	.60	.07	10	.70		1
Xylophanes tersa	.38	.06	9	.61		2
Xylophanes turbata	.45	.10	10	.62	.13	9
Xylophanes tyndarus	.78		1			
*Xylophanes sp.						
Range		.14–3.28			.35–4.58	

Table 3

Saturniidae larval hosts in nature in Santa Rosa National Park (as of December 1983).

Arsenurinae

Arsenura armida	*Bombacopsis quinatum* (Bombacaceae)	large tree crown
Caio championi	*Bombacopsis quinatum* (Bombacaceae)	large tree crown
Copiopteryx semiramis	*Manilkara chicle* (Sapotaceae)	large tree crown
Dysdaemonia boreas	*Ceiba pentandra* (Bombacaceae)[1]	large tree crown
Titaea tamerlan	*Bombacopsis quinatum* (Bombacaceae)	large tree crown

Ceratocampinae

Adeloneivaia isara	*Lysiloma divaricata* (Leguminosae)	large tree crown
	Lysiloma auritum (Leguminosae)	large tree crown
Citheronia bellavista	*Phoradendron quadrangulare* (Loranthaceae)[2]	parasite in crown of large tree
Citheronia lobesis	*Cochlospermum vitifolium* (Cochlospermaceae)	large saplings
	Bursera simaruba (Burseraceae)	large tree crown
	Spondias mombin (Anacardiaceae)	large saplings
	Psidium guajava (Myrtaceae)[3]	shrubby treelet
	Calcyophyllum candidissimum (Rubiaceae)	large tree crown
	Phoradendron quadrangulare (Loranthaceae)	parasite in crown of large tree
Eacles imperialis	*Cochlospermum vitifolium* (Cochlospermaceae)	large saplings and large tree crown
	Bursera tomentosa (Burseraceae)	large tree crown
	Astronium graveolens (Anacardiaceae)	large tree crown
	Cedrela odorata (Meliaceae)	large tree crown
Othorene purpurascens	*Manilkara chicle* (Sapotaceae)	large tree crown
Othorene verana	*Quercus oleoides* (Fagaceae)	large tree crown
Ptiloscola dargei	*Acacia tenuifolia* (Leguminosae)	saplings and large vine crown
Schausiella santarosensis	*Hymenaea courbaril* (Leguminosae)	large tree crown

Syssphinx colla	Pithecellobium saman (Leguminosae)	large tree crown
Syssphinx mexicana	Acacia collinsii (Leguminosae)	sapling to adult treelet crown
	Acacia cornigera (Leguminosae)	sapling to adult treelet crown
Syssphinx molina	Pithecellobium saman (Leguminosae)	large tree crown
	Cassia grandis (Leguminosae)[3]	large tree crown
	Albizzia adinocephala (Leguminosae)	large tree crown
Syssphinx quadrilineata	Acacia collinsii (Leguminosae)[2]	laboratory
Hemileucinae		
Automeris io	Crescentia alata (Bignoniaceae)[3]	large tree crown
	Mimosa pigra (Leguminosae)	shrub
	Cassia biflora (Leguminosae)	shrub
	Rhynchosia reticulata (Leguminosae)	herbaceous vine
	Gliricidia sepium (Leguminosae)	sapling
Automeris rubrescens	Inga vera (Leguminosae)	sapling
	Rourea glabra (Connaraceae)	scandent shrub
	Guazuma ulmifolia (Sterculiaceae)	large tree crown
	Cassia biflora (Leguminosae)	shrub
	Quercus oleoides (Fagaceae)	sapling
	Cordia alliodora (Boraginaceae)	sapling
	Lonchocarpus minimiflorus (Leguminosae)	sapling
	Calycophyllum candidissimum (Rubiaceae)	large tree crown
	DHJ 12175 (Bignoniaceae)	sapling vine
	Zuelania guidonia (Flacourtiaceae)	large tree crown
	Crescentia alata (Bignoniaceae)[3]	large tree crown
	Cassia grandis (Leguminosae)	large tree crown
Automeris zugana	Annona purpurea (Annonaceae)	large tree crown
	Lonchocarpus costaricensis (Leguminosae)	large tree crown
	Quercus oleoides (Fagaceae)	large tree crown
	Cydista heterophylla (Bignoniaceae)	large woody vine
	Calycophyllum candidissimum (Rubiaceae)	sapling to large tree crown

	Food plant	Growth form
	Hymenaea courbaril (Leguminosae)	sapling
	Solanum hazenii (Solanaceae)	large herb
	Lantana camara (Verbenaceae)[3]	large herb/shrub
	Lonchocarpus eriocarinalis (Leguminosae)	large tree crown
	Centrosema pubescens (Leguminosae)	herb vine
	Cassia hayesiana (Leguminosae)	shrub/treelet
	Inga vera (Leguminosae)	sapling
	Serjania atrolineata (Sapindaceae)	large vine
Dirphia avia	Hymenaea courbaril (Leguminosae)	large tree crown
	Cedrela odorata (Meliaceae)	large tree crown
Hylesia dalina	Casearia arguta (Flacourtiaceae)	treelet
	Malvaviscus arboreus (Malvaceae)	shrub
	Tabebuia rosea (Bignoniaceae)	sapling
Hylesia lineata	Bombacopsis quinatum (Bombacaceae)	large tree crown
	Cordia alliodora (Boraginaceae)	treelet
	Hirtella racemosa (Chrysobalanaceae)	treelet
	Muntingia calabura (Elaeocarpaceae)	treelet
	Casearia arguta (Flacourtiaceae)	treelet
	Casearia sylvestris (Flacourtiaceae)	treelet
	Casearia corymbosa (Flacourtiaceae)	treelet
	Zuelania guidonia (Flacourtiaceae)	large tree crown
	Acacia tenuifolia (Leguminosae)	large vine crown
	Cassia biflora (Leguminosae)	shrub
	Diphysa robinioides (Leguminosae)	sapling
	Enterolobium cyclocarpum (Leguminosae)	large tree crown
	Hymenaea courbaril (Leguminosae)	sapling
	Inga vera (Leguminosae)	treelet
	Lonchocarpus minimiflorus (Legumin.)	treelet
	Lonchocarpus costaricensis (Legumin.)	sapling
	Lysiloma auritum (Leguminosae)	large tree crown

Periphoba arcaei

Machaerium kegelii (Leguminosae)	sapling large vine
Mimosa pigra (Leguminosae)	shrub
Myrospermum frutescens (Leguminosae)	treelet
Pithecellobium lanceolatum (Legumin.)	treelet
Hyptis pectinata (Labiatae)	large herb
Malvaviscus arboreus (Malvaceae)	shrub
Banisteriopsis muricata (Malphighiaceae)	low vine
Byrsonima crassifolia (Malpighiaceae)	treelet
Stigmaphyllon ellipticum (Malphighiaceae)	low vine
Psidium guineense (Myrtaceae)	shrub
Ouratea lucens (Ochnaceae)	shrub
Gouania polygama (Rhamnaceae)	low vine
Calycophyllum candidissimum (Rubiaceae)	sapling
Chomelia spinosa (Rubiaceae)	treelet
Guettarda macrosperma (Rubiaceae)	treelet
Xanthoxylum setulosum (Rutaceae)	sapling
Allophyllus occidentalis (Sapindaceae)	treelet
Cupania guatemalensis (Sapindaceae)	treelet
Paullinia cururu (Sapindaceae)	low vine
Serjania schiedeana (Sapindaceae)	low vine
Urvillea ulmacea (Sapindaceae)	low vine
Byttneria aculeata (Sterculiaceae)	shrub
Byttneria catalpaefolia (Sterculiaceae)	low vine
Guazuma ulmifolia (Sterculiaceae)	medium tree
Luehea speciosa (Tiliaceae)	sapling
Lantana camara (Verbenaceae)[3]	shrub
Erythroxylum havanense (Erythroxylaceae)	shrub
Calliandra emarginata (Leguminosae)	shrub
Eugenia salamensis (Myrtaceae)	medium tree crown
Cassia biflora (Leguminosae)	shrub

Guazuma ulmifolia (Sterculiaceae)   large tree crown
Lysiloma auritum (Leguminosae)   large tree crown
Spondias mombin (Anacardiaceae)   large tree crown
Rourea glabra (Connaraceae)   scandent shrub
Annona purpurea (Annonaceae)   treelet crown
Calycophyllum candidissimum (Rubiaceae)   large tree crown
Bombacopsis quinatum (Bombacaceae)   large tree crown
Cassia alata (Leguminosae)[3]   large tree crown
Inga vera (Leguminosae)   medium tree crown
Ardisia revoluta (Myrsinaceae)   treelet
Astronium graveolens (Anacardiaceae)   sapling
Hymenaea courbaril (Leguminosae)   sapling
Quercus oleoides (Fabaceae)   large tree crown
Miconia argentea (Melastomataceae)   sapling

Saturniinae
Copaxa moinieri   *Ocotea veraguensis* (Lauraceae)   saplings and lower branches of treelet
Rothschildia erycina   *Exostema mexicanum* (Rubiaceae)   large tree crown
    Coutarea hexandra (Rubiaceae)   treelet crown
Rothschildia lebeau   *Exostema mexicanum* (Rubiaceae)   large tree crown
    Spondias mombin (Anacardiaceae)   large tree crown
    Spondias purpurea (Anacardiaceae)   treelet
    Casearia corymbosa (Flacourtiaceae)   treelet
    Zuelania guidonia (Flacourtiaceae)   large tree crown
    Xanthoxylum setulosum (Rutaceae)   large tree crown

[1] Not found in nature but accepts readily and dies on other Santa Rosa Bombacaceae. [2] Not found in nature but accepts readily and has the appropriate colour and behaviour to use this host. [3] Plant introduced to Santa Rosa within past several hundred years.

determined by both immediate environmental factors and internal calendars, and larval size is highly variable within a species at the time of pupation. Sex ratios of first instar larvae and of wild-caught caterpillars are one to one.

For the purpose of this essay the focal characteristics of saturniids are that they do not feed as adults, are short-lived as adults, and have caterpillars with diverse and sometimes lengthy host lists. The adult males are primarily specialists at locating females, and the females are specialized for oviposition (and staying alive long enough to do so). They both experience selection for escape from predators, but the selective pressures are probably different because of differences in weight, size, habitat needs, rate of potential fitness loss with age, *etc.*

Sphingid caricature

Body weights of adult sphingid moths of Santa Rosa (Figs. 3–4) are distributed over about the same range as are those of the saturniids (Table 2). The 63 species that breed in the Park (and the 16 transient species) also have about the same aggregate geographic range (e.g., Schreiber 1978) as do the saturniids, except that the sphingids also occur on many Caribbean and Pacific Islands (e.g., Cary 1957, Curio 1965) while saturniids are generally absent from the islands in the New World. While the three species of *Aellopos* are diurnally active, the remaining Santa Rosa sphingids are nocturnal, as are the saturniids. All the nocturnal and crepuscular species are highly cryptic when at rest in the daytime (bark and damaged leaf colours and patterns, just as with saturniids), but all display red, yellow or white presumed flash colours on the hind wings and body when fleeing. Both sexes regularly drink with a long proboscis from many kinds of flowers while hovering in front of them (e.g., Haber and Frankie 1984, Bullock and Pescador 1983), presumably to obtain water as well as nutrients. Females generally weigh one to two times as much as do males at the time of eclosion, but owing to variation in the amount of oviposition and nectar uptake, middle-aged adult conspecific sphingids of both sexes are often of similar body weight (Table 2). Newly eclosed adults climb upward a few decimetres to hang and expand their wings, but generally do not fly on the night of eclosion. Mating probably occurs some days later, and is multiple for females (W. Haber, personal communication) and probably males. Oviposition ranges from rapid production of eggs, such that all the eggs may be laid within as short a time as a week (e.g., *Aellopos titan*, Janzen 1984b) to an oviposition period of weeks to months with only a few eggs maturing nightly (W. Haber, personal communication). Fecundity is unknown but probably in the hundreds if the female can feed freely.

The eggs hatch in four to eight days and are never the stage that passes the Santa Rosa five-month dry season. Larval host plants (Table 4) range from annual herbs to the crowns of large trees and vines; many are vines, small plants and juveniles of large plants. Caterpillars of many species of

Table 4

Sphingidae larval hosts in Santa Rosa National Park (as of December 1983).

Species	Host plant (family)	Growth form
Aellopos clavipes	*Randia karstenii* (Rubiaceae)	sapling to treelet
Aellopos fadus	*Genipa americana* (Rubiaceae)	sapling to large tree
	Alibertia edulis (Rubiaceae)	shrub
Aellopos titan	*Randia karstenii* (Rubinaceae)	sapling to treelet
	Randia subcordata (Rubiaceae)	sapling to treelet
Agrius cingulatus	*Merremia umbellata* (Convolvulaceae)	herb vine
	DHJ 12071 (Convolvulaceae)	herb vine
Aleuron carinata	*Doliocarpus dentatus* (Dilleniaceae)	low perennial vine
Aleuron iphis	*Tetracera volubilis* (Dilleniaceae)	low perennial vine
Amplypterus gannascus	*Ocotea veraguensis* (Lauraceae)	sapling to treelet
Amplypterus ypsilon	*Ocotea veraguensis* (Lauraceae)	sapling to treelet
Callionima falcifera	*Stemmadenia obovata* (Apocynaceae)	sapling to treelet
Cautethia spuria	*Exostema mexicanum* (Rubiaceae)	sapling to large tree
	Coutarea hexandra (Rubiaceae)	treelet
Cautethia yucatana	*Exostema mexicanum* (Rubiaceae)	treelet
Cocytius duponchel	*Annona purpurea* (Annonaceae)	sapling to treelet
	Annona reticulata (Annonaceae)	sapling to treelet
Enyo ocypete	*Tetracera volubilis* (Dilleniaceae)	low perennial vine
	Ciccus rhombifolia (Vitaceae)	herb vine
Erinnyis ello	*Sebastiana confusa* (Euphorbiaceae)	sapling to treelet
	Sapium thelocarpum (Euphorbiaceae)	sapling
	Manilkara chicle (Sapotaceae)	large tree
Erinnyis lassauxii	*Sarcostemma glauca* (Asclepiadaceae)	low vine
Erinnyis oenotrus	*Forsteronia spicata* (Apocynaceae)	low perennial vine
Eumorpha anchemola	*Cissus rhombifolia* (Vitaceae)	low perennial vine
	Cissus sicyoides (Vitaceae)	low perennial vine

Moth	Host plant	Growth form
Eumorpha satellitia	*Cissus rhombifolia* (Vitaceae)	low perennial vine
	Cissus sicyoides (Vitaceae)	low perennial vine
Eupyrrhoglossum sagra	*Chomelia spinosa* (Rubiaceae)	sapling to treelet
	Guettarda macrosperma (Rubiaceae)	sapling to treelet
Isognathus rimosus	*Plumeria rubra* (Apocynaceae)	large tree
Manduca barnesi	*Godmania aesculifolia* (Bignoniaceae)	sapling
Manduca corallina	*Cordia alliodora* (Boraginaceae)	sapling to large tree
Manduca dilucida	*Sapranthus palanga* (Annonaceae)	sapling to treelet
	Annona reticulata (Annonaceae)	sapling to treelet
Manduca florestan	*Pithecoctinium crucigerum* (Bignoniaceae)	low perennial vine
	Cydista heterophylla (Bignoniaceae)	low perennial vine
	Tabebuia ochracea (Bignoniaceae)	sapling
	Callichlamys latifolia (Bagnoniaceae)	low perennial vine
	Arrabidaea chica (Bignoniaceae)	low perennial vine
	Cornutia grandifolia (Verbenaceae)	shrub
	Ceratophytum tetragonolobum (Bignoniaceae)	low perennial vine
	Pleonotoma variabilis (Bignoniaceae)	low perennial vine
	Stachytarpheta frantzii (Verbenaceae)	shrub
Manduca lefeburei	*Casearia sylvestris* (Flacourticeae)	sapling to treelet
	Casearia corymbosa (Flacourtiaceae)	sapling to treelet
Manduca muscosa	*Verbesina gigantea* (Compositae)	giant herb
	Lantana camara (Verbenaceae)[1]	shrub
	Lasianthaea fruticosa (Compositae)	shrub
	Baltimora recta (Compositae)	herb
	Melanthera aspera (Compositae)	herb
	Wedelia calycina (Compositae)	herb
Manduca occulta	*Solanum ochraceo-ferrugineum* (Solanaceae)	herb
	Solanum hazenii (Solanaceae)	herb
	Solanum accrescens (Solanaceae)	herb
	Cestrum DHJ 12029 (Solanaceae)	shrub

Manduca rustica	*Lantana camara* (Verbenaceae)[1]	shrub
	Stachytarpheta frantzii (Verbenaceae)	shrub
	Cordia panamensis (Boraginaceae)	sapling
	Pithecoctenium crucigerum (Bignoniaceae)	low perennial vine
	Amphilophium paniculatum (Bignoniaceae)	low perennial vine
	Merremia umbellata (Convolvulaceae)	herb vine
	DHJ 12071 (Convolvulaceae)	herb vine.
	Hyptis verticillata (Labiatae)	herb
Manduca sexta	*Capsicum annuum* (Solanaceae)	herb
	Lycopersicon esculentum (Solanaceae)[1]	herb
	Piper marginatum (Piperaceae)	shrub
Neocoytius cluentius	*Calcyophyllum candidissimum* (Rubiaceae)	sapling to large tree
Nyceryx coffeae	*Doliocarpus dentatus* (Dilleniaceae)	low perennial vine
Pachygonia drucei	*Ficus insipida* (Moraceae)	sapling to large tree
Pachylia ficus	*Ficus cotinifolia* (Moraceae)	sapling to large tree
	Ficus obtusifolia (Moraceae)	sapling to large tree
	Ficus ovalis (Moraceae)	sapling to large tree
	Brosimum alicastrum (Moraceae)	sapling
	Chlorophora tinctoria (Moraceae)	sapling to large tree
	Castilla elastica (Moraceae)	sapling
Pachylia syces	*Ficus ovalis* (Moraceae)	large tree
Pachylioides resumens	*Forsteronia spicata* (Apocynaceae)	low perennial vine
Perigonia lusca	*Calcophyllum candidissimum* (Rubiaceae)	sapling to large tree
	Guettarda macrosperma (Rubiaceae)	sapling to treelet
Protambulyx strigilis	*Astronium graveolens* (Anacardiaceae)	sapling to large tree
	Spondias mombin (Anacardiaceae)	sapling to large tree
Pseudosphinx tetrio	*Plumeria rubra* (Apocynaceae)	large tree
Sphinx merops	*Lantana camara* (Verbenaceae)[1]	shrub
	Hyptis pectinata (Labiatae)	herb

Unzela pronoe	*Tetracera volubilis* (Dilleniaceae)	low perennial vine
Xylophanes anubus	*Psychotria nervosa* (Rubiaceae)	shrub
	Psychotria horizontalis (Rubiaceae)	shrub/herb
Xylophanes ceratomioides	*Hamelia patens* (Rubiaceae)	shrub
Xylophanes chiron	*Psychotria pubescens* (Rubiaceae)	shrub
	Psychotria horizontalis (Rubiaceae)	shrub
	Faramea occidentalis (Rubiaceae)	sapling
Xylophanes juanita	*Psychotria pubescens* (Rubiaceae)	shrub
	Psychotria horizontalis (Rubiaceae)	shrub/herb
	Psychotria nervosa (Rubiaceae)	shrub
Xylophanes maculator	*Psychotria horizontalis* (Rubiaceae)	shrub/herb
Xylophanes pluto	*Hamelia patens* (Rubiaceae)	shrub
Xylophanes porcus	*Hamelia patens* (Rubiaceae)	shrub
Xylophanes turbata	*Hamelia patens* (Rubiaceae)	shrub to treelet
	Psychotria mecrodon (Rubiaceae)	shrub/herb
Xylophanes tyndarus	*Faramea occidentalis* (Rubiaceae)	treelet

[1] Host plant introduced to Santa Rosa National Park.

sphingids eat both young and mature leaves. If a Santa Rosa sphingid has two or more larval host species, they are almost always closely related at the level of the family or genus (Table 4). None has legumes as host plants, and in general they eat a different subset of the Santa Rosa flora than do the saturniids. The Santa Rosa sphingids not only have enormous latitudinal ranges, but also most occur in many other Costa Rican habitats (as is the case with the saturniids); over these ranges they tend to have the same or closely related larval host plants (e.g., Moss 1912, 1920, Hodges 1971, W. Haber, personal communication). Larvae use two to five weeks for larval development and are subject to the same kinds of mortality as are saturniids, but in different proportions. Sphingid larvae occasionally defoliate individuals or populations of their larval hosts (e.g., Janzen 1981, 1984b). All but *Pseudosphinx tetrio*, which is either aposematic or a coral snake mimic (Janzen 1983), are highly cryptic at rest; a few (*Xylophanes* spp., *Hemeroplanes triptolemus*, *Eumorpha labruscae*, *Erinnyis ello*, *Agrius cingulatus*) become mimetic of vertebrate eyes when attacked. Almost all cryptic species have larval polymorphisms within and among instars (e.g. Schneider 1973). The last instar makes its pupation chamber underground or in the litter. The pupal stage lasts two to many weeks, is variable in length within a species and season, and is the stage that passes the dry season except for those sphingids that have continuous generations throughout the year (e.g., *Pachylia ficus*, *Protambulyx strigilis*, *Cautethia spuria*) or leave the Park for part of the year (e.g., *Aellopos titan*, Janzen 1984b). Larval duration is variable and determined by both environmental factors and internal calendars. Primary sex ratios are as in saturniids, one to one.

The key sphingid trait, in contrast with saturniids, is that adult sphingids feed heavily over a long period and possess the mental and flight machinery to do it. Sphingids of opposite sexes and of different species therefore have a major activity in common – finding flowers, hovering in front of those flowers, using the resources so gained, and remembering where those flowering plants are the next night.

Santa Rosa as a saturniid and sphingid habitat

The Park (10 degrees north Latitude) is a fine-scale mosaic of deciduous to evergreen forest ranging from newly abandoned grassy pastures and old fields to virtually pristine forests. Plant species richness ranges from nearly monospecific tree stands (mangroves, evergreen *Hymenaea* or *Quercus* forest) to 20–30 species of woody plants per ha (dry rocky cactus-rich ridges) to 100-plus species of woody plants per ha (late succession on good soil); there are about 650 breeding dicot plant species in the Park (Janzen and Liesner 1980). Spanning 0–350 m elevation, it is primarily a habitat and climate representative of the pre-Columbian Central American Pacific coastal plain with intrusions from the more moist volcanic foothills immediately adjacent to the Park (Boza and Mendoza 1981, Hartshorn 1983). The five-month long rain-free dry season ends with varying suddenness in May, a variably light and short dry season occurs in late

July–early August, and the rains terminate between late November and early January. Between 900 and 2200 mm of rain fall during the rainy season, and the dry season is generally so windy and sunny that it can kill an exposed first instar saturniid caterpillar by desiccation in a single day.

Santa Rosa's deciduous forest climate (and the 4000-plus km^2 of similar Costa Rican climate in which it is embedded) contrasts strongly with the wetter evergreen rainforest habitats covering most of the remainder of the country (Hartshorn 1983, Coen 1983). The deciduous forest vegetation of Costa Rica likewise differs from the rainforest in that the former has been almost entirely replaced by the biological deserts of croplands and pastures, while there is still enough of the latter to make a conservation effort worthwhile.

The saturniid (Janzen 1982) and sphingid (Haber 1983) faunas of Santa Rosa are very similar in species richness, composition and relative abundance to those of other Central American and lowland tropical Mexican deciduous forest habitats (e.g. Beutelspacher 1978, 1981, Hoffman 1942). They differ from those of the lowland rainforest parts of Costa Rica by being about 20 per cent less species rich, proportionately and absolutely richer in what are traditionally thought of as extra-tropical and arid-land species and genera of moths, and much more seasonal in periodicity of abundance. For example, there are 12 species of Ceratocampinae breeding at Santa Rosa but only 10 breeding Hemileucinae; at Costa Rican lowland rainforest sites, there are usually eight to 10 Ceratocampinae and 15–20 Hemileucinae. Likewise, at rainforest sites most species are present as adults year round, while all Santa Rosa saturniid populations are dormant from January to the end of April.

Santa Rosa has a substantial fauna of carnivores that feed on saturniid and sphingid caterpillars and adults. In addition to the generally insectivorous birds, bats, insectivores and small rodents found in any mesic forest, there are squirrel cuckoos (*Piaya cayana*) that specialize on finding and eating large urticating caterpillars (e.g., *Hylesia lineata, Dirphia avia, Automeris zugana*), armadillos (*Dasypus novemcinctus*) and coatis (*Nasua narica*) that plough up the litter in search of caterpillars and pupae, white-faced capuchin monkeys (*Cebus capucinus*) that glean the forest from about four metres to the tops of the tallest crowns, and arboreal mice (e.g., *Reithrodontomys gracilis*) that glean larvae, pupae and adults at night. However, in contrast with extra-tropical moth-rich forests, there is no massive invasion of migrant insectivorous small birds during the rainy (caterpillar breeding) season. In addition to the expected fauna of spiders, scorpions, predacious bugs, ants, wasps, tettigoniid grasshoppers and crickets, there is an abundant but species-poor fauna of parasitic Hymenoptera and tachnid flies. Viral, bacterial and fungal diseases are conspicuous sources of caterpillar death (e.g., Janzen 1984a).

Some of the key quantitative features of Santa Rosa as a saturniid and sphingid habitat are, then, a five- to seven-month rainy season that is long enough for two to three generations of most species, a dry season sufficiently severe to cause most species to be dormant (saturniids and sphingids) or migrate (some sphingids) even if they feed on evergreen hosts, hundreds of broad-leaved plant species within normal flight range of an individual of any moth species, a rich carnivore array, and highly variable timing of the onset and intensity of the rainy season. The abrupt and dramatic change in weather with the onset of the rains in late April or early May serves as a major synchronization cue for moth populations, a cue somewhat analogous to an extra-tropical spring. Each moth species is accompanied by an array of confamilials as great as that to be found in half of North America north of Mexico.

Differential attraction to lights

When saturniids and sphingids are collected throughout the year at a bright light (a 15 watt fluorescent and a 15-watt ultra violet-rich black light placed one metre apart on a white background) at Santa Rosa in or over a forested habitat, each of the families has a different pattern of appearance at the light. 90 per cent of the female saturniids arrive during the first four hours of the night and the females of no saturniid species regularly arrive after midnight. Except for the saturniid species whose females call in the first few hours after dark (*Dirphia avia*, *Adeloneivaia isara*, probably *Automeris zurobara*), the males arrive almost entirely during the second half of the night. On the same nights, provided a sphingid migration is not occurring, half or more of the species of sphingids arrives before midnight and females continue to arrive throughout the night. If a migration of sphingids is occurring (as opposed to a local population high), sex ratios may be equal or even strongly biased toward females. After coming to rest at the light, neither saturniids nor sphingids are likely to leave, but sphingids are more likely to leave than are saturniids. Throughout the rainy season the saturniids as species and in aggregate display stronger peaks and troughs in density and have less lunar phobia (as measured by arrival at lights). Saturniid fluctuations in numbers at lights correlate better with the density of adults in the habitat than is the case with sphingids. If saturniids and sphingids are marked at a light and released 50–100 m distant at dawn, the saturniids are more likely to reappear at the light during the next few nights than are the sphingids, but some of the sphingids will reappear as long as two to four weeks later.

Such differences as these, potentially mere artifacts since they are components of the larger artifact of arriving at a light, suggest major and revealing differences in the biology of saturniids and sphingids. To make this suggestion, I discuss a hypothesis on why moths arrive at lights and differences in the details of saturniid and sphingid natural history that could generate different arrival patterns.

Why do moths arrive at lights?   This question is two questions. First, why does an adult moth released within one to five metres of a light often fly directly to it and come to rest nearby (Hienton 1974, Weiss *et al.* 1941, Hsiao 1972)? All the Santa Rosa saturniids and sphingids that come to light display this behaviour, though certain individuals of certain species may also ignore a light (e.g., *Pachyliodes resumens* may fly in a controlled manner up to a light and then fly away from it; a saturniid following a pheronome plume may fly right past a light, and a male saturniid going at full speed may careen so far past a light that it is carried into the dark before it can turn around and return). Despite some attempts at constructing a working hypothesis for this question (Hsiao 1972), there is neither a traditional nor avant-garde reasonable explanation of this behaviour. I have no convincing hypothesis to offer. This behaviour does not appear to be a disconnected fragment of moth biology, is generally not shown by diurnally active moths or butterflies (or caterpillars), and is exhibited by only a very small proportion of the non-lepidopteran insect species in the area of the light. Whatever the cause, this response is so useful for collectors and ecologists that moths should long ago have become one of the most studied of wild insects.

Second, why do (so many) moths arrive at the site of the light (at which point they are then directly attracted)? The thousands of moths of hundreds of species that often arrive at a light in one night at Santa Rosa certainly would not have accidentally flown that night through any one randomly placed two to five metre diameter hemispherical area of direct attraction. The current hypothesis, developed by R. R. Baker and foreshadowed by Robinson and Robinson (1950), is that a moth that needs to fly in a straight line can do this best by flying at a constant angle to a very distant landmark (e.g., moon, star, bright cloud) (Wehner 1984, Baker and Mather 1982; see also Baker and Sadovy 1978, Sotthibandhu and Baker 1979). If, however, the landmark is a bright light hung in the forest (and therefore very near), the moth flying at a constant angle will trace a spiral path to it. It is striking that the lights used at Santa Rosa are indistinguishable to my eye from a bright star at a distance of 0.5–5 km.

A simpler edition of the above hypothesis is that the moth wishing to fly in a straight line selects the landmark which is directly ahead and homes on that. In this case a much smaller subset of the moths in the habitat would arrive at the light than if a more complex angular orientation were being used.

I accept that the light is a landmark to the moth as a working paradigm. The most biologically relevant question to this essay then becomes, why should a non-migratory adult saturniid or sphingid wish to fly in a straight line when not following an odour plume or wind current? I discuss this question only for saturniids and sphingids, but I assume that to some degree the discussion applies to other moths as well.

Why do Santa Rosa saturniids arrive at lights?   This question is really a query about what determines the frequency with which saturniids fly in a straight line while using a landmark such as the light and also, just happen to fly through the hemisphere of direct attraction while doing other things. In other words, how do male saturniids search for females and how do females search for oviposition sites?

In the most direct sense male saturniids presumably find virgin female saturniids by flying upwind along a pheromone plume, just as do other moths (e.g., Kennedy *et al.* 1980, 1982, Collins and Weast 1961, Cardé and

Hargaman 1979, Tobin and Bell 1982, Baker and Kuenen 1982). But what is unknown is how insects in general, and saturniids specifically, search for pheromone plumes. For a moth with a short and fixed adult life, the worst method would be to sit and wait for the odour plume to arrive, and probably the next worst is to fly about at random. I therefore assume that male saturniids have species-specific search patterns for pheromone plumes. The searching male is faced with the following conditions. The plume lies downwind, turbulence is an inevitable consequence of wind flow through and over vegetation, competition is severe among males since there are many fewer virgin females than males on any given night (each night of the population's eclosion period adds more males but the nightly cohort of virginal females is removed by mating), and the pheromone plume is diluted with distance. The optimal search machine should fly rapidly at right angles to the general direction of the wind until a pheromone plume is encountered, and they fly upwind to the source with maximum haste. If no plume is encountered during a transit across the appropriate habitat, the moth should then drop downwind and repeat the process back across the same habitat. The distance downwind will depend on such things as the maximum distance at which a female can be perceived (considering the usual amount of turbulence and the consistency of the wind direction), the relative importance of finding the plume versus being able very quickly to move up it (the closer to the source the intersection, the quicker he can get to her), the patchiness of female-containing habitats, etc. Santa Rosa male saturniids have sustained flight airspeeds of 20–60 km per hour (the former speed is based on free-flying *Rothschildia lebeau* males released in calm air at dawn, and the latter speed is based on a free-flying male *Eacles imperialis* fortuitously flying parallel to a moving car in early dawn light). Capture-recapture records of males in traps baited with virgin females show numerous movements of two to six kilometres. I envision a given male regularly coursing over an area of several square kilometres during the second half of each night of its life (unless it finds a mate). If a bright light is placed on the horizon of that male's habitat, the moth should arrive at that light while searching, largely because it is using the light as a reference for flying a straight line at right angles to the general direction of the wind. However, it may also occasionally arrive at a light because its path just happens to intersect the tiny hemisphere of direct light influence.

Saturniid males are famous for eventually arriving at traps baited with virgin females after being released many kilometres away (e.g., Brower *et al.* 1967, Jeffords *et al.* 1980, Waldbauer and Sternburg 1982b, Rau and Rau 1929). This leads to the potentially deceptive impression that the males are 'attracted' to the females over these distances (Rau and Rau 1929, Riddiford 1974). The search-pattern hypothesis developed in the previous paragraph suggests that male saturniids might well be attracted only over quite short distances but have an effective and/or wide-ranging search pattern that eventually leads them to pass near the trap female even if released far away.

The proposed search pattern, and the moth's use of the light as a landmark, is compatible with many of the heterogeneities in arrivals of saturniids at lights at Santa Rosa. For example, the arrival time of male saturniids is synchronous with the calling times of their respective females. *Dirphia avia* begin to call just after sunset and the males arrive at the lights almost entirely within three hours after sunset. Females of the close relative *Periphoba arcaei* call shortly after midnight and the males arrive about that time. *Rothschildia lebeau* and *R. erycina* call during the two to three hours before dawn, and their males arrive at lights then. However, just as Waldbauer and Sternburg (1979) have observed with *Hyalophora cecropia* males in Illinois, the majority of Santa Rosa male saturniids that mate after midnight are also on the wing during the first couple of hours after sunset. They are not searching for females at this time (there are none calling), I favour Waldbauer's and Sternburg's (1979) hypothesis that they are moving to avoid mating with sisters, and they almost never arrive at the light at this time. I hypothesize that the occasional male of these species that arrives before 2200 hours (about three per cent of all males to arrive) is one that just happened to fly through the hemisphere of direct attraction by the light during its dispersal flight.

A second prominent heterogeneity is that except for *Rothschildia erycina* tens (*Adeloneivaia isara, Caio championi*) to hundreds (*Automeris zugana, Othorene purpurascens*) of males arrive for each female that arrives. Why are so many more male than female saturniids encountered at lights (as has also been observed elsewhere, e.g., Worth 1979, van den Berg 1973, 1974c)? First, males fly much farther than do females, and therefore any kind of point trap will intercept more per night. Second, many males will arrive at a light because they are using it as a landmark. Third, I do not expect the female saturniids to use the light for flight orientation.

Since the female pupates and mates directly below her larva's host plant, I assume that she first searches for larval food plants largely by flying a very local search pattern (e.g., by flying up host plant odour plumes even if quite faint). When less heavily egg-laden, she may fly farther but still very locally. Since saturniid females usually oviposit in the crowns of large adult perennials (the non-hemileucines and some hemileucines) or a few times per female in multi-species assemblages of large and small plants (some hemileucines), there is likely to be one or more host plants within a few metres of where mating occurred and others are likely to be within a 50–100 m radius. In such a scenario female saturniids should arrive at a light only if they happen to fly through its zone of direct influence; they should also arrive only during the first four to five hours of the evening, which is the case (in the laboratory, all 27 species of Santa Rosa saturniids observed oviposit in the first three hours after sunset). Only zero to three females of a particular species should be captured per light per night (unless there is a population high, e.g., *Hylesia lineata*, Janzen 1981, 1984a) because the local density of females is very low. Their numbers at lights may be even further reduced if they are as strongly attracted to a nearby oviposition site as are males to a nearby virgin female; such a male can sometimes fly within a metre of the light without being attracted. In effect, the light is a very local census device for female saturniids but it censuses males over a much larger area.

I have no reason to expect any of the above processes to change with age of the male, since he cannot learn where his resources are clumped locally; virgin females will appear at different microsites each night, and he should at best only encounter one per night with even the best of luck. He should be just as susceptible to being pulled into the light on his first as his last night of flight. However, as his body weight declines (e.g., Waldbauer *et al.* 1984), he may be able to fly faster (further per night) with the result of more old males appearing at the light than young ones; such a numerical result will, however, be confounded by the fact that a cohort is always largest the night of its eclosion. The process might change with age of the female if she flies further as her egg load becomes lighter. However, so few females arrive at Santa Rosa lights (average about one per night per light, summed over all 30 species, during the rainy season) that it will require many more years of data for a picture to emerge.

Nevertheless, I do expect different species of saturniids to conform differently to this process of arrival at the lights. There should be species-specific variation in distance of direct attention, use of visual landmarks (is this why *Rothschildia erycina* males almost never come to the light at Santa Rosa?), distance flown in searching, fidelity to the microhabitat in which the light happens to be placed, etc.

What factors may be responsible for the frequent strong intra-specific night-to-night variation in numbers of male saturniids to arrive at Santa Rosa lights? Migration effects can be disregarded as there is no hint of migratory movements like those of the sphingids. First, if a virgin female happens to be calling within a few tens of metres of the light, an exceptional number of males may appear at the light. For example, during the 1981 population explosion of *Copaxa moinieri*, a forest understory light attracted one to five males each night of a three week period, except for three non-consecutive nights of 21, 37 and 34 males each (Janzen 1984d). During two of those nights I had hung a virgin female *C. moinieri* in deep shadow eight metres from the light. While many of the males arrive at a virgin female calling near a light ignore that light, they later end up perched at it.

Second, there should be a decline in numbers of males at lights on the nights of heavy female eclosion, since these males will spend more time flying upwind on pheronome plumes and will be trapped by the virgin females they encounter. On nights after most of the virgin females have eclosed and mated, there should be an excess of males searching the habitat.

Third, short-term inimical bad weather will generate heterogeneity, a heterogeneity that a male saturniid can not afford to conquer by inactivity, since it has so few days to live. On the one hand the more natural landmarks are obscured (by clouds, rain, fog, etc.), the more important is the light as a landmark (hence the huge catches at lights on a heavily foggy night). On the other hand a starry sky or bright moon offers many landmarks to compete with the artificial light. Saturniids do display the phenomenon of lunar phobia, but not nearly as strongly as do sphingids (see below), If the air is very still, or the wind changes direction so frequently that pheromone plumes are chaotic in direction, there may be no advantage to straight flight and the male moths may use a different search pattern. Finally, the heterogeneity in time and space of eclosion cues will generate inter-night heterogeneity of the number of moths available to arrive at the lights; the shorter the life of the male moths, the more consequential will be this effect.

An arrival hypothesis helps to explain strong inter-site heterogeneity in numbers of moths arriving at several lights, even when they are only a few tens of metres apart. A light that is positioned near the horizon of the visual fields for a maximum number of searching males is likely to attract more males than will a light placed in other parts of the moths' visual fields. A light within the habitat in which males search for females will capture more males than will one that is visible to the moths in that habitat yet outside of it. A light placed among the crowns of potential larval hosts will catch more females than will one placed at a site that is often flown across by males. For example, one of the Santa Rosa lights is on a cliff top at the level of the crowns of nearby large *Bombacopsis quinatum* trees; this light captures more female *Caio championi* than male *C. championi*, presumably because the females fly near it when moving among the crowns of their sole species of host tree. On the other hand, a light placed in or near a migratory flyway – such as in the pass in a mountain chain (e.g., the famed Rancho Grande moth collecting site in Venezuela, Fleming 1947) – should capture migratory species of moths in enormous numbers (see below), but will not collect exceptional numbers of saturniids.

Why do Santa Rosa sphingids arrive at lights?   In general the Santa Rosa sphingids should arrive at lights for the same behavioural reasons as do saturniids. However, sphingids differ from saturniids in several aspects of their natural history that should cause their arrival patterns to be quantitatively different. The relevant differences are that sphingids feed extensively at spatially particulate resources that are relatively fixed in location, live for weeks to months as adults, lay few eggs per night, probably oviposit on many host individuals and repeatedly visit many of them, have less synchronous eclosion during the rainy season, migrate, and are 'smarter' than are saturniids.

When the rains begin at the end of the long dry season in Santa Rosa's dry forests, a large number of sphingid individuals and species appear at the lights; one light may nightly attract several hundred individuals including 10–20 species. Within a few weeks, the numbers for each species declines to zero or to the low but fluctuating numbers that arrive at the lights throughout the remainder of the rainy season. There are two causes for the decline in numbers, only one of which also affects saturniids. Some of the species have laid their eggs and died, and the species is represented in the habitat by caterpillars (the saturniid life-style, albeit somewhat attenuated). However, from observations of caterpillar density, pupal dormancy, and adults at flowers, it is clear that many of the species that cease to appear at the lights are still present as adults. For example, at one of the regular light stations there is a patch of *Stachytarpheta frantzii* (a verbenaceous heavily-visited shrubby nectar source for sphingids at Santa Rosa). It is 20–50 m behind the light and from it the light is clearly visible. At a time when *Erinnyis, Xylophanes, Enyo, Eumorpha, Pachylioides* and *Perigonia* have fallen to zero or very low density at this light, adults of both sexes of these species can be collected at the pre-dawn darkness while they drink nectar in the *S. frantzii* patch. On the other hand, these species and others whose nectar hosts are unknown to me continue to appear as very low numbers of newly eclosed individuals throughout the rainy season.

I hypothesize that for many of the Santa Rosa species of sphingids, individuals search widely at all hours of the night for the first few nights after eclosion, using lights for orientation but quickly learning where to find resources. Once they have established flight paths (using contour, odours, wind, ambient light and memory as cues), specific light landmarks are no longer used. It is striking that females become much scarcer than males at the lights very shortly after a species first appears seasonally; it may be that the males do search for females somewhat as do saturniid males. However, I suspect that they also use other search methods such as hill-topping familiar with butterflies and flies, repeated visits to areas where females are active (as in bees), patrolling mating territories (as in dragonflies), etc. When using a variety of chemical, memory and non-light landmarks to arrive at resources, both sexes of sphingids should become essentially immune to the distant attractiveness of an artificial light. As suggested by the common event of seeing a sphingid simply fly by a bright light at night with hardly any deviation, such experienced moths may even be immune to the close attractiveness of an artificial light. The above hypothesis is consistent with the observations that sphingids at Santa Rosa lights are often in fresh condition while conspecifics taken at flowers can be very worn as well as fresh. However, even the most experienced local sphingid may periodically become susceptible to an artificial light if it periodically undertakes straight-line exploratory flights to replenish fading resources or if a dense fog obliterates essentially all of its usual orientation cues.

The above model should be least applicable to species of sphingids that have relatively short adult life spans (e.g., some *Manduca*) and those that do not rely so heavily on nectar (e.g., perhaps *Amplypterus* and *Protambulyx*). From a practical viewpoint, such a model suggests that the most effective way to capture all the species of attractable sphingids in a habitat is to move the light from night to night, while for male saturniids there may be some best place to leave the light night after night.

At Santa Rosa, a number of crepuscular, matinal, and even fully nocturnal sphingids rarely or never appear at a light (e.g., six species of *Enyo, Aleuron, Eupyrrhoglossum* and *Pachygonia*). While the adults of these species are generally viewed as rare, the caterpillars can be annually or seasonally abundant. For example, I have found caterpillars of *Pachygonia drucei* and *Aleuron carinata* on *Doliocarpus dentatus* vines growing only 40 m from a fixed light site at Santa Rosa; the females of these two species had to have been staring straight at the light as they oviposited yet the adults of these two species have never been found at any Santa Rosa light during about six light-years of maintaining the light. Over 2000 males and only one female of *Cautethia yucatana* have been recorded at Santa Rosa lights in the same period. Such 'invisible' species are usually small and somewhat crepuscular or matinal; this may give them the ability to ignore the light and mean that they use dimly visible habitat contour as a primary means of orientation. Nevertheless, other small crepuscular sphingids, such as *Perigonia lusca* and *Enyo ocypete*, commonly arrive at the Santa Rosa lights during the night.

Sphingids conspicuously display lunar phobia as measured by numbers taken in light traps through the lunar cycle (Bowden and Church 1973, Robertson 1977, Harling 1968). Santa Rosa sphingids are not exceptions. However, I suspect that the effect is more due to the moon obliterating the attraction or arrival effects of the artificial light than through cessation of sphingid activity. Certainly some species of Santa Rosa sphingids can be observed to forage at flowers under a full moon (e.g., those mentioned above visiting *Stachytarpheta frantzii*). If it is eventually shown that sphingids curtail flight activity during lunar illumination, they will then be quite different from the saturniids at Santa Rosa. While there is a noticeable decline in numbers of saturniids arriving at lights during lunar illumination, no such decline appears in catches of males at traps baited with calling females, even if she is calling with a full moon nearly overhead. Likewise, a female saturniid with only a few days to live could hardly cease her oviposition activities to wait days for a substantial reduction in lunar illumination; the female sphingid, however, does have this option.

There is mounting evidence that Costa Rican sphingids regularly migrate tens of kilometres (W. Haber, personal communication); there are no suggestions of migratory behaviour by saturniids, though waif male saturniids do occasionally appear far from their birthplace (seven individuals of four species in six light-years at Santa Rosa). It is commonplace for large numbers of sphingid individuals of a few species to be taken at a very exposed light far from anything that approximates breeding habitat for these species. For example, on 4 December 1983, at a 1800 m elevation pass in the mountains between the Pacific coastal lowlands of Costa Rica and the Atlantic rainforested coastal lowlands, a light such as the Santa Rosa lights, placed on a prominent grassy knoll, attracted a minimum of 403 males and 741 females of 12 sphingid species. All 12 were species that breed at Santa Rosa and not at the elevation of the light, and all were species that disappear from the Santa Rosa lights during the dry season but occur throughout the year in the Atlantic rainforests of Costa Rica. The same light also attracted ten males and one female of four species that breed in the wet forests at the collecting site. It seems reasonable to hypothesize that these lowland sphingids arrived at the light in the pass not because they just happened to fly haphazardly through the zone of direct attraction, but rather because when migrating, they use a bright star as an orientation landmark or as a direct beacon; the artificial light was simply a star mimic, and one that would have been of no interest to these individuals in the sky at Santa Rosa or other Pacific lowland site. In the 1800 m pass, my light was probably an exceptional star mimic since there were heavy clouds and occasional drizzle. This aspect of migratory arrival at lights is simply missing from saturniid biology, but can be an important aspect of sphingid arrival at Santa Rosa lights both when migrants are incoming and initiating a journey.

Sphingid generations at Santa Rosa are initially quite asynchronous due to variable responses to cues to break pupal dormancy. They become even more asynchronous as the rainy season progresses due to long-lived ovipositing adults and variable pupal durations. While there should be a few newly eclosed naive adults (and exploring experienced adults) available to arrive at lights on any rainy season night, the number of adults arriving should be a very poor estimator of the total numbers present. When migrants arrive (or leave), they may arrive at the lights in numbers proportional to their true numbers, but their rapid subsequent decline in numbers at the light says little or nothing about their actual density in the habitat. This suggests that in contrast with saturniids, census of sphingids at lights (e.g., Wolda 1980, Owen 1969) is only partly understandable without detailed corroborative data from other sources such as larval density. Light traps are very convenient, but like sweep samples, are highly suspect census devices. Certainly the presence of male or female sphingids, even if regular in occurrence, cannot be used as firm proof that there is a breeding population in the vicinity of the light. On the other hand, when female saturniids occur at a light there is very likely to be a breeding population in the immediate vicinity while male saturniids are less good indicators unless they occur in large numbers on a regular basis.

In closing this section I wish to leave the reader with the caricature that saturniid males, in their single-minded pursuit of female pheronome plumes, are fairly stupid flying machines that can be behaviourally derailed by a light. They have neither the time for extensive learning of the habitat, orientation needs that change in space and seasonal time, nor resources in a fixed pattern that can be learned. Sphingids, on the other hand, must possess a fairly complex learning capacity such that each individual can finely tune itself to its local nightly harvest of resources. While the adult is still young it is susceptible to false landmarks such as an artificial light, but with advancing age and experience becomes relatively immune as it settles into a routine of resource harvest. However, even an experienced sphingid may again become susceptible to capture at light when important traditional cues are obliterated such as when there is a dense fog or heavy drizzle, which should generate both the blackest night and the most odour-free atmosphere. Likewise, migration and exploration off established foraging routes may render the experienced sphingid again dependent on lights. However, both drizzle and long migration flights may cause sustained wing wear, rendering age evaluations somewhat problematical (R. Peigler, personal communication).

Why are adult saturniids so polymorphic?

Figs. 1–4 will acquaint the reader with two of the three ways that adult Santa Rosa saturniids are conspicuously more polymorphic than are adult sphingids: between sexes, among species, within a sex. First, the males can be easily distinguished from their mates by colour, size and/or wing shape (e.g., compare Fig. 1.1 with 1.2–1.3, 1.4 with 1.5–1.6, 2.18 with 2.19, 2.20 with 2.21). The sexes can be distinguished in flight, if illuminated, while sitting at the light among other moths, and while at rest in foliage. Sphingids, on the other hand, usually require close scrutiny to distinguish the sexes even when spread and well illuminated; *Amplypterus ypsilon* and *Protambulyx strigilis* are perhaps the most easily sexed of the sphingids in Figs. 3–4, and only two other Santa Rosa sphingids are slightly more dimorphic in wing size (*Pseudosphinx tetrio* and *Madoryx oiclus*, both with very heavy-bodied and broader-winged females). Four species of Santa Rosa sphingids can be sexed by small differences in the variegated bark-like patterns on their wings. Sphingid sexes can be distinguished with practice by noting fine differences in the curvature of wing margins, wing maculation, body thickness, etc. However, as a group, the Santa Rosa sphingids are in general aspect much more similar between the sexes than are Santa Rosa saturniids. These differences are not a unique local phenomenon, as saturniid sexual dimorphism is prominent in other parts of the world (e.g., Tams 1924, Peigler 1976a, 1983, Ferguson 1972) while the most dimorphic extra-tropical sphingid appears to be the North American poplar sphinx, which does not feed as an adult.

Second, saturniids vary strongly among the species in wing shape, while sphingids have quite similar shapes among the species. It is easy to draw a silhouette that will almost exactly cover each sphingid in Figs. 3–4 just by shrinking or expanding; no such universal shape can be drawn for the saturniids in Figs. 1–2. This is true whether the silhouette is made for one sex or for all individuals. Adding the remainder of the Santa Rosa saturniid and sphingid species to Figs. 1–4 would not invalidate the generalization.

The third form of polymorphism is visible in Figs. 1–2 only in *Adeloneivaia isara*, *Copaxa moinieri*, *Rothschildia lebeau*, and *Hylesia lineata*. However, 17 of the 30 saturniids that breed in Santa Rosa have two to four colour morphs within the adults of one or both sexes. Among adult Santa Rosa sphingids there are none. In the world fauna of saturniids, intra-sex colour polymorphisms are commonplace (e.g., Peigler 1976a), while the poplar sphinx mentioned above is the only sphingid example known to me. There are, however, examples of sphingids that vary geographically in colour, such as the (apparently) non-migratory *Amplyterus gannascus* at Santa Rosa which are lighter in colour (and smaller) than their Costa Rican rainforest counterparts (W. Haber, personal communication).

There is something quite different about the biology of wing function of saturniids and that of sphingids. I hypothesize that the basic difference is due to saturniids not feeding as adults, with various degrees of directness in the causality. The effect of this difference should be more pronounced in a tropical dry or strongly seasonal habitat such as Santa Rosa than in lowland tropical rainforests such as those found in other parts of Costa Rica. Whether the trait of non-feeding as an adult should be viewed as a cause or consequence of the saturniid life style will be discussed later.

Sexual dimorphism. A male saturniid is a flying machine specialized primarily for one activity, finding females – fast. And he does it while carrying only the weight of the machine and the fuel and water needed for five to 10 days survival. His female is a flying machine specialized primarily for a very different activity – locating host plants and laying eggs. She does it carrying not only the weight of the flying machine and its fuel, but also an egg load weighing more than half her initial body weight and diminishing rapidly as her potential fitness declines through oviposition and wing wear. A male saturniid wins by getting to females fast over long distances; a few seconds of flight time can make the difference between expressing zero or one fifth of the male's potential fitness. There is no second place prize money. A female saturniid wins by finding a few large host plants and getting rid of her eggs quickly, but she can afford more short term delay, at least within a night. Yes, both sexes avoid predators and desiccation, but each sex does this in different, even if overlapping, microhabitats. Such different functions should select for quite different flying machines, and appear to have done so.

Male sphingids also search for females. However, they also regularly hover in front of flowers to harvest fuel and water with their long proboscises. Female sphingids also search for oviposition sites. However, like the males, they nightly hover in front of flowers to drink. In short, male and female sphingids have a major kind of activity in common. If they belong to a migratory species, they have even a second major kind of activity in common. Such communality of flight activity should be a major barrier to the evolution of quite different morphological phenotypes, even if other aspects of the life history are selecting for them.

What aspects of saturniid biology may lead to more exaggeration of the male/female differences then is found in sphingids (remaining within the confines of an intra-specific comparison)? The male saturniid has its one and only harvestable resource available for only that (short) time when females of its species are calling with pheromones; its flight behaviour and aerial predator avoidance should be evolutionarily engineered to match primarily the challenges that occur during that one period (it is unknown how much flight occurs during the post-sunset dispersal flight, but I suspect it to be only a few minutes). Female saturniids also have a narrow activity period, but it is at a different time of night than the males fly (except for those few species that both mate and oviposit during the first few hours of the night). A pair of sphingids, however, probably has flower resources available throughout the night and therefore may be experiencing the same challenges from predators and weather. If the species migrates, both sexes probably migrate and are shaped by the same selective pressures for migration ability.

Assuming that a male saturniid is competitively functional for only five nights, it can mate only a maximum of five times and its potential fitness must steadily decline with age (assuming that it stays in copula all night if a mate is found, as is true for at least 66 per cent of the Santa Rosa saturniids). Fast accurate flight irrespective of obstruction is paramount. Loss of 20 per cent of a mate's fitness may occur by using a few seconds to carefully negotiate a vine tangle around a female rather than by blasting through it irrespective of wing damage, or by hesitating to examine a potential predator near the calling female. For the saturniid female, however, wing-tattering speed and oblivion to obstructions may be less important than is accuracy of finding a few large hosts each night. Whether she finds a host at 1900 or 1910 hours may not be very critical. Her ability to flutter (helicopter) through the foliage while bearing several grams of eggs is paramount. She even hangs on the foliage with (sometimes) lightly beating wings while ovipositing; sphingid females oviposit in hovering flight that is just slightly supported by extended legs in contact with the foliage. If a saturniid's aerial caution or clumsiness slows her oviposition rate, it need not lower her potential fitness if she is not taken by a predator before the next oviposition bout and/or if she can compensate by laying more eggs in the next tree crown.

The male sphingid, however, uses its wings for weeks to months for resource harvesting as well as mate location. Care of the wings and caution in flying can increase potential fitness through lengthened life span and greater flight competence later in that life span. The female sphingid is subject to the same suite of selective pressures, and even uses her wings as does the male when she is hovering for oviposition and evaluation of oviposition sites.

Since saturniids have a fixed and very short period in which to express their potential fitness, I expect selection to result in bizarre solutions to how to do it fast. Such solutions are less likely to be evolutionarily invented by sphingids with their longer time to act and therefore more ways to integrate compensatory and antagonistic activities. For example, *Hylesia lineata* (Fig. 2.7–2.10) has carried its speed of oviposition to the extreme of putting all of its eggs in one basket (a single ball of 100–450 eggs covered with an elaborate felt pad constructed of interlocking abdominal hairs, Janzen 1984a). Its potential fitness goes from high and nearly constant (the adult female is well protected from vertebrate predators by urticating hairs) to zero in one act; the flying machine has only to function under the stress of a full load, and never has to function at a light body weight of a male. A second example is that a *Syssphinx molina* female seems to have a probability of near unity of getting a male the night she ecloses and a host tree the following night; she often begins to lay sterile eggs on the night of eclosion if not quite literally plugged by a male, and she lays as many as two-thirds of her (sterile or fertile) 200–400 eggs the following night even if confined to a plastic bag with no host plant odours. Such oviposition behaviour strongly selects for, or could only evolve in the presence of, highly reliable mating and a female phenotype associated with rapid location of a few host plants (such as the huge crowns of *Pithecellobium saman*, the primary *S. molina* hosts at Santa Rosa). Such behaviour is also only compatible with the traits of a small subset of the Santa Rosa plants that might be physiologically suitable pablum for *S. molina* caterpillars (assuming them to be monophagous or narrowly oligophagous). The male *S. molina* is, on the other hand, confronted with the task of coursing widely over the relatively dry kinds of open and low forest where *S. molina* is common in the Neotropics. *S. molina* seems to require little more than open pastureland dotted with huge adult *P. saman* to stay in the game in the face of human habitat destruction.

Perhaps the most extreme dichotomy of selective regimes acting on conspecific male and female saturniids is absent from Santa Rosa – that of diurnal males in pursuit of calling (stationary) females and nocturnal ovipositing (flying) females. Such pairs are well known in extra-tropical regions. Their males have colours and wing shapes quite distinct from those of their females; the phenomenon is apparently generated by inter-specific competition among congeners for a time of day (or night) free of allospecific males (e.g., Toliver *et al.* 1979, Brown 1972, Peigler 1976a, 1981, Ferguson 1972). While diurnal saturniids are abundant extra-tropically, all but one of the few Neotropical ones are in high and cold and/or dry habitats (R. Peigler, C. Lemaire, personal communication). The exceptional deep tropical diurnal saturniid is *Automeris phrynon*, whose males arrive like high-speed bright yellow and brown butterflies in full morning daylight to the calling females in Costa Rican rainforest (Marquis 1984). The females fly to oviposit at night, come to lights occasionally (the males never do), and weigh four to five times as much as the males at the time of eclosion. *A. phrynon* is the only diurnal *Automeris* and the most sexually dimorphic. Reminiscent of the postulated cause of the diurnality (and hence strong sexual polymorphism) of the saturniid *Callosamia* in the eastern US, *A. phrynon* co-occurs with at least 10 species of *Automeris* in Costa Rican rainforest. Competition for pheromonally clean airspace must be severe, especially since there is a suggestion that all *Automeris* males are at least physiologically capable of reacting to each other's allospecific females' pheromones (Priesner 1968).

In fact, perhaps the most puzzling aspect of saturniids is that the males and females resemble each other at all. Intra-specific phylogenetic inertia is the likely dominant cause, but that jargon phrase for being stranded on the top of a steep-sided adaptive peak does not disclose the actual processes. It is likewise not a very satisfying reply when, even within the wild population of a Santa Rosa saturniid, there can be functional males weighing as little as 10 per cent of the weight of a newly eclosed conspecific female. For example, the ordinary-sized *Othorene purpurascens* male in Fig. 1.5 weighed 1.02 g while his wild-caught male congener in Fig. 1.6 weighed 0.23 g but was functional if I may infer from controlled matings in other Santa Rosa species such as *Rothschildia lebeau*. The same applies to the contrasting *R. lebeau* males in Figs. 1.10 and 1.11. It might also be argued that the male saturniid rests in the same ecologically similar diurnal habitat as does the female (but see below under intra-sex polymorphism) and therefore if they both start on the same cryptic adaptive peak, they are likely to remain there. Likewise at night, while he flies at different speeds and with a different goal than she does, they both fly through the same general habitat at least part of the time.

Yet why does he not live longer than she does (longevity trials at Santa Rosa give no hint of this) by accumulating as much resource while a caterpillar as she does? He would, however, then be a slower (heavier) flier and perhaps be more awkward. Additionally, since female saturniids are often very pulsed in their seasonal availability, greater male longevity might be of less value than it would be to a moth with a more even temporal distribution of receptive females. An answer to the question of why saturniids are not more dissimilar between the sexes will require more knowledge of their biology than is at hand.

Interspecific variation.   No Santa Rosa saturniid species feeds as an adult or migrates; the freedom from these constraints allows species, as it does sexes of one species, to go its own evolutionary way according to differences in flight demands of the habitats occupied, oviposition host spacings and physical structures, predator avoidance, diurnal roosting sites, etc. This may even be at the root of why saturniids are sufficiently different among species that there has been considerable argument over whether they should be split into several families and why saturniids have so many distinctive subfamilies (as compared with sphingids). A pair of saturniid species of recent mutual derivation may diverge strongly if in quite different habitats while a pair of sphingids with the same evolutionary proximity in time and in equally dissimilar habitats may remain morphologically much more similar than will the saturniids for two reasons. First, the sphingid species will have hovering flight and (perhaps) migratory flight in common. Second, with their long adult life spans and ability to gather food and water as adults, they can have more kinds of physiological, ecological and behavioural solutions to dissimilar habitat challenges, instead of expressing solutions in readily visible wing traits. In short, a set of 30 species of similar-appearing sphingids may have as divergent biologies as do 30 species of quite different-appearing saturniids in the same habitat. However, it is not clear that one can argue that a major constraint such as a fixed wing shape in an aerial organism can result in fewer solution options when the remainder of the life cycle has many other facets that may be stretched in compensation. For example, sphingids as a group can make use of many more species, life forms, specific ages, and abundances of oviposition sites than can adult saturniids, if for no other reason than that they have the adult time, brains and flight agility to search them out.

It is easy to conclude that the wing shape so characteristic of adult sphingids is somehow one of the 'right' ones for fast and accurate hovering flight (and in this, conspicuously convergent on that of hummingbirds, Casey 1976). However, I cannot be firmly specific about the function of the various interspecifically different wing shapes of the Santa Rosa saturniids. A few guesses may be illuminating, however. Of the five arsenurine saturniids at Santa Rosa, the males of three of them fly unharried, and when escaping, as does the male of *Titaea tamerlan* (Fig. 2.19) – with a fast and flapping wing beat, erratic trajectory when threatened, and high speed. *Arsenura armida* males remain immobile and display their yellow body ornaments when attacked, have the most rounded and tailless wings, and fly straight with a hemileucine-like very fast wing beat. The fifth arsenurine, *Copiopteryx semiramis* (Fig. 2.11), flies slowly to fast in a nearly straight trajectory with a moderately rapid wing beat, and the long tails stream out behind with the tip of each tracing a five to 10 cm diameter circle in a plane at right angles to the trajectory of the moth. I suspect that the tails render this moth, the smallest (lightest) of the arsenurine saturniids at Santa Rosa, the largest saturniid in the Park in the sonar imagery of a bat.

The ceratocampine saturniid males (Figs. 1.5, 1.6, 1.8, 2.4–2.6, 2.13, 2.14, 2.15, 2.17) are the fastest-flying saturniids in the Park. I cannot distinguish individual wing beats in flight; ceratocampine males arrive at a light at about the speed of a thrown rock, and as mentioned earlier, a male *Eacles imperialis* was clocked with a speedometer at 60 km/hr. They have the longest and narrowest (most sphingid-like) wings, are disproportionately species-rich in dry and open sites like Santa Rosa, have arid-land plants primarily as larval hosts (e.g., Table 3), and are easily caricatured as specialists at flying long distances in clear airspace (as mentioned earlier for the ceratocampine *Syssphinx molina*).

Hemileucine saturniids (Figs. 1.12, 2.7–2.10, 2.20–2.21) tend toward more rounded wings, fly with a very buzzing and controlled flight (though erratic trajectory if fleeing), moderate forward speed, and extreme agility in and around dense foliage at high speed. I cannot help but note that practically all the increase in saturniid species richness in moving from Santa Rosa's dry forests to the wetter lowlands of Costa Rica is due to hemileucines and/or *Copaxa* spp. (e.g., Fig. 1.1–1.3), which very much resemble a hemileucine when in flight. However, this observation is confounded by the observation that hemileucine caterpillars, being urticating, are the best-protected against vertebrate predators and are the most polyphagous of the saturniid caterpillars. To proceed further and more authoritatively in these directions will require considerably more natural history information on neotropical moths than we have at present.

Intra-sex polymorphisms.   While the Santa Rosa adult sphingids display no within-sex polymorphism, over half of the Santa Rosa saturniids do so. The saturniid polymorphism is of two types, with compatible and overlapping causes. First, there is a conspicuous seasonal polymorphism, whereby light-coloured morphs predominate during dry spells during the rainy season and in the dry weather around the beginning of the rainy season. *Adeloneivaia isara*, *Othorene verana* and *O. purpurascens*, and *Rothschildia lebeau* display the trait most clearly. Greater than 95 per cent of any large sample of newly eclosed *R. lebeau* taken at lights or with virgin female-baited traps during the week before the rains start to a week after (late April to late May) range from nearly orange to a bright rusty red in background colour (Fig. 1.9). During a month of rainy weather, better than 80 per cent range from dark chocolate brown to dark rusty brown

(Fig. 1.10). Both sexes display the changes in about equal proportion, but the females achieve the lightest colours and the males the blackest. *Adeloneivaia isara* displays the same seasonal change in the proportions of the colour morphs in Fig. 2.1–2.6. I have postulated (Janzen 1984c) that these highly edible moths are basically mimics of hanging dead leaves during daylight hours and have been selected to resemble a light-coloured dry dead leaf during dry weather and a dark wet mouldy leaf during rainy weather. The colour differences are cued or caused by the temperatures of the pupal environment. It is tempting to suggest that at least one reason why Santa Rosa sphingid do not have this kind of seasonal polymorphism is that a sphingid is designed to live for enough weeks that its colours will have to serve in long periods of both dry and wet weather.

Second, there is a type of polymorphism whereby the males have two to four different but variously intergrading colour morphs, and the females no more than two. Here there is no apparent relationship of season to preponderance of any one colour, though all colour morphs for a particular species are not equally abundant. *Syssphinx quadrilineata, Automeris zugana, Hylesia lineata* (Fig. 2.8–2.10), *Copaxa moinieri* (Fig. 1.2–1.3), *Caio championi* and *Titaea tamerlan* all display this kind of aseasonal polymorphism. The seasonal polymorphisms can be added back into the system at this point, since all of their morphs are present in any large sample of adults.

I suspect that the primary cause of the aseasonal saturniid polymorphism at Santa Rosa is the large number of adults that occur at periodic and aperiodic intervals, due to seasonal cueing of adult eclosion, synchronized timing of larval and pupal duration of subsequent generations within the season, and occasional population highs. Such pulses of high density of edible adults quite probably result in rapid formation of search images by individual vertebrate predators for whatever morph they first encounter in abundance, resulting in selective favouring of the other morph. The peaks can be enormous. During a population high of *Hylesia lineata* as many as several hundred males came to a single light in one night (Janzen 1984a); in a different year, 174 male *Automeris zugana* arrived at one light one night. On 23 May 1982, 19 female *Caio championi* arrived at a single light in response to a uniformly perceived start of the rainy season. Sphingids at Santa Rosa are more uniform in their abundance than are saturniids, or at least less commonly reach such spectacular peaks in density. When there has been an exceptional density of sphingids (e.g., *Aellopos titan* defoliating *Randia*, Janzen 1984b), the adults leave the habitat immediately after eclosion. However, there could well be other aspects of sphingid biology that nullify any selection that there might be for aseasonal polymorphism in sphingids.

Habitat gradients.   Several changes pertinent to the biology of Costa Rican saturniid polymorphisms are encountered when moving from the dry seasonal forests of Santa Rosa to the more uniformly wet low elevation rainforests of Costa Rica. First, the saturniid species in common between the two sites (94 per cent of the Santa Rosa saturniids) are invariably monomorphic at the rainforest sites and the morph is as dark or darker than is the Santa Rosa darkest morph. This generalization applies to all the different patterns of adult polymorphisms mentioned above and to all the moths mentioned except *Adeloneivaia isara*, which in Costa Rica occurs only in dry forests. It is striking that the other three species of Costa Rican *Adeloneivaia* (*A. jason*, *A. boisduvalii*, *A. subangulata*) are all monomorphic and are all rainforest species (in South America, where these species occur in both wet and dry sites, there are dry season light-coloured morphs, C. Lemaire, personal communication). At least part of the answer to why Santa Rosa saturniids are seasonally polymorphic rather than simply generally of a lighter colour than their rainforest relatives is that the dry forest is in fact seasonally as dark as is the rainforest and the dry forest also contains strips and islands of evergreen forest.

Second, the drier the site, the more pulsed will be the density of saturniid adults because the more accurately and thoroughly can be perceived the weather cues. A given annual number of adults at a dry site will present better conditions for selection for colour polymorphisms than will the same number of eclosions spread throughout the year at a rainforest site. The same effect is generated by the more frequent saturniid population highs at dry sites than at rainforest sites. The very low density between successive population highs should not select against extant polymorphisms (assuming all to be equally cryptic), but the conditions during the peak are excellent for selection for adult polymorphisms in non-migratory species.

Wings have other uses.   While my emphasis has been on wings as flight devices and the major cryptic structure when sessile, there are other selective pressures on wings that may lead to differences between saturniids and sphingids. First, sphingids are singularly unimaginative in their initial dash for freedom when approached or fumbled by a vertebrate predator. Santa Rosa diurnal temperatures are generally warm enough (27–32 C) for the moth to attempt to fly away with rapid wing beats, becoming more rapid as the flight muscles warm up. In contrast, Santa Rosa saturniids are highly variable in diurnal escape behaviour and many of the ways relate to wing shape and colour. Male *Rothschildia lebeau*, *Copaxa moinieri*, *Caio championi* and *Titaea tamerlan* launch into instant fast and erratic flight, achieving this with relatively few beats of their large wings. Fleeing males then come to an abrupt halt on contact with vegetation, once again achieving the hanging dead leaf pose, complete with a faint and temporary side-to-side oscillation like that of a breeze-disturbed leaf. The females of these species, however, respond to a touch by locking their wings in a nearly spread position and letting go of the substrate. The appearance and dynamics of the gliding and falling moth matches exactly that of a large leaf falling generally downward while side-slipping such as to trace out a zig-zag trajectory. Landing on the litter with the upper surface of the wings upward, or hanging up as she passes through a tangle of vines, the moth is an excellent behavioural mimic of a falling leaf (whose colour pattern it also possesses). Both sexes of *Eacles imperialis* also fall this way,

Fig. 1. Representative Saturniidae breeding in Santa Rosa National Park, Guanacaste Province, Costa Rica. All specimens were wild-caught. Rule is 4 cm long. 1. *Copaxa moinieri*, female. 2. *C. moinieri*, male. 3. *C. moinieri*, male. 4. *Othorene purpurascens*, female. 5. *O. purpurascens*, male. 6. *O. purpurascens*, male. 7. *Eacles imperialis*, female. 8. *E. imperialis*, male. 9. *Rothschildia lebeau*, female. 10. *R. lebeau*, male. 11. *R. lebeau*, male. 12. *Dirphia avia*, male.

Fig. 2. Representative Saturniidae breeding in Santa Rosa National Park, Guanacaste Province, Costa Rica. All specimens were wild-caught. Rule is 4 cm long. 1. *Adeloneivaia isara*, female. 2. *A. isara*, female. 3. *A. isara*, female. 4. *A. isara*, male. 5. *A. isara*, male. 6. *A. isara*, male. 7. *Hylesia lineata*, female. 8. *H. lineata*, male. 9. *H. lineata*, male. 10. *H. lineata*, male. 11. *Copiopteryx semiramis*, male. 12. *Syssphinx mexicana*, female. 13. *S. mexicana*, male. 14. *S. mexicana*, male. 14. *Schausiella santarosensis*, male. 16. *Ptiloscola dargei*, female. 17. *P. dargei*, male. 18. *Titaea tamerlan*, female. 19. *T. tamerlan*, male. 20. *Automeris rubrescens*, female. 21. *A. rubrescens*, male.

Fig. 3. Representative Sphingidae breeding in Santa Rosa National Park, Guanacaste Province, Costa Rica. All specimens were wild-caught. Rule is 4 cm long. 1. *Manduca lefeburei*, female. 2. *M. lefeburei*, male. 3. *Xylophanes pluto*, female. 4. *X. pluto*, male. 5. *Aellopos titan*, female. 6. *A. titan*, male. 7. *Erinnyis obscura*, female. 8. *E. obscura*, male. 9. *Amplypterus ypsilon*, female. 10. *A. ypsilon*, male. 11. *Manduca corallina*, female. 12. *M. corallina*, male. 13. *Xylophanes ceratomioides*, female. 14. *X. ceratomioides*, male. 15. *Eupyrrhoglossum sagra*, female. 16. *E. sagra*, male. 17. *Enyo ocypete*, female. 18. *E. ocypete*, male. 19. *Callionima falcifera*, female. 20. *C. falcifera*, male. 21. *Manduca sexta*, male.

Fig. 4. Representative Sphingidae breeding in Santa Rosa National Park, Guanacaste Province, Costa Rica. All specimens were wild-caught. Rule is 4 cm long. 1. *Aleuron iphis*, male. 2. *Xylophanes tersa*, female. 3. *X. tersa*, male. 4. *Agrius cingulatus*, female. 5. *A. cingulatus*, male. 6. *Cautethia yucatana*, male. 7. *Cautethia spuria*, female. 8. *C. spuria*, male. 9. *Nyceryx coffeae*, female. 10. *N. coffeae*, male. 11. *Perigonia lusca*, female. 12. *P. lusca*, male. 13. *Protambulyx strigilis*, female. 14. *P. strigilis*, male. 15. *Pachylia ficus*, female. 16. *P. ficus*, male. 17. *Cocytius lucifer*, female. 18. *C. lucifer*, male. 19. *Celerio lineata*, female. 20. *Xylophanes porcus*, female. 21. *X. porcus*, male. 22. *Aleuron chloroptera*, male.

Fig. 1

Fig. 2

Fig. 3

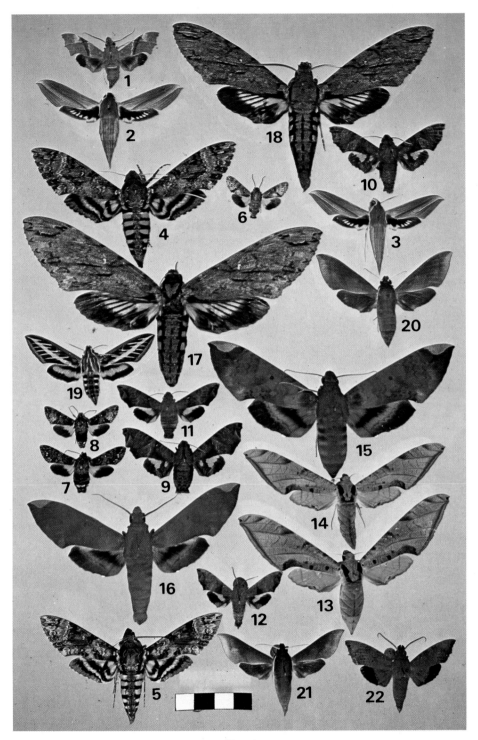

Fig. 4

but after a few minutes of invisibly warming up its flight muscles, the male launches into extremely fast flight up through the general forest canopy. When the males of *Citheronia* become motionless (see below) they often let go of the substrate and fall with no attempted flight; however, the stereotyped posture, the heavy body attached to the four tightly appressed wings (erect, over the back), creates a device that spins in the air and looks exactly like a large falling samara. Selection for wings and body weights that function in escapes such as these can be partly responsible for saturniid sexual dimorphisms, especially since the female has to weigh much more than does the male because all her egg resources have to be with her from the beginning.

Rather than flee from vertebrate predators, at least 50 per cent of the Santa Rosa saturniids raise the wings above the body and display a ringed (orange, yellow, red, black) abdomen and/or large eye mimics on the hind wings when molested (and see Blest 1957a, 1957b, 1960, Gardiner 1967, for description and ethological analysis of this behaviour). Except for two species of *Automeris* and one *Hylesia*, there is a striking *lack* of colour and aspect polymorphism within each of these aposematic/mimetic species. Why *Automeris* (and *Hylesia lineata*, which looks like a little *Automeris*) should differ is not evident, unless perhaps it is more edible than the others.

There is still the puzzle of why female saturniids are generally less polymorphic than are the males, especially in intra-sexual aseasonal polymorphism. It could be caused by the males being subject to more kinds of predators than are the females; some predators should favour a different pair of morphs than would others, through the particular way they form search images. Additionally, females may well roost in a more restricted subset of the habitat sub-sites than do the males; certainly all females spend their first day (the most important one) in the shadiest part of the habitat only a few tens of centimetres above the ground and often in copula. Females may also roost in the vicinity of the crowns of their ovipositional host plants, while males are likely to roost in a greater variety of sites since in their search for calling females they will have to cross virtually all habitat types and move through all heights of vegetation.

Why do saturniid and sphingid caterpillars eat different plants?

Saturniid and sphingid caterpillars are the big ones at Santa Rosa just as they are in other parts of the world. A last instar female *Eacles imperialis* caterpillar weighs 25–30 g, as does a last instar *Eumorpha anchemola* or *Neococytius cluentis*. Medium-sized saturniids and sphingids have caterpillars that are as heavy before they pupate as are those of the largest noctuids, notodontids, megalopygids, etc. Saturniid and sphingid caterpillars have the same general goal – eat leaves in such a manner as to grow rapidly large enough to pupate, without being found by a carnivore. One might therefore expect the caterpillars of each family collectively to consume about the same subset of the vegetation, the one that is best for this goal. However, for the most part each group does not consume the same plant species, combinations of plant species, or life forms (Tables 3–4). This difference occurs with no hint of character displacement over larval food plants, either as evidenced with outcomes or as indicated by the existence of inter-specific interfaces appropriate for its evolution (though there are many indirect and inconspicuous ways that saturniid and sphingid caterpillars can influence each other, such as by sharing parasitoids). The larval food plant patterns suggest to me that saturniid and sphingid caterpillars have different goals and that their different adult biologies may dictate different optima for their caterpillars (and vice versa).

I have already briefly caricatured the caterpillars of Santa Rosa saturniids and sphingids in the introduction and have mentioned them in the previous two sections. Saturniid caterpillars are slower-growing and less cryptic with a more fixed development time on apparently lower quality food selected from a larger subset of the available plant species and families but a smaller subset of the life forms, than is the case with sphingids. Not only do the saturniids feed on a distinctive and different set of plant families than do sphingids, but Santa Rosa saturniids (especially the hemileucines) display a greater degree of polyphagy than do the sphingids. In general at Santa Rosa, saturniid caterpillars eat phenol-rich and/or aromatic foliage of big trees and/or smaller perennials (Table 3); sphingid caterpillars eat foliage that is traditionally viewed as rich in toxic small molecules, almost entirely in the Solanaceae, Apocynaceae, Asclepiadaceae, Euphorbiaceae, Bignoniaceae, Flacourtiaceae, Rubiaceae, Verbenaceae, Labiatae, Convolvulaceae, Moraceae, Vitaceae, Boraginaceae, Dilleniaceae, Anacardiaceae and Lauraceae (Table 4). The saturniids also feed on foliage significantly less water-rich than do the sphingids at Santa Rosa (Janzen and Waterman 1984).

There are therefore at least two ways to grow a big caterpillar that eats leaf blades. I have not the space or expertise to discuss these two ways for the world fauna of saturniids and sphingids but in closing will briefly mention some ways that the Santa Rosa fauna seems to depart from that of other tropical areas. Below I will focus on what seem to be some of the major aspects of saturniid and sphingid biology that have led their caterpillars to feed on different subsets of plants: amount of time available for oviposition, compatibility of crypticity with polyphagy, physiology of fast caterpillar development, and what is wrong with small life forms as host plants.

How to oviposit in a short time.   There are at least three ways that a saturniid may get her eggs to the right places in a short time: have a conspicuous host, lay eggs in large batches, and/or have polyphagous caterpillars. First, she may be a specialist at locating a single plant species that is, from her viewpoint, conspicuous because its density is high, it is very odoriferous, and/or it is very large. There are a number of consequences of following this route. For such a monophagous moth species, there is no selection on the larvae to be either capable of digesting other species of plants or cryptic on them. There should be few impediments to the caterpillar evolving digestive abilities as efficient (or thorough) as are biochemically possible and also evolving to be quite cryptic on the host. Additionally, the plant species that are initially evolutionarily chosen by the moth may well be those that are especially digestible to a saturniid by virtue of being both low in digestion inhibitors and toxins (e.g., *Bombacopsis quinatum*, the sole local host of three of the five monophagous Santa Rosa arsenurines, has no indication of foliar toxins and has low foliar phenolics (Janzen and Waterman 1984); *Manilkara chicle*, the host of *Copiopteryx semiramis*, has latex-rich foliage and would therefore appear to group with the many latex-rich sphingid host plants – however, its latex is so innocuous that it was the original base for chewing gum). Similarly, plants offering exceptional freedom from carnivores should be evolutionarily chosen by such saturniids (e.g., the ant-acacias as the sole larval hosts of *Syssphinx mexicana*; the crowns of large trees).

The Santa Rosa saturniids contain a number of examples of saturniid-host pairs that seem to conform to the above generalizations. *Copaxa moinieri* is an exceptional saturniine saturniid in having only one host, which is also a small plant (and furthermore, the caterpillar is restricted to saplings and the lower parts of large adult plants). However, *Ocotea veraguensis* is an abundant understory shrub and like other Lauraceae (e.g., bay leaves) it has very odoriferous foliage. Furthermore, the large genus *Copaxa* seems to be a lauraceous specialist (Janzen 1984d) and if there were other species of Lauraceae at Santa Rosa, *C. moinieri* would likely have a longer host list (it is striking that several species of *Copaxa* can, however, be reared on *Crateagus* and *Salix* in Europe, C. Lemaire, personal communication). Only one Santa Rosa saturniid—*Dysdaemonia boreas* – is restricted (apparently, at least) to a very rare tree – *Ceiba pentandra*. However, the tree is huge and the moth is the rarest breeding saturniid in the Park. *C. pentandra* is (and especially, was) moderately common just outside the Park and throughout its range from Mexico to Brazil, which is also the range of *D. boreas* (Lemaire 1980). It is a fair guess that *D. boreas* would not be a member of the breeding fauna of Santa Rosa saturniids if the population had to persist on only the three known adult *C. pentandra* in the Park.

Second, a female may place her eggs in large batches, thereby substantially reducing the number of actual oviposition sites she has to find (and increasing the time that she has available to search for them). *Hylesia lineata*, putting all of her clutch in one felt-covered ball (Janzen 1984a) is the extreme form of this trait. Whether *H. lineata* can retain its position as the most polyphagous of the Santa Rosa saturniids remains to be seen as more records accumulate for *Automeris rubrescens*, *A. zugana*, and *Periphoba arcaei*. The other seven Santa Rosa hemileucines for which oviposition is known lay batches of 30–150 eggs (about 0.1–0.5 of a female's fecundity per batch). Such oviposition behaviour selects for either ovipositing in very large tree crowns (e.g., *Arsenura armida* oviposits about half its egg load in one place in a huge *Bombacopsis quinatum* crown), being a small caterpillar in small tree crowns (e.g., *Hylesia lineata* on any of its numerous hosts), and/or being so polyphagous that once all the food has been eaten off the plant, the caterpillars can move on to other species (e.g., *Automeris rubrescens, A. io, A. zugana, Periphoba arcaei, Hylesia lineata, H. dalinaa*). Oviposition in batches also sets the stage for the evolution of caterpillar group defences (e.g., as shown by *Hylesia*, Hogue 1972, Janzen 1984a) and feeding behaviour, and need not result in defoliation of individual host plants if there is very heavy carnivory of the young caterpillars. Looked at the other way around, group oviposition can be viewed as having been selected for by the various advantages of group living (e.g., larger aposematic displays when young), but the above constraints and advantages apply anyway.

Third, she may oviposit on any one of many host species. While this means that she can find a host plant more quickly, she must also either have a number of different cueing systems or the members of her multi-species oviposition list must have cues in common that enable her to distinguish them from the hundreds of species of plants on which the most polyphagous Santa Rosa saturniids are never found (or some combination of these two traits). The caterpillars must not only be able to develop on a greater variety of diet and chemical defence types, but also be able to withstand the carnivory regimes of those host plants with little aid from detailed crypticity or a short larval development time. It is possible that such a moth is acting like a plant – it hits some good development sites (host plants) with its offspring by distributing them in a pattern that has the intrinsic property that many are certain to die. When a female *Automeris io* places 30 eggs on a *Rhynchosia calycosa* vine (a very small plant), its evolutionary past is assuming that somewhere in the vicinity of that plant there are sufficiently edible other plants to sustain some of the 30 caterpillars. It is in the polyphagous species with many oviposition sites that I expect the longest development times and the greatest variation in intra-specific development time. At Santa Rosa, *Automeris rubrescens, A. io, A. zugana, Periphoba arcaei*, and *Hylesia lineata* are the most involved in this kind of biology. They are conspicuous in being able to starve for as much as four to six days with only a slowing in weight gain, being able to (usually) change hosts at any instar (among the hosts on which that species feeds), being urticating and aposematic, varying in development time as much as 2.5-fold within a clutch of siblings feeding on different host plants (but being similar in body weight at pupation), and being able to eat a large yet distinctly circumscribed set of species (e.g., Table 3).

Hemileucine caterpillars have a peculiar behavioural trait that relates strongly to their polyphagy. When attacked, they often let go of the substrate and fall. Being polyphagous, even if oligophagous, then they are more likely to be able to relocate at least one edible host than if they were monophagous. All the non-hemileucines at Santa Rosa will not voluntarily release their hold on the substrate even if being ripped to pieces by a wasp or bird (as is generally the case with sphingids as well). This behavioural trait should also contribute directly to the frequency with which the collector encounters hemileucine caterpillars on all their potential hosts and suggests that the long host list of a polyphagous hemileucine need not imply a long list of species suitable for oviposition (however, I have never found a batch of hemileucine eggs on the foliage of a species not eaten by that hemileucine).

By virtue of their short time available for oviposition, saturniids seem to be preadapted for continuous ecological, and hence evolutionary, sampling of the host plant offerings in a habitat. Sphingids appear to be the opposite since the unlucky female sphingid should wait until the next night or even leave the habitat to search for a good oviposition site. Since saturniid females lay all their eggs before dying, even in the laboratory with no host plants available, and since in the laboratory the absence of a host plant only deters saturniids from ovipositing for a few hours or days (if at all), I suspect that in nature a female saturniid must often place all or part of her night's eggs on atypical hosts. Yet the records in Table 3 include all wild living saturniid host records for over 800 different accessions over six years (a clutch of gregarious caterpillars is recorded as one accession). The stenophagy portrayed by the non-hemileucines in Table 3 suggests that even though they feed on many families of large plants, a given saturniid species is still rather tightly bound to its particular host(s) in a given habitat.

Incompatibility of crypticity with long or diverse host lists.   While I have already alluded to the incompatibility of crypticity and polyphagy at numerous places, it deserves explicit mention. Non-cryptic defences, such as extreme urtication, should be strongly selected for as companion traits to polyphagy. Polyphages should often find themselves on quite different leaf shapes, colours, sun exposures, etc., than those experienced by their siblings and conspecifics. Additionally, they may have to cross non-leafy surfaces in search of new host plants. Finally, by growing slowly, they are exposed to carnivores for a maximum time. Viewed the other way around, a caterpillar with a very effective defence against both vertebrate and invertebrate carnivores might well be able to eat almost anything, albeit while growing at some excrutiatingly slow rate on certain of these hosts.

There is an important but easily overlooked complexity in the relationship between crypticity and duration of the larval period. If a caterpillar relies totally on crypticity for its defence, the more days that it is a caterpillar, the more likely it is to be found while a caterpillar. If a caterpillar can rely totally on a violent and self-evident personal defence such as urtication, additional days of development will not only mean no additional risk, but may even lower the average daily risk of carnivory if the carnivores are local ones that learn about the presence of a particular individual caterpillar. The above dichotomy is blurred by the existance of certain vertebrates that can eat well-protected caterpillars, and by the fact that what deters a vertebrate may have no effect on a parasitoid fly or wasp. However, risk of being taken by a parasitoid may also not necessarily increase with larval duration. Certain parasitoids seem to oviposit successfully or find their hosts with ease only at specific times in the caterpillar developmental progression. If a parasitoid uses volatiles released at the time of moulting or cocoon spinning as host-location cues (see Marsh 1937 for a probable case with cecropia moths), the length of time between moults may be irrelevant to the intensity of its threat. Mimics of urticators (e.g., Santa Rosa saturniines and most ceratocampines) and of vertebrate eyes (e.g., *Xylophanes* spp., *Eumorpha labruscae, Agrius cingulatus, Hemeroplanes triptolemus*) are intermediate cases. However, this is probably less true of the mimics of urticators since no amount of visual inspection can tell a monkey if a spiny mimic is in fact an urticator.

In summary, a new immigrant species of hemileucine saturniid might well have the opportunity to choose evolutionarily or ecologically a host list taking into account only the nutrient traits, conspicuousness, and microclimate of its potential hosts, while a newly arrived sphingid might not ever use many nutritionally suitable hosts because the carnivory regime on them is too severe given a low crypticity on the backgrounds they provide. Alternatively, the sphingid may stay tied firmly to a small subset of the hosts it can develop on because other hosts do not offer a growth rate quite as fast as those used (see below), given that particular sphingid's fine-tuned detoxification system.

Physiology of fast development time.   Santa Rosa sphingid caterpillars are unexceptional in their development rates and variability in size at pupation. Even the largest only use four to five weeks for development, and the smallest (e.g., *Cautethia spuria*) as little as two weeks. Within a species there is little intra-sex variation in pupal weight (although by severe starvation bouts on low quality food in the laboratory, subnormal-size adults can be produced, and are found occasionally in nature as well). Santa Rosa saturniids differ from this pattern in three ways. They grow more slowly, the size of conspecifics at pupation is quite variable even on the best foods (except for hemileucines, which are more sphingid-like on this trait), and they appear to have an internal calendar that dictates the time of cessation of feeding (again, except in hemileucines). The non-hemileucines use 1.3–2.0 times as long to attain full-size as do sphingids of the same pupal weight. Hemileucine saturniids require as much as two to three times as long (up to 2.5 months) as do sphingids of the same body weight. For example, it takes 20 days of feeding to grow a 1.8 g female *Perigonia lusca* pupa on *Calycophyllum candidissimum* and 52 days of feeding to grow an *Automeris zugana* female pupa of the same weight on the same host plant side by side in the laboratory. A 20 g Puerto Rican *Pseudosphinx tetrio* caterpillar may be produced in as little as 24 days (J. A. Santiago-Blay, personal communication) while an *Eacles imperialis* caterpillar at Santa Rosa normally uses 30–40 days to attain this weight. As yet I do not know if such differences are due to the saturniids taking in less leaf material per 24 hours, getting less out of what they take in, or taking in overall lower quality materials (or all three). There is also the possibility that a living gram of saturniid pupa is more expensive than is a live gram of sphingid pupa because of different proportions of water, fats, etc., but I do not have the data to comment further on this point.

My working hypothesis is that saturniid caterpillars are often consuming phenol-rich foliage that yields relatively little assimilable material per bite because the leaf phenols have bound with the nutrients in the leaf and that the caterpillar has evolved food passage rates appropriate for such a low yield per bite kind of extraction. This stands in contrast to a sphingid caterpillar that can detoxify or otherwise avoid the primary defence chemicals of its food by, for example, enzymatically crunching up the toxin molecules or not assimilating them. It is then free to extract a much higher proportion of the nutrients in the meal (assuming that plants protected with toxic small molecules are low in foliar digestion inhibitors to bind with the nutrients). The caterpillar digestive physiology literature adds corroboration and complexity to such a view. Martin and Martin (1982, 1983) have quite appropriately emphasized that whether phenolic content of foliage is a reliable measure of how much of the leaf protein is unavailable to a caterpillar depends on the caterpillar gut pH as much as on the amount of phenolics and nutrients (and see Lawson *et al.* 1982). However, the fact remains that the Santa Rosa saturniids feed on some of the most phenol-rich plants in the Park whereas the sphingid hosts have very low phenolic levels and often contain alkaloids or other toxic small molecules (Janzen and Waterman 1984). In the saturniid hosts there is certainly the opportunity for nutrient binding (and indigenous gut chemical binding) by phenolics and apparently none for direct toxicity (except for *Copaxa* on *Ocotea*, see below), while the reverse is true for the sphingid hosts. Schroeder (1972) found growth efficiencies of the polyphagous cecropia caterpillar to be about half that of the sphingid *Manduca sexta*, and there is a growing body of examples that polyphagous caterpillars grow more slowly than do closely related monophagous caterpillars (e.g., Scriber 1979a, Scriber and Slansky 1981). While the causal relationship has yet to be discovered, it is also clear that caterpillars feeding on moister food have higher assimilation efficients and/or growth rates (Scriber 1977, 1978, 1979a, 1979b, 1979c, Scriber and Slansky 1981). The sphingid hosts at Santa Rosa have a significantly higher water content than do the saturniid hosts (Janzen and Waterman 1984).

The overlaps between the saturniid and sphingid host lists (between Table 3 and 4) are instructive. *Ocotea veraguensis* is perhaps the most confounding overlap, since it supports a monophagous saturniid and two monophagous sphingids. Furthermore, it is the only alkaloid-positive saturniid host discovered to date in the Park (a single record of *Automeris zugana* on *Solanum hazenii* is an exception, but *S. hazenii* is certainly not among the usual hosts of *Automeris zugana*). *O. veraguensis* has a very low leaf phenol content and I suspect that *C. moinieri* is behaving like a sphingid with respect to it (which is further evidenced by the apparent restriction of *Copaxa* to Lauraceae (Janzen 1984d), a sphingid-like generic oligophagy). *Calycophyllum candidissimum* is in the alkaloid-rich Rubiaceae and seemingly appropriately supports two sphingids. However, it is also a common host for *Automeris rubrescens* and *Periphoba arcaei*; its leaves are not alkaloid positive and are the most phenol-rich of the Rubiaceae tested, though still quite low in phenolics (Janzen and Waterman 1984). That *Automeris zugana* can eat *Solanum hazenii* along with the great variety of other things on its host list suggests that sphingids are, however, not the only large caterpillars that can detoxify or bypass alkaloids. The pest status of *Eacles imperialis* on Brazilian coffee leaves (Crocomo and Parra 1979) suggests the same.

If saturniids are tolerating a low rate of nutrient assimilation and thereby feeding on either many species of plants (hemileucines) or the leaves of large trees (low in water, high in phenolics, variable in nutrient content depending on where the leaf lies in the tree crown), there must be strong variation within and among species in the amount of nutrients that can be assimilated within the caterpillar stage. The Santa Rosa hemileucines express this by having highly variable growth rates and a consequence is that by the end of the rainy season their adult eclosions are poorly synchronized. The non-hemileucines express this by having a relatively fixed larval period and a variable pupal size with the consequence of relatively synchronous adult eclosions during the rainy season. In a group of *Rothschildia lebeau* siblings on the same individual host plant, for example, it is commonplace to obtain two-fold variation in male or female pupal weights yet have only three- to six-day variation in larval duration for most individuals. Size seems to depend on the luck of the particular leaves obtained. The caterpillars do not continue to grow until they reach some size near the average before pupating, and fortunate caterpillars do not bow out of larval life well before their thinner siblings. I suspect that the primary selection for such a pattern is the value of remaining in synchrony with the population, since the dis-synchronous saturniid cannot simply wait around until other adults eclose, or migrate to a different habitat. Sphingids, with their longer adult lives and ability to obtain nutrients as adults, should place less value on synchrony and more on getting through the larval stage rapidly.

Saturniid avoidance of small life forms. In contrast with sphingid caterpillars – which as a group are found on all sizes and ages of plants of all life form (Table 4) – Santa Rosa saturniid caterpillars are usually found in the crowns of adult and large host plants (non-hemileucines and some hemileucines) or host plants of all sizes with emphasis on large ones and adults (hemileucines) (Table 3). This ecological statement has two aspects. Is the saturniid caterpillar distribution generated by the eggs being laid in many places but the caterpillars only surviving in tree or treelet crowns? Or, are the adults programmed to oviposit primarily in adult plant crowns? Both cases occur at Santa Rosa. *Rothschildia lebeau* eggs can be found on *Spondias mombin* and *Exostemma mexicanum* from one to 20 m in height, but the caterpillars almost never survive carnivory on plants under about four m in height. On the other hand, there is no indication that *Syssphinx molina* and *S. colla* ever oviposit on sapling *Pithecellobium saman* trees; however, when the caterpillars are experimentally placed on saplings, they are almost invariably removed by carnivores before reaching pupation.

What is the difference between saplings and other small plants on the one hand, and adults and large plants on the other? At least for the 26 Santa Rosa saturniids reared to date, the foliage of saplings of their host plants is quite adequate fodder, whether it is cut foliage in the laboratory or foliage on the tree inside a protective net.

To the ovipositing moth, saplings and little plants are much smaller targets than are adult crowns. A sapling is usually mixed in with many other plant species and produces a much smaller odour cue than does an adult tree. Once the target has been found, a sapling only has the resources for a few larvae; the female will have to locate many more of them (or her caterpillars will have to do the searching).

To the caterpillar the sapling or small plant offers limited choices for safe feeding and resting sites. Saplings often bear relatively sparse foliage and a large caterpillar is more conspicuous there than in dense clusters of leaves in a large tree crown. A sapling is also likely to be defoliated if several larvae are present. Defoliation not only threatens larvae with starvation but exposes the caterpillars to visually-orienting carnivores. Being inter-mingled with other species-rich and fast-growing vegetation, the sapling and small plant crown will be foraged through by carnivores more intensely than will be an equal volume of vegetation in the relatively sterile foliage of a large tree crown occupying as much as 0.5 ha. It seems appropriate that some of the strongly urticating and polyphagous hemileucines are the saturniids that have come to occupy the tangles of small plants so rich in carnivores at Santa Rosa. An exception is *Syssphinx mexicana*, a ceratocampine saturniid that feeds only in ant-acacias, shrubs and treelets of fast-growing secondary succession; however, *S. mexicana* may be unambiguously viewed as the most urticating saturniid of all, since the plants it lives on are heavily occupied by strongly stinging *Pseudomyrmex* ants.

But if life is so dangerous in low vegetation and on small plants, how do the sphingids survive there? First, many sphingids match their backgrounds extremely well and add dramatic larval colour polymorphisms to the mix as well (e.g. Schneider 1973). Second, some leave their hosts during the day to hide in the litter or on shaggy-barked stems (e.g., *Sphinx merops, Isognathus rimosus, Xylophanes anubus, X. ceratomioides, Aleuron carinata*). Third, by laying single eggs, the female sphingid gets more tries at finding locally carnivore-free micro-sites than does a saturniid laying the same number of eggs in large batches. Fourth, the sphingid caterpillar is exposed for a shorter time; a 0.7 g adult female *Perigonia lusca* may spend slightly less than three weeks on a *Calycophyllum candidissimum* sapling as a caterpillar while an urticating *Automeris zugana* weighing as much will be there six weeks (or longer). Fifth, if the right situation for oviposition does not present itself, the sphingid can delay oviposition or migrate out of the habitat. Finally, it may be that many of the cryptic sphingids are immune to repeated predation by vertebrates owing to having a gut full of toxic foliage. A small bird (e.g., *Campylorynchus rufinuchus*, F. Joyce personal communication) may repeatedly search a *Calycophyllum* crown for *Perigonia lusca* caterpillars but pass up search opportunity for the very similar green caterpillars of *Callionima falcifera* on *Stemmadenia* simply because the later sphingid has a gut full of alkaloid-rich foliage and would be a lethal lunch for a baby bird. *Isognathus rimosus* and *Callionima falcifera* also squirt very bitter fluids from glands on the body when molested (Haber 1983b, A. Pescador, personal communication).

In closing

This attempt to dichotomize saturniids and sphingids brings to mind several background questions of widespread application. Should we view the large-bodied moths termed Saturniidae as having evolved from a smaller non-feeding moth (as there are many of in the Bombycidae, Mimallonidae, Limacodidae, Lymantriidae, Lasiocampidae, Megalopygidae – moths that have many if not all of the traits attributed to saturniids in this essay) or from a large moth that feeds as an adult and has many other sphingid attributes? Does the dichotomy shed light on why most continental but local moth faunas contain roughly twice as many species of sphingids as saturniids, be they extra-tropical or tropical? Is it more reasonable to speak of a local fauna of saturniids than sphingids (or neither)? In general I think we do not yet know enough of the natural history of these moths to construct elaborate or definitive answers to questions such as these. However, a small try may be of value in encouraging the gathering of relevant data by those around the world with the moths in their hands.

The evolution of a large saturniid from a small saturniid-like moth is neither difficult to imagine nor particularly helpful in understanding the evolution of the non-feeding adult habit in the first place. However, the evolution of non-feeding has two possible interesting routes. On the one hand it may have occurred in a habitat exceptionally favourable to larval survival, creating a situation that favoured mutants that remained longer as larvae and enclosed as more egg- and fat-laden adults. Such adults would be able to give rise to the next larval stage faster and perhaps even be less competent as resource gatherers and exacting ovipositors. On the other hand it may have occurred in a habitat exceptionally unfavourable to adult survival. Selection would be intense for larval traits that allowed a long stay in this resource-gathering stage. The ideal habitat for the evolution of a saturniid-like organism out of a sphingoid lineage would then be one with both exceptionally good conditions for larval survival and exceptionally harsh conditions for adults. In the progression from deserts to tropical rainforests, arid lowland forest would seem the most ideal for such an evolutionary event (with, for example, a quick-flushing deciduous legume tree as the host), though not the habitat in which the most species could co-occur once the life form is evolutionarily established.

Such reasoning is also pertinent to the question of why there are about twice as many sphingid as saturniid species in most lowland continental habitats. One way to create favourable conditions for a large adult moth is to give the adult the ability to search widely for local good conditions, and sphingids have this ability. In a certain sense, Santa Rosa does not have a breeding population of 61 species of sphingids, since many of those that breed in Santa Rosa seem to leave for at least part of the year. Understanding their species richness in Santa Rosa requires knowledge of all of Costa Rica, and were Santa Rosa an isolated island, its breeding species richness of sphingids would be severely reduced. Saturniids, in contrast, maintain a breeding population at Santa Rosa without migration, though it is quite possible that the strong-flying males move genes about over an area considerably greater than that of the Park and that local extinction occasionally occurs but the population is re-established by local movements of females. It is then more reasonable to speak of a local fauna of saturniids than of sphingids.

Such an inquiry brings to mind the age-old question of whether a widespread species is made up of many local populations specialized to local conditions or of a sufficiently plastic phenotype and all-purpose genotype that its members' responses to locally different ecological circumstances are sufficient for survival (Fox and Morrow 1981). In the case at hand, saturniids appear to have the lack of vagility which predisposes them for the former, while sphingids appear to be the opposite. However, a closer look at saturniid biology suggests the reverse. Many, with hemileucines at the top of the list, should be able to drop into just about any habitat and find some plant, among a variety of families, on which the larvae can feed. In contrast with sphingids, adult hosts are not needed. Barriers to geographic range extension should be based on climate and the balance of carnivory against the output from the particular edible hosts. Likewise, sphingids may be doing the opposite trick of laboriously seeking out the relatives of some suite of closely related plants in each new habitat invaded; given that such a relative and adult nectar resources can be found, the moth can persist. While it certainly has to deal with the climate and carnivory regimes, it has the option of vacating the habitat for part of the year, and both its caterpillars and adults may be able to survive under an overall greater intensity of carnivory than can the saturniids. Such a scenario is consistent with the observation that many sphingids have taxonomically narrow host lists (though perhaps containing many species) over tens of degrees of Latitude (e.g., the larval host records of Moss (1912, 1920) in Peru and Brazil, and mine in Santa Rosa are almost identical at the genus and family level). In contrast, the aggregate host list of a widespread saturniid may contain tens of families of plants or be as narrow as one of a sphingid.

If ever-sharpening focus on the Santa Rosa saturniid and sphingid faunal portrait bears out the general pattern that I think I perceive at this beginning, are there reasons to believe that a similar close look at these moths in some other tropical area will reveal a different portrait? Certainly even a pristine tropical island fauna cannot show the Santa Rosa contrast since the saturniids are largely missing from islands. The upper part of a tropical continental mountain range will likewise be of no use as it will lack sphingids (except for migrants passing through) at the 2500 m-plus elevations that still have one to five breeding saturniids. As already emphasized, a lowland rainforest site will lack the strong seasonal element that gives the Santa Rosa portrait part of its distinctive complexity. While the species richness ratios of saturniids to sphingids tend to be about 1:2 for most lowland neotropical sites for which there are data, taken as a whole, large tropical land masses have equal numbers of each family or even more saturniids (e.g., Mexico appears to have about 148 species of saturniids and 154 species of sphingids (Hoffmann 1942); C. Lemaire (personal communication) estimates 850 saturniids and 500 sphingids for the New World).

A quick glance at other continents suggests important similarities and differences. Three African saturniids have beaten the mating game by becoming parthenogenic (Lemaire 1969, Pinkey 1972). The life forms of old world adult tropical sphingids and saturniids contain many close copies of those of the Neotropics; old world tropical saturniid caterpillars are often urticating (or apparent mimics) and the sphingid caterpillars bear the same close similarity to their substrates as do the Neotropical ones. However, there is at least one conspicuous cautionary difference. Not only do the 61 species of breeding Santa Rosa sphingids not use legumes as larval hosts (despite the fact that the Santa Rosa flora is 20 per cent legumes (Janzen and Liesner 1980)), but legumes are conspicuously missing from all New World sphingid larval host lists. In contrast, of 135 sphingids whose larval hosts were recorded in India, Sri Lanka and Burma (Bell and Scott 1937), 10.4 per cent fed on legume foliage. Likewise there are several legume-eating sphingids in Ivory Coast foliage (Vuattoux 1978). A second example of discordance is that the saturniid:sphingid species ratio in this rainforest is 27:62 (Vuattoux 1978, 1981) and therefore consistent with this ratio in lowland Costa Rican rainforest sites (Haber 1983a, sphingids; Janzen collection records, saturniids). However, it also appears that 42 per cent of the Ivory Coast rainforest sphingids do not come to light (Vuattoux 1978), as compared with four per cent at Santa Rosa. While neotropical islands characteristically lack saturniids, those of the Asian tropics have a small but conspicuous saturniid fauna (Peigler 1983).

The saturniid-sphingid comparison should differ in various ways outside the tropics. Extra-tropically there are more diurnal special in both families, less species-rich and life-form-rich vegetation types from which the moths may choose their larval hosts, more kinds of and longer severely inimical seasons, and more pulsed carnivore regimes. In areas sufficiently extra-tropical that there can be only one generation per growing season, with the inimical season serving as an omnipresent synchronization event, the saturniid larva and pupa are not under selection for the use of an internal calendar and I expect the consequence to be larval and pupal stages that are more intra-specifically variable in duration (e.g., Worth et al. 1979).

At the end, I can only lament that it is already too late to explore the kinds of questions I have raised in this essay. An attempt to understand extra-tropical saturniid and sphingid faunas in the eco-evolutionary context presented here will be almost entirely an act of reconstruction, a reading of post-Columbian anachronisms. How does one move from Waldbauer and Sternburg's elegant and detailed examination of cecropia moth urban ecology to understanding how that moth evolved and in concert with what other saturniids and sphingids. Illinois is only a zoo with no feeding and heating bill. As long as tropical patches of relatively pristine habitat still remain, it is tempting to think that there is some chance. However, the reality is that they will be gone within a few decades and the small dots that will be saved by intensive efforts will have quite different ecologies from those that they had for millennia before. Imagine how many migrant moths would have been attracted to that light that I placed in the 1800 m Costa Rican pass on 4 December 1983, were I to have put it there when 90 per cent of the source area was not pasture and crop fields as it is today. Yes, Santa Rosa will remain as a National Park, but from where are the migrant sphingids going to come at the beginning of each rainy season when their source area is lush agricultural land providing a high standard of living for this relatively well-to-do tropical country?

Acknowledgements

This study was supported by NSF grants DEB 77-04889, DEB 80-11558, and BSR 83-08388, and by the Servicio de Parques Nacionales de Costa Rica. The following people were especially helpful in discussing the ideas and commented constructively on the manuscript: W. A. Haber, C. Lemaire, G. P. Waldbauer, J. G. Sternburg, R. S. Peigler, G. Stevens, W. Hallwachs, and M. O. Johnston. R. S. Peigler aided greatly in locating pertinent references. I was substantially aided in field work by W. A. Haber, M. O. Johnston, W. Hallwachs, R. Espinosa, G. Vega, T. Gush, R. Glass, M. L. Higgins, T. Fleming, F. Joyce, J. Howard, E. Arce, P.. J. DeVries, Santa Rosa park guards, and others who have brought me caterpillars. I dedicate this essay to all those future tropical generations who will never see many of the things discussed here unless some severe and dramatic changes occur in tropical social attitudes on how much of the remaining forest should be converted to money, children and hamburgers.

References

Baker, R. R. and Sadovy, Y. (1978). The distance and nature of the light-trap response of moths. *Nature* **276**: 818–821.

Baker, R. R. and Mather, J. G. (1982). Magnetic compass sense in the large yellow underwing moth, *Noctua pronuba*. *Animal Behaviour* **30**: 543–548.

Baker, T. C. and Kuenen, L. P. S. (1982). Pheromone source location by flying moths: a supplementary non-anemotactic mechanism. *Science* **216**: 424–427.

Bell, T. R. D. and Scott, F. B. (1937). Appendix B. *Food-plants of the Indian hawk-moths*. The fauna of British India. Moths. Sphingidae. Taylor and Francis Ltd., London, pp. 507–519.

Beutelspacher, C. R. (1978). Familias Sphingidae y Saturniidae (Lepidoptera) de las Minas, Veracruz, México. An. Inst. Biol. Univ. Nal. Autón. México 49, Ser. *Zoología* **1**: 219–230.

Beutelspacher, C. R. (1981). Lepidopteros de Chamela, Jalisco, Mexico. II. Familias Sphingidae y Saturniidae. Anales del Instituto de Biologia Universidad Nacional Autonoma de Mexico 52, Ser. *Zoologica* 1: 389–406.

Blest, A. D. (1957a). The function of eyespot patterns in the Lepidoptera. *Behaviour* 11: 209–255.

Blest, A. D. (1957b). The evolution of protective displays in the Saturnioidea and Sphingidae (Lepidoptera). *Behaviour* 11: 257–310.

Blest, A. D. (1960). A study of the biology of saturniid moths in the Canal Zone Biological Area. *Smithsonian Report for 1959*: 447–464.

Blest, A. D. (1963). Relations between moths and predators. *Nature* 197: 1046–1047.

Bowden, J. and Church, B. M. (1973). The effect of moonlight on catches of insects in light traps in Africa. Part II – the effect of moon phase on light trap catches. *Bulletin of Entomological Research* 63 129–142.

Boza, M. A. and Mendoza, R. (1981). *The national parks of Costa Rica.* I.N.C.A.F.O., Madrid, Spain, 310 pp.

Brower, L. P., Cook, L. M. and Croze, H. J. (1967). Predator response to artificial Batesian mimics released in a neotropical environment. *Evolution* 21: 11–23.

Brown, L. N. (1972). Mating behaviour and life habits of the sweet bay silk moth (*Callosamia carolina*). *Science* 176: 73–75.

Bullock, S. B. and Pescador, A. (1983). Wing and proboscis dimensions in a sphingid fauna from western Mexico. *Biotropica* 15: 292–294.

Capinera, J. L. (1980). A trail pheromone from silk produced by larvae of the range caterpillar *Hemileuca oliviae* (Lepidoptera: Saturniidae) and observations on aggregation behaviour. *Journal of Chemical Ecology* 6: 655–664.

Capinera, J. L., Wiener, L. F. and Anamosa, P. R. (1980). Behavioural thermo-regulation by late-instar range caterpillar larvae *Hemileuca oliviae* Cockerell (Lepidoptera: Saturniidae). *Journal of the Kansas Entomological Society* 53: 631–638.

Cardé, R. T. and Hagaman, T. E. (1979). Behavioural responses of the gypsy moth in a wind tunnel to air-borne enantiomers of disparlure. *Environmental Entomology* 8: 475–484.

Carolin, V. M. and Knopf, J. A. E. (1968). *The pandora moth.* U.S.D.A. Forest Service Pest Leaflet 114: 1–7.

Cary, M. M. (1957). Distribution of Sphingidae (Lepidoptera: Heterocera) in the Antillean-Caribbean region. *Transactions of the American Entomological Society* 77: 63–129.

Casey, T. M. (1976). Flight energies of sphinx moths: power input during hovering flight. *Journal of Experimental Biology* 64: 529–543.

Coen, E. (1983). Climate. In *Costa Rican Natural History*, D. H. Janzen, ed. University of Chicago Press, Chicago, pp. 35–46.

Collins, M. M. and Weast, D. (1961). *Wild silk moths of the United States.* Collins Radio Company, Cedar Rapids, Iowa, 138 pp.

Crocomo, W. B. and Parra, J. R. P. (1979). Biologia e nutricao de *Eacles imperialis magnifica* Walker, 1856 (Lepidoptera, Attacidae) em cafeeiro. *Revista Brasileira de Entomologia* 23: 51–76.

Cryan, J. F. and Dirig, R. (1977). The moths of autumn. Pine Bush Preservation Project, Inc., Albany, New York, 16 pp.

Curio, E. (1965). Die Schutzanpassungen dreier Raupen eines Schwärmers (Lepidoptera, Sphingidae) auf Galapagos. *Zool. Jb. Syst. Bd.* 92: 487–522.

Dillon, P. M., Lowrie, S. and McKey, D. (1983). Disarming the 'evil woman': petiole constriction by a sphingid larva circumvents mechanical defenses of its host plant, *Cnidoscolus urens* (Euphorbiaceae). *Biotropica* 15: 112–116.

Ferge, L. A. (1983). Distribution and hybridization of *Hyalophora columbia* (Lepidoptera: Saturniidae) in Wisconsin. *The Great Lakes Entomologist* **16**: 67–71.

Ferguson, D. C. (1972). Bombycoidea, Saturniidae. In *The Moths of American North of Mexico*, (eds. R. B. Dominick, *et al.*,) E. W. Classey Ltd. and R. B. D. Publications Inc., London, Fascicle 20.2, 275 pp.

Fleming, H. (1947). Sphingidae (moths) of Rancho Grande, north central Venezuela. *Zoologica* **32**: 133–145.

Fleming, R. C. (1970). Food plants of some adult sphinx moths (Lepidoptera: Sphingidae). *The Michigan Entomologist* **3**: 17–23.

Fox, L. R. and Morrow, P. A. (1981). Specialization: species property or local phenomenon. *Science* **211**: 887–893.

Gardiner, B. O. (1967). The life history of *Periphoba hircia* (Saturniidae) with a note on distribution and larval variation. *Journal of the Lepidopterists' Society* **21**: 198–204.

Grant, K. J. (1937). An historical study of the migrations of *Celerio lineata lineata* and *Celerio lineata livornica* Esp. (Lepidoptera). *Transactions of the Royal Entomological Society of London* **86**: 345–357.

Gregory, D. E. (1963). Hawkmoth pollination in the genus *Oenothera*. *Aliso* **5**: 357–384.

Giles, P. H. (1968). The relative abundance and seasonal distribution of hawk-moths (Lepidoptera: Sphingidae) attracted to mercury vapour lights in Samaru, northern Nigeria. *Nigerian Journal of Science* **2**: 45–54.

Haber, W. A. (1983). Checklist of Sphingidae. In *Costa Rican Natural History*, (ed. D. H. Janzen,) University of Chicago Press, Chicago, Illinois, pp. 645–650.

Haber, W. A. (1983b). *Callionima falcifera*. In *Costa Rican Natural History*, (ed. D. H. Janzen,) University of Chicago Press, Chicago, pp. 704–705.

Haber, W. A. and Frankie, G. W. (1984). Characteristics and organization of a tropical hawkmoth community. *Ecology* (in press).

Harling, J. (1968). Meteorological factors effecting the activity of night flying macro-Lepidoptera. *Entomologist* **101**: 83–93.

Hartshorn, G. S. (1983). Plants. Introduction. In *Costa Rican Natural History*, (ed. D. H. Janzen,) University of Chicago Press, Chicago, Illinois, pp. 118–157.

Hienton, T. E. (1974). Summary of investigations of electric insect traps. U.S.D.A. Technical Bulletin 1498, Washington, D.C.

Hintze-Podufal, C. (1977). The larval melanin pattern in the moth *Eudia pavonia* and its initiating factors. *Journal of Insect Physiology* **23**: 731–737.

Hodges, R. W. (1971). Sphingoidea. In *The Moths of America North of Mexico*, (eds. R. B. Dominick, *et al.*,) E. W. Classey Ltd. and R. B. D. Publications Inc., London, Fascicle 21, 158 pp.

Hoffman, C. C. (1942). Catalogo sistematico y zoogeografico de los lepidopteros Mexicanos. *Anales del Instituto de Biología de la Universidad Nacional de México* **13**: 213–256.

Hogue, C. L. (1972). Protective function and sound perception and gregariousness in *Hylesia* larvae (Saturniidae: Hemileucine). *Journal of the Lepidopterists' Society* **26**: 33–34.

Hogue, C. L., Sala, F. P., McFarland, N. and Henne, C. (1965). Systematics and life history of *Saturnia* (*Calosaturnia*) *albofasciata* in California (Saturniidae). *Journal of Research on the Lepidoptera* **4**: 173–184.

Hsiao, H. S. (1972). *Attraction of moths to light and to infrared radiation*. San Francisco Press Inc., San Francisco, 89 pp.

Janzen, D. H. (1981). Patterns of herbivory in a tropical deciduous forest. *Biotropica* **13**: 271–282.

Janzen, D. H. (1982). Guia para la identificacion de mariposas nocturnas de la familia Saturniidae del Parque Nacional Santa Rosa, Guanacaste, Costa Rica. *Brenesia* **19/20**: 255–299.

Janzen, D. H. (1983). *Pseudosphinx tetrio*. In *Costa Rican Natural History*, (ed. D. H. Janzen,) University of Chicago Press, Chicago, Illinois, pp. 764–765.

Janzen, D. H. (1984a). Natural history of *Hylesia lineata* (Saturniidae: Hemileucinae) in Santa Rosa National Park, Costa Rica. *Journal of the Kansas Entomological Society* **57**: 490-514.

Janzen, D. H. (1984b). A host plant is more than its chemistry. *1983 Symposium of the Illinois Natural History Society*, Urbana, Illinois (in press).

Janzen, D. H. (1984c). Seasonal colour polymorphism of *Rothschildia lebeau* (Saturniidae) in a Costa Rican deciduous forest. *Bulletin of the Entomological Society of America* **30(2)**: 16–20.

Janzen, D. H. (1984d). Natural history of *Copaxa moinieri* (Saturniidae) in Santa Rosa National Park, Costa Rica. *Journal of the Kansas Entomological Society* (submitted).

Janzen, D. H. and Liesner, R. (1980). Annotated check-list of plants of lowland Guanacaste Province, Costa Rica, exclusive of grasses and non-vascular cryptogams. *Brenesia* **18**: 15–90.

Janzen, D. H. and Waterman, P. G. (1984). A seasonal census of digestion-inhibitors and alkaloids in foliage of forest trees in Costa Rica: some factors influencing their distribution and relation to host selection by Sphingidae and Saturniidae. *Biological Journal of the Linnean Society* **21**: 439–454.

Jeffords, M. R., Waldbauer, G. P. and Sternburg, J. G. (1980). Determination of the time of day at which diurnal moths painted to resemble butterflies are attacked by birds. *Evolution* **34**: 1205–1211.

Kennedy, J. S., Ludlow, A. R. and Sanders, C. J. (1980). Guidance system used in moth sex attraction. *Nature* **288**: 475–477.

Kennedy, J. S., Ludlow, A. R. and Sanders, C. J. (1982). Reply. *Nature* **295**: 263.

Laroca, S. and Mielke, O. H. (1975). Ensaios sobre ecologia de comunidade em Sphingidae na Serra do Mar, Paraná, Brasil (Lepidoptera). *Revista Brasileira de Biologia* **35**: 1–19.

Lawson, D. L., Merritt, R. W., Klug, M. J. and Martin, J. S. (1982). The utilization of late season foliage by the orange striped oakworm, *Anisota senatoria*. *Entomologia Experimentata et Applicata* **32**: 242–248.

Lemaire, C. (1969). Un cas de pathénogenèse chez les lépidoptères Attacidae: *Goodia kuntzei* (Dewitz). *Alexanor* **5**: 47–48.

Lemaire, C. (1974). Révision du genre *Automeris* Hübner et des genres voisins. Biogéographie, éthologie, morphologie, taxonomie (Lep. Attacidae). Mémoires du Museum National d'Histoire Naturelle, N.S., Ser. A., *Zoologie* **92**: 423–576.

Lemaire, C. (1978). *Les Attacidae Americains*. Attacinae. C. Lemaire, Neuilly-sur-Seine, France, 238 pp.

Lemaire, C. (1980). *Les Attacidae Americains*. Arsenurinae. C. Lemaire, Neuilly-sur-Seine, France, 199 pp.

Lemaire, C. (1982). Trois Saturniidae inedits du Costa Rica et du Perou (Lepidoptera). *Rev. Franc. Ent. (N.S.)* **4**: 79–85.

Lemaire, C. (1985). Les Saturniidae Americains. Ceratocampinae. *Museo Nacional de Costa Rica* (in press).

Marquis, R. J. (1984). Natural history of a tropical daytime-flying saturniid: *Automeris phrynon* Druce (Lepidoptera: Saturniidae: Hemileucinae). *Journal of the Kansas Entomological Society* (in press).

Marsh, F. L. (1937). Ecological observations upon the enemies of *cecropia*, with particular reference to its hymenopterous parasites. *Ecology* **18**: 106–112.

Martin, J. S. and Martin, M. M. (1982). Tannin assays in ecological studies: lack of correlation between phenolics, proanthocyanidins and protein-precipitating constituents in mature foliage of six oak species. *Oecologia* **54**: 205–211.

Martin, J. S. and Martin, M. M. (1983). Tannin assays in ecological studies. *Journal of Chemical Evolution* **9**: 285–294.

Michener, C. D. (1949). Parallelisms in the evolution of the saturniid moths. *Evolution* **3**: 129–141.

Michener, C. D. (1952). The saturniids (Lepidoptera) of the Western Hemisphere, morphology phylogeny and classification. *Bulletin of the American Museum of Natural History* **98**: 335–502.

Miller, T. A. (1978). Oviposition behaviour of colonized *Hyalophora gloveri gloveri* (Saturniidae). *Journal of the Lepidopterists' Society* **32**: 233–234.

Miller, T. A. and Cooper, W. J. (1977). Oviposition behaviour of colonized *Callisamia promethea* (Saturniidae). *Journal of the Lepidopterists' Society* **31**: 282–283.

Moss, A. M. (1912). On the Sphingidae of Peru. *Transactions of the Zoological Society of London* **20**: 73–134.

Moss, A. M. (1920). Sphingidae of Para, Brazil. *Novitates Zoologicae* **27**: 333–424.

Owen, D. F. (1969). Species diversity and seasonal abundance of tropical Sphingidae (Lepidoptera). *Proceedings of the Royal Entomological Society of London (A)* **44**: 162–168.

Owen, D. F. (1972). Species diversity in tropical Sphingidae and a systematic list of species collected in Sierra Leone. *Journal of Natural History* **6**: 177–194.

Peigler, R. (1975). The geographical distribution of *Callosamia securifera* (Saturniidae). *Journal of the Lepidopterists' Society* **29**: 188–191.

Peigler, R. S. (1976a). Wing colour variation in *Callosamia* (Saturniidae). *Journal of the Lepidopterists' Society* **30**: 114–115.

Peigler, R. S. (1976b). Observations on host plant relationships and larval nutrition in *Callosamia* (Saturniidae). *Journal of the Lepidopterists' Society* **30**: 184–187.

Peigler, R. S. (1976c). Collecting cocoons of *Callosamia securifera* (Saturniidae). *Journal of the Lepidopterists' Society* **30**: 111–113.

Peigler, R. S. (1981). Demonstration of reproductive isolating mechanisms in *Callosamia* (Saturniidae) by artificial hybridization. *Journal of Research on the Lepidoptera* **19**: 72–81.

Peigler, R. S. (1983). *A revision of the Indo-Australian genus Attacus (Lepidoptera: Saturniidae)*. Unpublished Ph.D. Dissertation, Texas A and M University, College Station, Texas, 322 pp.

Pinhey, E. (1972). *Emperor moths of South and South Central Africa*. C. Struik, Cape Town. 150 pp.

Priesner, E. (1968). Die interspezifischen Wirkungen der Sexuallockstoffe der Saturniidae (Lepidoptera). *Zeit. Vergl. Physiologie* **61**: 263–297.

Quezada, J. R. (1973). Insecticide applications disrupt pupal parasitism of *Rothschildia aroma* populations in El Salvador. *Environmental Entomology* **2**: 639–641.

Rau, P. and Rau, N. L. (1913). The fertility of cecropia eggs in relation to the mating period. *Biological Bulletin* **24**: 245–250.

Rau, P. and Rau, N. L. (1929). The sex attraction and rhythmic periodicity in the giant saturniid moths. *Transactions of the Academy of Science of St. Louis* **26**: 83–221.

Riddiford, L. M. (1974). The role of hormones in the reproductive behaviour of female wild silkmoths. In *Experimental analysis of insect behavior*, (ed. L. B. Browne,) Springer-Verlag, Berlin, pp. 278–285.

Rivnay, E. and Yathom, S. (1965). Phenology of Sphingidae in Israel. *Z. Agnew. Entomol.* **59**: 372–384.

Rivnay, E. and Sobrio, G. (1967). The phenology and diapause of *Saturnia pyri* Schiff. in temperate and subtropic climates. *Zeitschrift für Angewandte Entomologie* **59**: 59–63.

Robertson, I. A. D. (1977). Records of insects taken at light traps in Tanzania. VI-seasonal changes in catches and effect of the lunar cycle on hawkmoths of the subfamily Semanophorinae (Lepidoptera: Sphingidae). *Center for Overseas Pest Research, Miscellaneous Report* 37, 20 pp.

Robinson, H. S. and Robinson, P. J. M. (1950). Some notes on the observed behaviour of Lepidoptera in flight in the vicinity of light-sources together with a description of a light trap designed to take entomological samples. *Entomologists' Gazette* **1**: 3–20.

Rothschild, W. and Jordan, K. (1903). A revision of the lepidopterous family Sphingidae. *Novitates Zoologicae 9 (supplement)*: 1–972.

Scarbrough, A. G., Waldbauer, G. P. and Sternburg, J. G. (1974). Feeding and survival of cecropia larvae on various plant species. *Journal of the Lepidopterists' Society* **28**: 212–219.

Schneider, G. (1973). Uber den Einfluss verschiedener Umwelfactoren auf den Färbungspolymorphänismus der Raupen des tropisch-amerikanischen Schwärmers *Erinnyis ello* L. (Lepidoptera: Sphingidae). *Oecologia* **11**: 351–370.

Schreiber, H. (1978). *Dispersal centres of Sphingidae (Lepidoptera) in the neotropical region*. W. Junk, The Hague, Holland, 195 pp.

Schroeder, L. A. (1972). Energy budget of cecropia moths, *Platysamia cecropia* (Lepidoptera: Saturniidae), fed lilac leaves. *Annals of the Entomological Society of America* **63**: 367–372.

Scriber, J. M. (1977). Limiting effects of low leaf-water content on the nitrogen utilization, energy budget, and larval growth of *Hyalophora cecropia*. *Oecologia* **28**: 269–287.

Scriber, J. M. (1978). The affects of larval feeding specialization and plant growth form on the consumption and utilization of plant biomass and nitrogen: an ecological consideration. *Entomologia Experimentata et Applicaca* **24**: 694–710.

Scriber, J. M. (1979a). The effects of sequentially switching foodplants upon biomass and nitrogen utilization by polyphagous and stenophagous *Papilio* larvae. *Entomologia Experimentata et Applicata* **25**: 203–215.

Scriber, J. M. (1979b). Effects of leaf-water supplementation upon post-ingestive nutritional indices of forb-, shrub-, vine-, and tree-feeding Lepidoptera. *Entomologia Experimentata et Applicata* **25**: 240–252.

Scriber, J. M. (1979c). Post-ingestive utilization of plant biomass and nitrogen by Lepidoptera: legume feeding by the southern armyworm. *New York Entomological Society* **87**: 141–153.

Scriber, J. M. and Slansky, F. (1981). The nutritional ecology of immature insects. *Annual Review of Entomology* **26**: 183–211.

Smith, W. E. and Turner, R. B. (1979). Effects of age and temperature on the calling behaviour of the female range caterpillar moth, *Hemileuca oliviae* (Lepidoptera: Saturniidae). *The Southwestern Entomologist* **4**: 254–257.

Sotthibandhu, S. and Baker, R. R. (1979). Celestial orientation by the large yellow underwing moth, *Noctua pronuba*. *Animal Behaviour* **27**: 786–800.

Sternburg, J. G. and Waldbauer, G. P. (1969). Bimodal emergence of adult cecropia moths under natural conditions. *Annals of the Entomological Society of America* **62**: 1422–1429.

Sternburg, J. G. and Waldbauer, G. P. (1978). Phenological adaptations in diapause by cecropia from different latitudes. *Entomologia Experimentata et Aplicata* **23**: 48–54.

Sternburg, J. G., Waldbauer, G. P. and Scarbrough, A. G. (1981). Distribution of cecropia moth (Saturniidae) in central Illinois: a study in urban ecology. *Journal of the Lepidopterists' Society* **35**: 304–320.

Stewart, P. A. (1969). House sparrows and a field infestation of tobacco hornworm larvae infecting tobacco. *Journal of Economic Entomology* **62**: 956–957.

Stewart, P. A. (1975). Observations on flights of released tobacco hornworm moths (*Manduca sexta*, Order Leipdoptera, Family Sphingidae). *Ohio Journal of Science* **75**: 83–84.

Tams, W. H. T. (1924). Notes on *Heliconisa pagenstecheri* Hübn. in the Argentine. *The Entomologist* **57**: 243–245.

Thurston, R. and Prachuabmoh, O. (1971). Predation by birds on tobacco hornworm larvae infesting tobacco. *J. Economic Entomology* **64**: 1548–1549.

Tobin, T. R. and Bell, W. J. (1982). Guidance system for pheronome orientation in moths. *Nature* **295**: 263.

Toliver, M. E., Sternburg, J. G. and Waldbauer, G. P. (1979). Daily flight periods of male *Callosamia promethea* (Saturniidae). *Journal of the Lepidopterists' Society* **33**: 232–238.

van den Berg, M. A. (1974a). Natural enemies and diseases of the forest insect *Nudaurelia cytherea clarki* Geertsema (Lepidoptera: Saturniidae). *Phytophylactica* **6**: 39–44.

van den Berg, M. A. (1974b). Pouoogmotte (Lepidoptera: Saturniidae) van die Nasionale Krugerwildtuin. *Koedoe* **17**: 159–172.

van den Berg, M. A. and van den Berg, M. M. (1974). Frass sampling to determine the population densities and instars of Saturniidae (Lepidoptera) in pine plantations. *Phytophylactica* **6**: 105–108.

van den Berg, M. A., Catling, H. D. and Vermeulen, J. B. (1973). The distribution and seasonal occurrence of Saturniidae (Lepidoptera) in Transvaal. *Phytophylactica* **5**: 111–114.

Vuattoux, R. (1978). Plantes hôtes et durée de developpement de Lépidoptères Sphingides élevés à la station de Lamto (Côte d'Ivoire). *Ann. Univ. Abidjan, série E (Ecologie)* **11**: 53–87.

Vuattoux, R. (1981). Les Lépidoptères Attacides élevés à la station d'écologie de Lamto (Côte d'Ivoire). *Ann. Univ. Abidjan, série E (Ecologie)* **14**: 83–106.

Waldbauer, G. P. and Sternburg, J. G. (1967). Differential predation on cocoons of *Hyalophora cecropia* (Lepidoptera: Saturniidae) spun on shrubs and trees. *Ecology* **48**: 312–315.

Waldbauer, G. P. and Sternburg, J. G. (1973). Polymorphic termination of diapause by cecropia: genetic and geographical aspects. *Biological Bulletin* **145**: 627–641.

Waldbauer, G. P. and Sternburg, J. G. (1979). Inbreeding depression and a behavioural mechanism for its avoidance in *Hyalophora cecropia*. *American Midland Naturalist* **102**: 204–208.

Waldbauer, G. P. and Sternburg, J. G. (1982a). Cocoons of *Callosamia promethea* (Saturniidae): adaptive significance of differences in mode of attachment to the host tree. *Journal of the Lepidopterists' Society* **36**: 192–199.

Waldbauer, G. P. and Sternburg, J. G. (1982b). Long mating flights by male *Hyalophora cecropia* (L.) (Saturniidae). *Journal of the Lepidopterists' Society* **36**: 154–155.

Waldbauer, G. P., Sternburg, J. G. and Janzen, D. H. (1984). Free-flying male cecropia moths: in what direction do they go, how long do they live, and how much weight do they lose? *Great Lakes Entomologist* (in press).

Wangberg, J. K. (1983). Defoliation of sand shinnery oak (*Quercus havardii* Rydb.) in western Texas by *Hemileuca* sp. (Lepidoptera: Saturniidae) larvae. *The Southwestern Naturalist* **28**: 383–384.

Wehner, R. (1984). Astronavigation in insects. *Annual Review of Entomology* **29**: 277–298.

Weiss, H. B., Soraci, F. A. and McCoy, E. E. (1941). Insect behaviour to various wave lengths of light. *Journal of the New York Entomological Society* **51**: 117–131.

White, T. C. R. (1972). The distribution, dispersal and host range of *Antheraea eucalypti* (Lepidoptera: Saturniidae) in New Zealand. *Pacific Insects* **14**: 669–673.

Wolda, H. (1980). *Fluctuaciones estacionales de insectos en el tropico: Sphingidae.* Memorias del VI Congreso de la Sociedad Colombiana de Entomologia, pp. 11–58. Mimeo.

Worth, C. B. (1979). Captures of large moths by an ultraviolet light trap. *Journal of the Lepidopterists' Society* **33**: 261–264.

Worth, C. B., Williams, T. F., Platt, A. P. and Bradley, B. P. Differential growth among larvae of *Citheronia regalis* (Saturniidae) on three genera of foodplants. *Journal of the Leipdopterists' Society* **33**: 162–166.

Young, A. M. (1972). Notes on community ecology of adult sphinx moths in Costa Rican lowland tropical rainforest. *Caribbean Journal of Science* **12**: 151–163.

Size inequalities and fitness in plant populations

OTTO T. SOLBRIG AND DOROTHY J. SOLBRIG

In a population of plants, individuals vary in size. The size differences may be due to differences in age, or in the physical environment, or in the biological environment such as distance to nearest neighbour or effects of herbivores. Since in plants, size is related to seed production, the distribution of sizes in a population can have important effects on individual fitness and genetic structure of the population, and ultimately may affect the persistance of the species in the community.

The problem

Yield (in grams dry weight) of monospecific, even-aged experimental plant populations is constant over a range of densities. This is the so-called competition-density effect (Kira *et al.* 1953a, b, 1954), which states that

$$w \cdot d = K$$

where w = plant weight, d = density of plants (number per unit area) and K = constant. From this formula it can be deduced that as density increases, average plant size diminishes and *vice versa*; that is, density and plant weight are inversely correlated in even-aged, monospecific plant populations.

Nevertheless, although the average individual size (or weight) is predictable from a knowledge of the density (for a given environment), individual plant size (or weight) is not. This is due to the fact that even under the most controlled conditions certain individuals grow larger than others, that is, a size hierarchy is inevitably established.

As seedlings in an even-aged, monospecific population grow, they eventually reach the maximal average size that corresponds to their density. Any further increase in average size must be accompanied by a reduction in density if the competition-density effect is to be maintained. This process of mortality has been called self-thinning (Shinozaki and Kira 1956; Koyama and Kira 1956; Yoda *et al.* 1957, 1963; White and Harper 1970; White 1977). It has been shown that in high density stands seed production is arrested unless self-thinning takes place. Self-thinning is then a regulatory process that insures an adequate seed production.

In a population subjected to self-thinning, mortality takes place preferentially among the smallest individuals, which has been interpreted as indicating that self-thinning is the result of intra-specific competition (Yoda *et al.* 1957). Since mortality is higher among small individuals, self-thinning affects the size distribution in the population.

In a population of even-aged plants, large individuals produce more seeds than small individuals. Fecundity being an important fitness component, it follows that the form of the size distribution in a population and the effect of self-thinning will have important implications for the genetic structure of the population and its evolution.

Given the implications of the existence of size hierarchies, it is very important to determine what factors are responsible for the development of size hierarchies and what forces maintain or modify size hierarchies, not only in artificial, but also in natural populations. Furthermore, we must determine to what extent results from experimental, even-aged, mono-specific populations are transferable to naturally growing populations.

Before entering into a more detailed description of the phenomenon we would like first to define what we mean by size and by a size hierarchy.

By 'size' we will refer in this paper to an undetermined quantity representing the plant's volume, height, girth, or weight. In populations of the same species growing in similar environments, these parameters are correlated. However, because plants grow by the accretion of individual parts (leaves, branches, roots) – not all necessarily of the same size – the best way of measuring size differences is probably individual dry weight. However, in order to obtain its dry weight the plant must be sacrificed, making this measure inadequate if changes in a population over time are to be observed. Height or girth (in trees) may be substituted for weight, or number of parts (such as the number of leaves in rosette plants).

The term 'hierarchy' has different meanings in different disciplines. Consequently confusion can arise unless it is carefully defined. Hierarchy is defined by the Shorter Oxford Dictionary (third edition) as a 'body of persons or things ranked in grades, orders or classes' (Weiner and Solbrig 1984). The greater the number of orders, the more hierarchical a population, according to this definition. We shall use the term 'size hierarchy' to refer to the existence of individuals of different sizes in a population. The reason for using the particular word hierarchy in this context will become clear when we explain a statistical method derived from the economics of inequalities in income. The term 'size hierarchy' is normally used in biology to refer to the existence of individuals of different sizes in a population. All plant populations are hierarchical, although the degree of hierarchy, i.e. the number of size classes or orders into which a population can be classified, varies.

The relative number of individuals in each of the classes of a size hierarchy is another important characteristic of a size distribution. Since sizes in a population are usually not normally distributed, and they seldom conform to any distribution easily transformed into a normal distribution, (such as a log-normal distribution), various measures of skewness are used to determine the degree of hierarchy and for comparative purposes. However, by themselves such measures are incomplete characterizations of hierarchy, since populations with different ranges and size classes (and consequently different degrees of hierarchy) can have the same degree of skewness. An ideal measure of hierarchy must combine both an indication of the number of classes and their relative frequency.

Most plant populations are characterized by a size hierarchy formed by many small individuals and a few large ones. That is, they differ from a

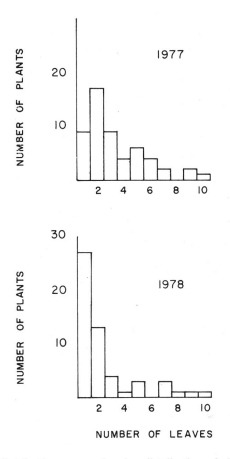

Fig. 1. Left-skewed distribution curves showing distribution of plant size based on number of leaves in a population of *Viola fimbriatula* in August 1977 and August 1978.

normal distribution by being skewed to the left (Fig. 1). The skewness is determined through standardized measures based on the third moment around the mean (e.g. $g_1 = n (x_1 - x)^3 / (n-1) (n-2)s^3$; Sokal and Rohlf 1981). These measures have been criticized by Weiner and Solbrig (1984) as being insufficient to describe differences in size hierarchies between populations. In effect, two populations within a species can have the same value of g_1, but in one the difference in size between the largest and the smallest individual may be much greater. That is, absolute degree of size difference between the smallest and largest individual in the population (range) as well as degree of deviation from a normal distribution (kurtosis) are important attributes of a size hierarchy. The range and the skewness together must be used to characterize a size distribution, but seldom have been since there are no good satatistical measures to compare ranges.

A measure of size hierarchy is the Lorenz curve and the Gini coefficient used in economic science to measure inequalities in income distribution (Lorenz 1905; Weiner and Solbrig 1984). To obtain a Lorenz curve, individuals are ranked according to the measure of size used (weight, girth, etc.) from the smallest to the largest, and the percentage of the total size (i.e. biomass, girth, etc.) that each represents is calculated by dividing its size by the sum of all sizes in the population. A graph is then drawn, where the abscissa represents the cumulative number of individuals ranked from the smallest to the largest and the ordinate the cumulative percentage of the total sizes represented by those individuals (Fig. 2).

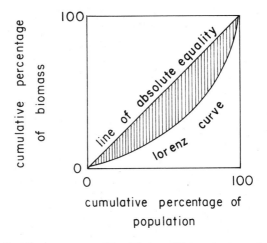

Fig. 2. A theoretical Lorenz curve. The Gini coefficient is the ratio of the shaded area to the area of the triangle under the diagonal.

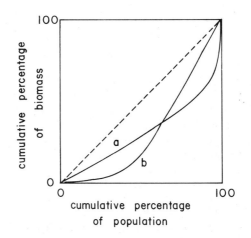

Fig. 3. Lorenz curves for populations with an excess of small individuals (a) or an excess of large individuals (b).

If all individuals are of the same size, the Lorenz curve will be a straight line of slope one; if the distribution of sizes is normal, the Lorenz curve will be symmetrical; if the size curve is skewed to the left (excess of small individuals) the Lorenz curve will have its inflection point to the right of center; if skewed to the right (excess of large individuals) the Lorenz curve will have its inflection point to the left of center (Fig. 3).

To evaluate the degree of inequality of two Lorenz curves the degree of deviation from the diagonal is assessed (Fig. 2). This can be quantified as the ratio of the area between the diagonal and the Lorenz curve, over the triangular area under the diagonal, and is called the Gini coefficient, G (Gini 1912; Ricci 1916; Weiner and Solbrig 1984). Thus G has a minimum value of 0 when all individuals are equal, and a theoretical maximum of 1 in an infinite population in which all individuals but one have a value of 0. The Gini coefficient is equivalent to one half of the relative mean difference, which is the arithmetic average of the absolute values of the differences between all pairs of individuals divided by the average size (Sen 1973).

$$G = \frac{\sum\limits_{i=1}^{n} \sum\limits_{j=1}^{n} |x_i - x_j|}{2 n^2 \bar{x}}$$

The value of the Gini coefficient does not change if each individual's size is raised in the same proportion. Thus populations of species of different sizes can be compared, or the same population over time. However different size hierarchies (especially those with different degrees of skewness) that result in different Lorenz curves, can have the same or very similar Gini coefficients.

CAUSES OF SIZE HIERARCHIES

Since size hierarchies are a universal characteristic of all populations of plants it is important to determine the factors that are responsible for them. Size hierarchies could result from genetically or environmentally determined inequalities in seed weight, germination time, and/or growth rate, or they can be the result of an unequal supply of resources (water, nutrients, light), or they may be the result of competition between the plants in the population. There is good evidence in favour of each of these factors, although there is strong disagreement among certain authors (Harper 1977; Rabinowitz 1979; Turner and Rabinowitz 1983; Weiner, in press) regarding the relative importance of competition. We now briefly review some of this evidence and discuss its significance.

Seed weights in a population are characteristically normally distributed (Fig. 4). A heavier seed may be an indication of a larger embryo, a greater amount of reserves, and/or thicker seed coats. Any of these factors can affect speed of germination as well as growth rate. Harper (1977) presents a very complete discussion of the effect that differences in seed

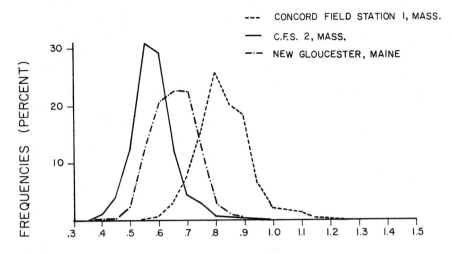

Fig. 4. Frequency distribution of seed weight (mg· 10^{-1}) in several populations of *Viola fimbriatula*.

characteristics and soil microtopography have on germination. Slight variations in seed characters and especially in soil microtopography determine the speed as well as the percentage of germination of a population of seeds. The principal factor controlling the speed of germination appears to be the time it takes for a seed to imbibe water, which in turn is affected by the thickness of the seed coats as well as by the closeness of the contact the seed makes with the soil. The latter is related to the shape of the seed and the texture of the soil. A flat seed will make better contact with a smooth soil, while a rough seed will fit better in the interstices of a soil with pores and lumps of about the same size as the seed (Harper 1977).

Available evidence (Harper 1977; Cook 1977; Turner and Rabinowitz 1983) indicates that in uniform environments the shape of the frequency distribution of seedling emergence is normal or slightly skewed to the right. Consequently germination time alone does not appear to be responsible for uneven size hierarchies in plant populations. Nevertheless it is indirectly an important factor.

Given a population of seedlings whose weights are distributed normally (either because of different seed weights or because uneven germination times allowed some more days to grow), and given that growth is an exponential process, over time a log-normal (right-skewed) size hierarchy will be produced. This was pointed out first by Koyama and Kira (1956) and Yoda et al. (1957) and has been confirmed by Rabinowitz (1979) and Turner and Rabinowitz (1983). It has also been pointed out by these authors that if there is variation in growth rate between individuals there need not be any variation in seedling size or germination time to develop a size hierarchy.

Another factor that can create a skewed size hierarchy is competition for resources. In effect, if resources (water, nutrients, light) are limited in the population, then those seedlings (presumably the ones that germinate first or are initially heavier) that can appropriate a greater than even share, will increase their growth rate at the expense of that of their nearest neighbours (Harper 1977). Competition for resources (or interference) can therefore be another factor that creates a right-skewed size hierarchy. Furthermore competition for resources will take place in crowded populations. It is in these populations where self-thinning occurs, and since it takes place primarily among the smallest individuals, self-thinning also can produce a right-skewed size hierarchy in a population which originally had a normal distribution of sizes.

It has been verified experimentally that a right-skewed size hierarchy appears with time, i.e. with growth of the plants, in populations grown singly in pots or in very low density so that no competition (or interference) takes place. It is therefore undeniable that as a population of seedlings grows, a right-skewed size hierarchy will appear. The unresolved question is whether competition increases or decreases the degree of inequality in the population.

Competition in its usual meaning is associated with unequal consumption of resources. It is usually assumed that in a competitive situation a 'winner' takes a greater than equal share of the resources at the expense of a 'loser'. Competition (or as Harper insists, interference) in plants is not necessarily of this form. According to Grime (1979) competition in plants exists when potentially they can use the same molecule of water, the same atom of nutrient, or the same quantum of light. Since plants are sessile competition (or interference) is primarily a neighbourhood effect. Furthermore, water and nutrient molecules will move in the soil. Provided that transpiration rates are more or less equal, neighbouring plants will absorb water and nutrients in proportion to their absorbing surfaces, and large plants will not be able to absorb a quantity greater than their proportion of biomass in the population. In other words, water and nutrients cannot be hoarded or easily sequestered. Not so with light. The unique unidirectional character of light allows a plant to remove light from another by shading even if it will not use that light itself for photosynthesis. This process of shading is not without costs (in increased transpiration) but since by shading its competitor the shaded plant will reduce its transpiration rate, the dominant plant will indirectly also gain water and nutrients. Consequently the results of competition for light are likely to be different from competition for nutrients and water, the former being more like 'competition' (in the classical sense of the word), the latter more like 'interference'.

The difference in the characteristics of the resource light (a form of energy) and the resources water and nutrients (chemical elements) may explain some of the apparently contradictory experimental results so far obtained when the relative effects of competition and growth as sources of the establishment of size hierarchies were tested.

Given that either a variation in growth rates within a population of seedlings or resource competition can in principle produce an uneven distribution of sizes, the question is to determine the relative importance of each. Since resource depletion reduces growth, competition for resources may actually slow down the establishment of size hierarchies.

The test of these hypotheses is simple and straightforward. Seedlings are grown at different densities and under different nutrient levels. Under the growth hypothesis, populations in low density and with high nutrients, that is, those with the highest growth rate, should have the most hierarchical size distribution. According to the dominance and suppression model, the greatest size hierarchy should be found where competition is greatest, i.e. high density, low nutrient populations.

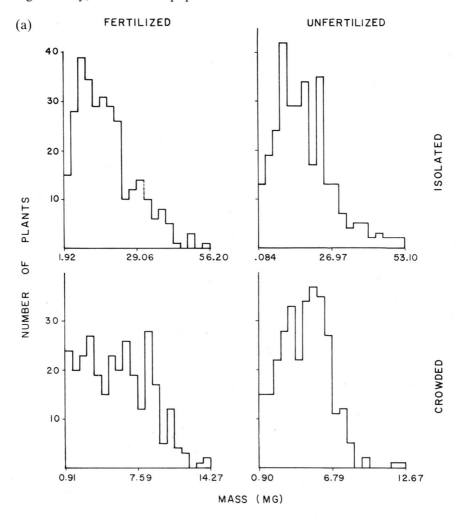

Fig. 5. Effect of density and fertilizer on populations of *Festuca paradoxa* 44 days after sowing. (a) Frequency distribution of sizes; (b) (p. 149) Lorenz curves. (Data from Turner and Rabinowitz 1983).

(b)

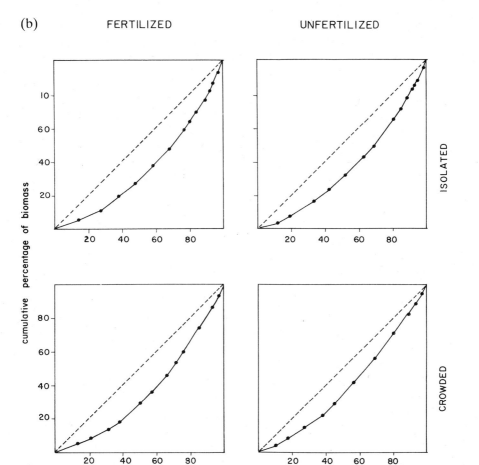

cumulative   percentage   of   population

These tests have been conducted recently by Turner and Rabinowitz (1983) and Weiner (in press), who arrive at opposite conclusions. In effect, Turner and Rabinowitz reach the conclusion that competition delays the establishment of a size hierarchy, while Weiner concludes that competition increases hierarchy! Given their different results, it is worth analysing these experiments in greater detail.

Turner and Rabinowitz (1983) grew seedlings of *Festuca paradoxa* from seeds collected in the wild under four different conditions: singly in small containers (5 × 5.5 × 5.5 cm) or in flats at a density of 8 seeds/cm², each without and with fertilizer (twice weekly with half strength Hoagland solution). Seedlings were harvested at five intervals, from 17 to 44 days after sowing. It was found that isolated plants were more skewed than crowded ones, and that fertilizer treatment had little effect.

Weiner (in press) grew seeds of *Trifolium incarnatum* and *Lolium multiflorum* both singly and under two other densities (200 and 1200 individuals/m^2), and two fertilizer treatments (with or without N-K-P fertilizer: no further details given). The experiment was conducted for 93 days at which time the populations were harvested. In addition the two species were grown together. Weiner did not calculate skewness, but used Lorenz curves and Gini coefficients as measures of inequality. These show that high density plots were more hierarchical than low density plots.

Because the experiments differ in degree of density, in time allowed for growth and in the statistical measure used, they are difficult to compare. We have calculated the Lorenz curves and Gini coefficients for the Turner and Rabinowitz experiments to facilitate comparative analysis. Weiner does not present his data in a way that allows the calculation of skewness indices.

Figs. 5 and 6 present the frequency distributions and Lorenz curves for the experiments of Turner and Rabinowitz and Weiner respectively. The Gini coefficients appear in Table 1. It can be seen that at 44 days the populations of *Festuca paradoxa* grown by Turner and Rabinowitz had very similar Lorenz curves and Gini coefficients under three out of four treatments; on the other hand populations of *Trifolium incarnatum* and *Lolium multiflorum* showed a significant effect of crowding as compared to singly grown plants. However the sample size for singly grown plants is very low, which makes this part of the experiment unreliable. This uncertainty is reinforced by the contradictory results of the density and

Table 1

Effect of density and fertilizer on the Gini coefficient (G)

Species	Density	Fertilizer Treatment	Days Grown	G
Festuca paradoxa	isolated	none	44	0.298
	„	fertilized	44	0.299
	8/cm^2	none	44	0.220 (0.241)
	„	fertilized	44	0.282
Trifolium incarnatum	isolated	none	92	0.235
	„	fertilized	92	0.088
	0.002/cm^2	none	92	0.377
	„	fertilized	92	0.376
	0.12/cm^2	none	92	0.621
	„	fertilized	92	0.482
Lolium multiflorum	isolated	none	92	0.080
	„	fertilized	92	0.147
	0.02/cm^2	none	92	0.368
	„	fertilized	92	0.459
	0.12/cm^2	none	92	0.382
	„	fertilized	92	0.489

(a)

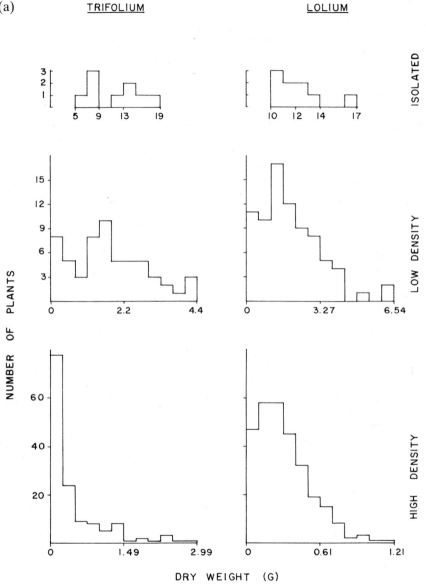

Fig. 6. Effect of density on low fertilizer treatments of *Trifolium incarnatum* and *Lolium multiflorum*. (a) Frequency distribution; (b) (p. 152) Lorenz curves. i = isolated; l = low density; h = high density. (Data from Weiner (in press)).

(b)

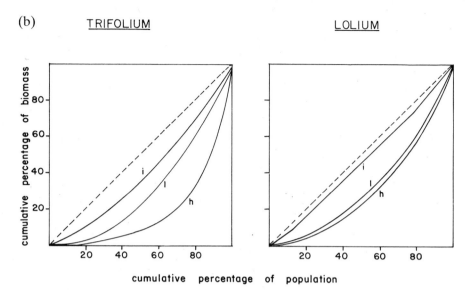

cumulative   percentage   of   population

fertilizer treatment on the two species. In *Trifolium incarnatum*, increases in density increased hierarchy significantly (as measured by the Gini coefficient), but not in *Lolium multiflorum*. On the other hand, fertilizer treatment had an effect on *Lolium* but not on *Trifolium*, probably because the latter is a legume.

These two experiments do not unambiguously refute either hypothesis. A size hierarchy is obviously established early on, regardless of the density of the plants, probably because of factors other than competition (as pointed out first by Koyama and Kira (1956) and verified by Burdon and Harper (1980)), such as the initial seed size (Black 1951), order of germination (Ross and Harper 1972; Abul-Fatih and Bazzaz 1979; Cook 1979, 1980), habitat heterogeneity (Solbrig 1981) and genetic variability (Schall and Levin 1976). It is however also clear from the experiments of Weiner (in press) that competition can increase the degree of hierarchy in the population by further enhancing the growth of large plants at the expense of small ones.

Competition *per se* does not establish the size hierarchy, and as argued by Rabinowitz (1979; Turner and Rabinowitz 1983), high density of seedlings, by slowing down growth, may actually delay the establishment of the size hierarchy. However, once the hierarchy is established, large plants can capture more light and further can deny light to smaller plants through shading, and thereby increase still more the hierarchy (and size skewness) of the population.

The effect of competition is shown best by the experiment of interspecific competition between *Lolium multiflorum* and *Trifolium incarnatum* performed by Weiner (in press). In the low nutrient experiments the Gini coefficients of *Lolium* and *Trifolium* when grown singly were very similar (Table 2), but they were more dissimilar when grown in mixtures,

Table 2

Effect of density, fertilizer, and competition on the Gini coefficient (G).

Species	Density	Fertilizer Treatment	G (single species)	G (mixed species)
Lolium multiflorum	low	none	0.368	0.297
	high	„	0.382/0.357*	0.333
	low	fertilized	0.459	0.368
	high	„	0.489/0.510*	0.496
Trifolium incarnatum	low	none	0.377	0.649
	high	„	0.621/0.341*	0.669
	low	fertilized	0.376	0.319
	high	„	0.482/0.437*	0.430

* Planted in a random and hexagonal pattern respectively

with *Lolium* populations having similar or lower values than when growing singly, and *Trifolium* having higher values. No such effect is seen in high fertility plots, where the Gini coefficients for both *Lolium* and *Trifolium* whether grown singly or in mixtures are very similar. However, as pointed out by Weiner, in these experiments mortality due to self-thinning was higher, especially among the suppressed *Trifolium* population, than in the low fertility experiments. This will have the effect of removing preferentially the smallest plants, which could reduce the size hierarchy.

In summary, the existence of size hierarchies in populations of plants is probably the result of the unequal exponential growth of seedlings, especially during the early phases of growth. Once the population reaches a high enough density for the competition-density effect to manifest itself, the larger plants will be able to shade smaller individuals, thereby maintaining their growth rate, while smaller plants stop increasing (the dominance-suppression effect, Harper 1977). As the larger individuals keep growing, smaller plants lose biomass (by shedding leaves) and eventually die (self-thinning). The exact effect of these two opposite phenomena (increase in size of the larger plants, loss of the smallest) on the size hierarchy is hard to predict, but it will depend on the initial size hierarchy and the distribution of plant sizes in space (since dominance-suppression is a neighbourhood effect). The longer-lived the population the greater the effect of competition.

So far we have been discussing primarily even-aged, monospecific populations. In natural communities with a mixture of species and different aged plants, seedlings are likely to be exposed from the time of germination to interference effects from congeners and non-congeners of different ages and sizes. In such situations establishment and growth depends on the number, the size and the distance to neighbours, and survival will not be possible unless there is an early period of growth free of competition (Harper 1977; Schellner, Newell and Solbrig 1982). In these situations, size hierarchy is almost entirely due to dominance and suppression.

SIZE AND FITNESS

The existence of size hierarchies in plants has important genetic and evolutionary implications. In effect it has been shown that in plants survivorship and fecundity, two important fitness components, are primarily related to size and not to age (Werner and Caswell 1977; Sohn and Policansky 1977; Solbrig et al. 1980; Solbrig 1981). Consequently large plants will leave more descendants than smaller plants. Solbrig et al. (in prep.) show that in populations of the perennial herb *Viola fimbriatula* that were analyzed demographically over four years, the 10 per cent largest plants produced from 50 to 80 per cent of the annual seed crop in the population. In addition these authors show that large plants have greater survival probability than smaller plants. As has been pointed out, the size hierarchy is established very early. Cook (1979; Cook and Lyons 1983) has followed cohorts of seedlings of *Viola fimbriatula* from germination to disappearance of the population and has shown that only a few large plants produced seeds, and these established their dominance very early in the life of the population. It also must be pointed out again, that self-thinning removes the smallest individuals from the population, usually before they bloom.

Species show great individual differences in their response to crowding. Some species (mostly annuals) can tolerate great differences in density. So, for example, *Chenopodium album* can bloom and produce some seed under very crowded conditions; other species, especially perennial trees and shrubs will not bloom until they attain a relatively large size, which may take several years and involve a great deal of self-thinning mortality if the initial seedling density was high (Ford 1975; Johnson and Bell 1975; Mohler, Marks, and Sprugel 1978; White 1980).

Plant species often show an increased reproductive effort with size (Solbrig and Rollins 1977). Consequently the relation between size and fecundity is often an exponential function (Solbrig et al. 1980; Solbrig 1981). As a result, distributions of seed contributions may be more hierarchical than biomass distributions.

If we define adaptation as the ability to survive the rigours of the environment and to reproduce (Solbrig 1982), and given that in plants survivorship and reproduction are closely related to attaining a certain size, then it can be stated that adaptation requires the ability to grow in an environment at a rate that maintains the individual in a size category above that subjected to self-thinning. Operationally this statement has statistical rather than absolute validity, since the growth rate of an individual plant depends on the particular neighbourhood composition. In a local situation with several large individuals a medium-sized plant may be outcompeted and die, while in another neighbourhood of smaller-sized plants, a medium-sized individual may survive. Nevertheless, even though the exact growth rate needed to survive in a particular environment cannot be predicted with precision, it is valid to say that adapted individuals (in the previously defined sense) are those that for a given physical and biological environment maintain a certain growth rate. We are accustomed to thinking of certain morphological and physiological characteristics as adaptations to different environments. It is likely that in many cases the significance of these characters lies in their effect on growth.

Within a population of interbreeding plants, a size hierarchy is established, and large individuals will produce proportionally more seed. The direct genetic effect of this phenomenon is to reduce the effective population number. Consequently, and provided that the environment does not change over several generations, strong selection for the genes or gene combinations producing high growth rate (especially in the early stages) will take place. Particularly since this selection is accompanied by inbreeding, populations should be fairly uniform genetically in terms of growth rate and observed differences should be due mostly to environmental and random phenomena. In other words, additive genetic variance for growth rate should be low.

There are few studies that have specifically looked at this. Gottlieb (1977) grew seeds produced by small and large wild individuals of *Stephanomeria exigua* var. *coronaria* in uniform environments and could detect no statistically significant difference in the average size of their progeny; Solbrig (1981 and unpublished) grew genetic families of *Viola sororia* and *V. fimbriatula* under various environmental and density conditions and partitioned the additive variance into genetic and environmental components and found the heritability for growth rate to be very low.

Because plants are sessile, and their pollen and seed shadows are very leptokurtic, they naturally have a tendency to inbreed and form distinct genetic neighbourhoods (Turner *et al*. 1982). The existence of size hierarchies may modify and delimit the genetic neighbourhoods, depending on which genotypes produce the fastest growth rate. In effect, if the environment is very uniform over the entire population, then it may be expected that the genotypic characteristics that are adaptive in terms of growth rate in that environment should be selected, countering any drift effects due to the peculiar effects of the sessileness and breeding systems of plants. On the other hand, if the environment is heterogeneous in space and over time, or the genetic component of growth rate is low, then we expect more drift, and consequently less uniformity.

Which kind of species should fit the former and which the latter category? In principle, the more a species forms monospecific, even-aged populations, the more we expect genetic uniformity for growth rate, i.e., the lower the expected heritability for growth rate. Species that fit this category are annual species of specialized habitats (such as desert annuals, or species of specialized soils, such as limestone outcrops), colonizers and early succession species. Most of these species tend to be short-lived. On the other hand, in late succession and climax species, growth rate may be less closely linked to survivorship. In these species, which characteristically grow in mixed species stands and have more complex age structures, survivorship is more a result of very local events and neighbourhood composition, and self-thinning in its true sense never takes place. Consequently, we expect much greater genetic heterogeneity for growth rate, as each genetic family is subject over time to different selection forces (Solbrig 1976).

No rigorous study of the degree of heritability for growth rate between species with different life histories exists. However the evidence from isozyme variation in plants (Hamrick 1979, Hamrick *et al.* 1979) indicates that long-lived trees have more variation than annuals and short-lived perennial species. Although this does not constitute proof of the model outlined, it does not contradict it.

Evolutionary implications

The first conclusion that can be derived from the existence of size hierarchies in plants is that growth rate during the early phases of life is a very important aspect of competition in species that tend to form monospecific, even-aged populations. This is not necessarily so in species that grow in mixed communities, where seedlings will by necessity be subordinated from an early age to larger individuals, and where survival depends more on mortality of existing individuals. Nevertheless, even in 'climax' forests, where establishment of new individuals is a replacement process after a gap is formed in the canopy as a result of the death of a tree, the individual or individuals that replace it are the ones that are fastest in closing the gap. A similar conclusion regarding the importance of growth rate has been reached by Grime (1979).

The second conclusion is that within interbreeding neighbourhoods there should be very low heritability for growth. An important corollary is that given the strong selection for growth rate, any linked characters – including nonadaptive ones – will also be selected and can become fixed in the population. On the other hand, the dynamics of size hierarchies also may explain why populations in plant species do not show more variability, given the short distances to which pollen and seeds flow. For any changes to become established within a population, they must confer a competitive advantage, which means faster seedling growth within the physical and biological context. The probability of establishment of a new mutation in a population where breeding and establishment is random is very low (Fisher 1930, Kimura and Ohta 1971). That probability will be even lower in a population where the advantage of the large individuals is as great as is the case in many species (i.e. the largest 10 per cent produce 50–80 per cent of the seed).

An example is provided by a pair of species of New England violets. We studied a pair of closely related species: the blue-flowered forest species *Viola sororia* and its field-inhabiting congener *V. fimbriatula*. The species are closely related and form fully fertile interspecific hybrids. Furthermore, transplant studies and observation show that both species are able to grow in both forest and field. In addition, detailed demographic and ecophysiological studies (Solbrig *et al.* in prep.) indicate that the two species do not differ very much in their phenology, life history, or physiology. They differ, however, quite markedly in their leaf morphology. This difference alters the growth rate of the species in the two environments. *Viola sororia* grows significantly faster than *V. fimbriatula* in shaded environments; the reverse situation exists in sunny environments. Although hybrids are formed where the two species meet in forest edges, no intermixing occurs in the main habitats.

A third and final conclusion is that size hierarchies may affect the process of speciation in plants. If size hierarchies through their effect on survivorship and fecundity have a cohesive effect on the population, so that it cannot be easily disrupted by the accumulation of gradual mutations, it follows that more drastic changes – genetic or evolutionary revolutions – may be required. In effect, when a species invades a new environment, one where the particular set of characteristics for fast seedling growth that it possesses no longer leads to fast growth, it probably will be eliminated. In the accepted jargon, that locality is outside its 'realized niche'. However, if such invasion is accompanied by a large change (such as that resulting from hybridization with other species, or a large chromosomal change), selection will operate quite quickly to select any genotype (if present) that can grow sufficiently fast to be competitive in the new environment. In other words, although normally the process is a conservative one (when variability is low), it has the potential of producing fast changes (if variability is high). This is akin to what Harlan Lewis has called catastrophic selection (Lewis 1962), and may provide the mechanism.

Acknowledgements

We would like to thank Jacob Weiner for the preprint of his article which we have quoted so copiously.

References

Abul-Fatih, H. A. and Bazzaz, F. A. (1979). The biology of *Ambrosia trifida* L. II. Germination, emergence, growth, and survival. *New Phytologist* **83**, 817–827.

Black, J. N. (1957). Early vegetative growth of three strains of subterranean clover (*Trifolium subterraneum* L.) in relation to size of seed. *Australian J. Agric. Res.* **8**, 1–14.

Burdon, J. J. and Harper, J. L. (1980). Relative growth rates of individual members of a plant population. *J. Ecol.* **68**, 953–957.

Cook, R. E. (1979). Patterns of juvenile mortality and recruitment in plants. In *Topics in Plant Population Biology*, (ed. O. T. Solbrig, S. Jain, G. B. Johnson and P. H. Raven) pp. 207–231. N.Y.: Columbia Univ. Press.

Cook, R. E. (1980). The biology of seeds in the soil. In *Demography and Evolution in Plant Populations*, (ed. O. T. Solbrig), pp. 107–129. Blackwell Sci. Oxford.

Cook, R. E. and Lyons, E. E. (1983). The biology of *Viola fimbriatula* in a natural disturbance. *Ecology* **64**, 654–660.

Fisher, R. A. (1930). *The Genetical Theory of Natural Selection*. Clarendon Press, Oxford.

Ford, E. D. (1975). Competition and stand structure in some even-aged plant monocultures. *J. Ecol.* **63**, 311–333.

Gini, C. (1912). *Variabilita e Mutabilita*. Bologna.

Gottlieb, L. D. (1977). Genotypic similarity of large and small individuals in a natural population of the annual plant *Stephanomeria exigua* spp. *coronaria* (Compositae). *J. Ecol.* **65**, 127–134.

Grime, J. P. (1979). *Plant Strategies and Vegetation Processes*. Wiley, Chichester.

Hamrick, J. L. (1979). Genetic variation and longevity. In *Topics in Plant Population Biology*, (ed. O. T. Solbrig, S. Jain, G. B. Johnson and P. H. Raven) pp. 84–114. Columbia Univ. Press, New York.

Hamrick, J. L., Linhart, Y. B. and Mitton, J. B. (1979). Relationships between life history characteristics and electrophoretically detectable genetic variation in plants. *Annu. Rev. Ecol. Syst.* **10**, 173–200.

Harper, J. L. (1977). *Population Biology of Plants*. Academic Press, London.

Johnson, F. L. and Bell, D. T. (1975). Size-class structure of three streamside forests. *Amer. J. Bot.* **62**, 81–85.

Kimura, M. and Ohta, T. (1971). *Theoretical Aspects of Population Genetics*. Princeton Univ. Press, Princeton, N.J.

Kira, T., Ogawa, H. and Hozumi, K. (1954). Intraspecific competition among higher plants. II. Further discussions on Mitscherlich's law. *J. Inst. Polytech. Osaka City Univ. D.* **5**, 1–7.

Kira, T., Ogawa, H. and Sakazaki, Y. (1953a). Intraspecific competition among higher plants. I. Competition-density-yield interrelationship in regularly dispersed populations. *J. Inst. Polytech. Osaka City Univ. D.* **4**, 1–16.

Kira, T., Hozumi, K., Ogawa, H. and Ueno, Y. (1953b). Spacing problem from the ecological viewpoint. *Studies from the Inst. Hort. Kyoto Univ.* **6**, 69–81. (in Japanese with English summary).

Koyama, H. and Kira, T. (1956). Intraspecific competition among higher plants. VIII. Frequency distribution of individual plant weight as affected by the interaction between plants. *J. Inst. Polytech. Osaka City Univ. D.* **7**, 73–94.

Lewis, H. (1962). Catastrophic selection as a factor in speciation. *Evolution* **16**, 237–271.

Lorenz, M. O. (1905). Methods for measuring the concentration of wealth. *Am. Stat. Assoc.* **9**, 209–219.

Mohler, C. L., Marks, P. L. and Sprugel, D. G. (1978). Stand structure and allometry of trees during self-thinning of pure stands. *J. Ecol.* **66**, 599–614.

Rabinowitz, D. (1979). Bimodal distributions of seedling weight in relation to density of *Festuca paradoxa* Desv. *Nature* **277**, 297–298.

Ricci, U. (1916). *L'indice di variabilita e la curve dei reddita*. Rome.

Ross, M. A. and Harper, J. L. (1972). Occupation of biological space during seedling establishment. *J. Ecol.* **60**, 77–88.

Schall, B. A. and Levin, D. A. (1976). The demographic genetics of *Liatris cylindrica* Michx. (Compositae). *Am. Nat.* **110**, 191–206.

Schellner, R. A., Newell, S. J. and Solbrig, O. T. (1982). Population biology of *Viola*. IV. Spatial pattern of ramets and seedlings in three stoloniferous species. *J. Ecol.* **70**, 273–290.

Sen, A. (1973). *On Economic Inequality*. Clarendon Press, Oxford.

Shinozaki, K. and Kira, T. (1956). Intraspecific competition among higher plants. VII. Logistic theory of the C-D effect. *J. Inst. Polytech. Osaka City Univ. D.* **7**, 35–72.

Sohn, J. J. and Policansky, D. (1977). The costs of reproduction of the mayapple *Podophyllum peltatum* (Berberidaceae). *Ecology* **58**, 1366–1374.

Sokal, R. R. and Rohlf, J. E. (1981). *Biometry*. Freeman, San Francisco.

Solbrig, O. T. (1976). On the relative advantages of cross and self-fertilization. *Ann. Mo. Bot. Gard.* **63**, 262–276.

Solbrig, O. T. (1981). Studies on the population biology of the genus *Viola*. II. The effect of plant size on fitness in *Viola sororia*. *Evolution* **35**, 1080–1093.

Solbrig, O. T. (1982). Energy, information and plant evolution. In *Ecological Physiology*. (ed. P. Calow and C. Townsend), Blackwell Scientific, Oxford.

Solbrig, O. T., Curtis, W. F., Kincaid, D. T., Malone, J. and Newell, S. J. In prep. Studies on the population biology of the genus *Viola*. VI. The demography of *V. fimbriatula* and *V. lanceolata*.

Solbrig, O. T., Newell, S. J. and Kincaid, D. T. (1980). Population biology of *Viola*. I. Demography of *Viola sororia*. *J. Ecol.* **68**, 521–546.

Solbrig, O. T. and Rollins, R. C. (1977). The evolution of autogamy in species of the mustard genus *Leavenworthia*. *Evolution* **31**, 265–281.

Turner, M. D. and Rabinowitz, D. (1983). Factors affecting frequency distributions of plant mass: the absence of dominance and suppression in competing monocultures of *Festuca paradoxa*. *Ecology* **64**, 469–475.

Turner, M. E., Stephens, J. C. and Anderson, W. W. (1982). Homozygosity and patch structure in plant populations as a result of nearest-neighbour pollination. *Proc. Natl. Acad. Sci. USA* **79**, 203–207.

Weiner, J. Size hierarchies in experimental populations of annual plants. *Ecology* (in press).

Weiner, J. and Solbrig, O. T. (1984). The meaning and measurement of size hierarchies in plant populations. *Oecologia* **61**: 334–336.

Werner, P. A. and Caswell, H. (1977). Population growth rates and age versus stage distribution models for teasel (*Dipsacus sylvestris* Huds.). *Ecology* **58**, 1103–1111.

White, J. (1977). Generalization of self-thinning of plant populations. *Nature* **268**, 373.

White, J. (1980). Demographic factors in populations of plants. In *Demography and Evolution in Plant Populations*, (ed. O. T. Solbrig), pp. 21–48. Blackwell Scientific, Oxford.

White, J. and Harper, J. L. (1970). Correlated changes in plant size and number in plant populations. *J. Ecol.* **58**, 467–485.

Yoda, K., Kira, T. and Hozumi, K. (1957). Intraspecific competition among higher plants. IX. Further analysis of the competitive interaction between adjacent individuals. *J. Inst. Polytech. Osaka City Univ. D.* **8**, 161–178.

Yoda, K., Kira, T., Ogawa, H. and Hozumi, K. (1963). Self-thinning in overcrowded pure stands under cultivated and natural conditions. *J. Biol. Osaka City Univ.* **14**, 107–129.

Dynamics of multilocus genetic systems

MICHAEL T. CLEGG

Introduction

Multilocus theory has been a major research area in population genetics during the past two decades. The mathematical problems posed by multilocus systems are complex and raise issues of mathematical as well as biological significance. Although it is sometimes asserted that multilocus theory is difficult to relate to the results of observation or experiment, there are in fact many important points of contact between empirical and theoretical research. The objective of this article will be to review work which connects theory with observation in the study of multilocus systems.

The scope of the article will be limited to random mating systems. (For an excellent review of plant population genetics where inbreeding systems are considered see Brown 1979). We begin by considering the necessity of a multilocus theory. We then consider the dynamics of multilocus systems and finally we consider ways in which multilocus transmission can be exploited to gain information about historical processes and population structure.

WHY HAVE A MULTILOCUS THEORY?

Theoretical population genetics grew out of an attempt to reconcile the apparent conflict of particulate Mendelian inheritance with the existence of the slight, continuous hereditary variation, fundamental to Darwinian natural selection (Provine 1971). The problem, as is often the case, was more apparent than real. It arose because the Mendelian methodology was based upon observing the transmission, in families, of major phenotypic discontinuities. The successors to Darwin – notably Galton, Weldon and Pearson – focused instead on a statistical description of the transmission of continuously varying phenotypic traits. Because of this methodological difference (and because of the personalities of the major participants) the view developed that Darwinian natural selection and Mendelian inheritance were inconsistent. The great achievement of theoretical population genetics (or mathematical genetics) was to erect an elaborate mathematical consistency argument, showing that the selection of variants producing small quasi-continuous phenotypic effects, was entirely consistent with the transmission of particulate genes.

The strategy used in constructing mathematical models had the following elements: first, it was recognized that selection acted on phenotypes and that the phenotype, as perceived by the environment, represented the totality of metabolic and developmental interactions affecting the character in question. Usually many loci – indeed most loci – could affect the phenotypic expression of the character of interest. However, it was assumed that one locus had a predominant effect, or alternatively, that the process of evolution could be regarded as taking place independently at each of the loci affecting the character. Wright (1931) expressed this view in the following terms: 'The selection coefficient for a gene is thus in general a function of the entire system of gene frequencies. As a first apoproximation, relating to a given population at a given moment, one may, however, assume a constant net selection coefficient for each gene.' The assumption that one locus could be studied in isolation can be regarded as the theoretical equivalent of the Mendelian methodological approach.

The second step in modelling Mendelian transmission with selection involved equating phenotypes to genotypes. This step was easy, once the assumption had been adopted that phenotypic variation could be reduced to variation at a single locus. The final step in the process of abstraction was to identify the transmission of genes, not genotypes or phenotypes, as the variable of interest. This was a natural choice because phenotypes and genotypes are ephemeral, being reconstituted each generation, while genes were regarded as the 'atoms of heredity'. Thus the process of evolution could be described in terms of changes in relative gene frequencies.

There are several grounds for criticizing the process of abstraction outlined above. Perhaps the most significant is that it is tantamount to constructing a theory based upon genetic transmission in populations of single locus organisms. Since single locus organisms do not exist, such a theory may be irrelevant to 'real world' observations. Lewontin (1974) has argued this view in detail. He makes the important point that a sufficient (in the sense of explaining empirical observations) population genetic theory must be framed in terms of the entire multilocus distribution. Single locus results can then be obtained as appropriate marginal sums from the complex system. Ewens and Thomson (1977) have made a start on constructing such a theory. This criticism, that context can not be ignored, or that single locus behaviour must be seen as part of a larger system, is susceptible to empirical investigation. A primary objective of this article is to review the results of experimental work where multilocus context is an explicit consideration.

WHY STUDY THE DYNAMICAL BEHAVIOUR OF MULTILOCUS SYSTEMS?

A second major trend in the development of population genetic theory has been the tendency to concentrate on statics, or the description of equilibrium states. Important exceptions to this trend can be found in the work of Kimura (1965), Nagylaki (1974, 1976) and Felsenstein (1965); however it is fair to say that the analysis of deterministic population genetic models has focused largely on the analysis of equilibria. At first this seems a strange preoccupation since evolution is a dynamic process.

The concern with equilibrium structures has an empirical motivation: A major problem in population genetics has been the maintenance of genetic variation in populations. A tenet of the synthetic theory of evolution is that most, if not all, selection response is based on a reservoir of pre-existing genetic variation in populations (Dobzhansky 1970). Consequently, the ability of populations to adapt to changing environmental circumstances is not limited by mutation rates (see Nei 1983 for a contrary view). The theoretical analysis of equilibrium structures, assuming various evolutionary forces, is therefore central to one of the basic tenets of evolutionary genetics. The study of statics has the additional attraction of presenting mathematically tractable and interesting problems.

While conceptually important and mathematically interesting, equilibrium theory presents formidable practical problems for the experimental population geneticist. It is virtually impossible to know, from a set of sample observations, whether the genetic system is at an equilibrium point, without knowledge of initial conditions and the history of frequency change. The difficulty arises because rates of change may be slow, in some cases of the order of the effective population size, and impossibly large samples are required to detect gene frequency changes due to reasonable selection (e.g. selection coefficients of the order of 0.001 to 0.01).

A second problem is that equilibrium systems are devoid of history. Usually no inferences can be made about the particular trajectories followed in reaching the equilibrium point. As a trivial illustration, consider the fact that two relative fitness values can not be estimated from the gene frequency equilibrium for a diallelic locus, assuming random mating. To estimate fitness values from population samples of genotype frequencies, one must draw samples from successive generations during the process of gene frequency change, as emphasized by Prout (1969). It is generally necessary to know initial conditions, and trajectories of change, to make inferences about the processes governing a dynamical system. For these reasons the major theme of this article is the dynamical behaviour of multilocus systems.

Two-locus selection theory

We begin with a brief review of two-locus selection theory. The objective of this review is to identify points of contact between empirical observation and theory. For more complete reviews from various perspectives, of the large body of mathematical work in multilocus theory see Karlin (1975), Nagylaki (1977), and Ewens (1979). As is typical, we assume two diallelic autosomal loci with gametic types A_1B_1, A_1B_2, A_2B_1 and A_2B_2, whose relative frequencies are x_1, x_2, x_3 and x_4, respectively. Loci A and B are assumed to recombine with probability r and random mating is assumed. Denote the relative viability of genotypes formed by the union of gametic types i and j by w_{ij} (i, j = 1,2,3,4). The discrete generation dynamics of the gametic types x_i are,

$$\bar{w} \, x_i = x_i w_i + \delta_i \, r \, D_w, \qquad i = 1,2,3,4, \qquad (1)$$

where $\delta_2 = \delta_3 = 1 = -\delta_1 = -\delta_4$, $D_w = w_{14}x_1x_4 - w_{23}x_2x_3$ is the linkage disequilibrium function, $w_i = \sum\limits_{j=1}^{4} x_j w_{ij}$ is the marginal fitness of gametic type

i, and $\bar{w} = \sum\limits_{i=1}^{4} x_i w_i$ is the mean fitness of the population.

The first issue to consider is the problem of context raised above: specifically, are the results of two-locus selection theory essentially contained in the analyses of equivalent one-locus models? There are at least three major grounds for answering in the negative. First, the system of equations (1) can exhibit stable limit cycles (Hastings 1981a; Akin 1982) which do not arise in the one-locus constant viability analogue. Second, marginal one-locus equilibria, when obtained in the context of two-locus models, may conflict with the predictions of one-locus theory. In particular, it is possible to have marginal underdominance at a stable equilibrium in a two-locus context (Hastings 1982), whereas under-dominance yields at unstable equilibrium in one-locus theory. Finally, two-locus models typically yield multiple equilibria because (1) is a nonlinear system of equations, while the equilibrium system for the analogous one-locus system of equations is linear, and the equilibrium for the fully polymorphic system is unique. To see this latter point consider the system of difference equations obtained from (1).

$$\Delta x_i = \bar{w}^{-1} \left[x_i (w_i - \bar{w}) + \delta_i r D_w \right] \qquad 1 = 1,2,3,4 \qquad (2)$$

where $\Delta x_i = x'_i - x_i$. Compare equations (2) to the system of difference equations for the multiallelic one-locus constant viability model,

$$\Delta p_i = \bar{w}^{-1} \left[p_i (w_i - \bar{w}) \right] \qquad i = 1,2,\ldots,k \qquad (3)$$

where p_i is the relative frequency of allele A_i ($i = 1,2,\ldots,k$), the w_{ij} are now

interpreted as the viability of genotype $A_i A_j$ and $w_i = \sum\limits_{j=i}^{k} p_j w_{ij}$, $\bar{w} = \sum\limits_{i=1}^{k} p_i w_i$.

Solutions for the polymorphic equilibrium system $\Delta p_i = 0$ and $p_i \neq 0$ (for all $i = 1,2,\ldots,k$) are obtained by solving the linear system,

$$\bar{w} = \sum_i w_{1i} p_i$$
$$\bar{w} = \sum_i w_{2i} p_i \qquad i = 1, 2, \ldots, k \qquad (4)$$
$$\bar{w} = \sum_i w_{ki} p_i.$$

Lewontin *et al.* (1978) discuss the constraints on fitness arrays $\|w_{ij}\|$ necessary to insure a fully polymorphic system.

Equations (2) and (3) are analogous except for the term $\delta_i r D_w$. In fact, for r in the neighbourhood of zero, the equilibrium structure of (2) can be inferred from solutions of the linear system (4). Karlin and Liberman (1976) have exploited this fact to obtain general equilibrium solutions for the two-locus system, for r in the neighbourhood of zero. From an empirical perspective, D is the quantity of primary interest because it introduces the nonlinearities into the system of equations (1). (We distinguish the estimate, $D = \hat{x}_1\hat{x}_4 - \hat{x}_2\hat{x}_3$, where the $\hat{x}_i$ are sample quantities, from the theoretical quantity D_w.) If, for example $D = 0$ usually obtains, then we may feel justified in concluding that one-locus theory provides a reasonable approximation to observable genetic systems. Conversely, if $D \neq 0$ occurs with reasonable frequency, then one-locus theory may not provide an appropriate framework for the interpretation of empirical observations.

A second reason for estimating the magnitude of D from population samples has been the belief that $D \neq 0$ provides a direct test for interaction in fitness (epistasis or coadaptation). The theoretical grounds for this belief derive from equilibrium analyses of the two-locus additive viability model (Table 1). In this model $D = 0$ at all equilibria (Bodmer and Felsenstein 1967; Karlin and Feldman 1970; Karlin and Liberman 1979a). If we define interaction in terms of deviations from additivity (nonadditive epistasis), then zero interaction implies $D = 0$ at equilibrium. Unfortunately the converse proposition, nonzero interaction implies $D \neq 0$, is not true in general. To develop this point, consider the symmetric viability model studied by Lewontin and Kojima (1960) and Karlin and Feldman (1970). The fitness array is given in Table 2 and the parameter measuring the

Table 1

Parameterization of additive viability model in terms of the array $\|w_{ij}\|$.

	Marginal fitness	B_1B_1 b_1	B_1B_2 b_2	B_2B_2 b_3
A_1A_1	a_1	$w_{11} = a_1+b_1$	$w_{12} + a_1+b_2$	$w_{22} = a_1+b_3$
A_1A_2	a_2	$w_{13} = a_2+b_1$	$w_{14} = w_{23} = a_2+b_2$	$w_{24} = a_2+b_3$
A_2A_2	a_3	$w_{33} = a_3+b_1$	$w_{34} = a_3 + b_2$	$w_{44} = a_3+b_3$

Table 2

Parameterization of the symmetric viability array of Lewontin and Kojima (1960) in terms of the array $\|w_{ij}\|$.

	B_1B_1	B_1B_2	B_2B_2
A_1A_1	$w_{11} = a$	$w_{12} = b$	$w_{22} = a$
A_1A_2	$w_{13} = b$	$w_{14} = w_{23} = 1$	$w_{24} = b$
A_2A_2	$w_{33} = a$	$w_{34} = b$	$w_{44} = a$

deviation from additivity of the viabilities is $E = a+1-2b$. The symmetric equilibria for this model of selection are $x_1 = x_4 = \frac{1}{4}, \pm \frac{1}{4} \sqrt{1-4r/E}$ and $x_2 = x_3 = \frac{1}{4}, \mp \frac{1}{4} \sqrt{1-4r/E}$. One equilibrium, $x_i = \frac{1}{4}$ ($i = 1,2,3,4$) is characterized by $D = 0$. The other two equilibria with $D = \pm \frac{1}{4} \sqrt{1-4r/E}$ exist and are stable when $E>4r$ and $a<1$. The condition $E>4r$ requires that the deviation from additivity be large relative to the recombination parameter. A variety of epistatic selection regimes may thus be characterized by $D = 0$ at equilibrium. Estimates of $D = 0$ from population samples do not imply zero epistasis. Strong interactions in fitness (relative to recombination) are necessary for permanent statistical associations to develop between polymorphic genes at a pair of loci (see also Hastings 1981b).

Selection in systems of three or more loci

If one-locus theory is not a natural reduction from two-locus theory, then two-locus results are also unlikely to be preserved when three or more loci are studied. Lewontin (1964) showed numerically that the conditions for stable $D_w \neq 0$ among pairs of loci are less stringent in the context of a five-locus system. Later Franklin and Lewontin (1970) simulated 36-locus models and showed that extreme pairwise linkage disequilibrium could develop, because the gametic frequency distribution evolved to a state characterized by two complementary gametic types in high frequency. From an empirical perspective these simulation results were very important for two reasons. First, and most importantly, they predicted an extreme genetic organization which was subject to direct empirical confirmation. (It is a rare thing in population genetics to have a theory which can be tested by direct observation.) The second important feature of this work was that the selection model simulated was weakly epistatic.

The two-locus measure of nonadditive interaction is $E = s^s$ for the Franklin and Lewontin simulation model. (The two-locus version of this model is given in Table 3.) Thus, E is a second order quantity in the multiplicative model relative to selection. Moreover, values of $s = 0.10$ and $r = 0.0025$ were employed in these simulations. Two-locus equilibria with $D = 0$ are $D = \pm \frac{1}{4} \sqrt{1-4r/s^2}$. It is easy to verify that $1-4r/s^2 = 0$ for

Table 3

Parameterization of the overdominant symmetric multiplicative selection model in terms of the array $\|w_{ij}\|$.

	Marginal fitness	B_1B_1 $1-s$	B_1B_2 1	B_2B_2 $1-s$
A_1A_1	$1-s$	$w_{11} = (1-s)^2$	$w_{12} = 1-s$	$w_{22} = (1-s)_2$
A_1A_2	1	$w_{13} = 1-s$	$w_{14} = w_{23} = 1$	$w_{24} = 1-s$
A_2A_2	$1-s$	$w_{33} = (1-s)^2$	$w_{34} = 1-s$	$w_{44} = (1-s)^2$

these parameter choices. One may therefore conclude that weak epistasis can produce high disequilibrium in a system of many loci and that the conditions for $D \neq 0$ at equilibrium are relaxed in a multilocus context relative to two-locus theory.

Subsequent theoretical work has provided an analytical framework for the results of Franklin and Lewontin (Slatkin 1972). In addition, algebraic investigations of a three-locus symmetric viability model provide direct confirmation for some of the simulation results (Feldman *et al.* 1974). Finally, a variety of multilocus simulations, positing different models of selection, have also shown high levels of linkage disequilibrium at equilibrium (Wills *et al.* 1970; Wills and Miller 1976; Yamazaki 1974; 1977). Based upon the results of multilocus simulation models, there seemed to be ample grounds for expecting linkage disequilibria to be common in populations of random mating organisms.

Experimental studies of multilocus organization

The usual approach to estimating D in populations has been to sample two-locus genotypes and then to estimate D, subject to the assumption of random mating (see Weir 1979; for a discussion of statistical considerations). This procedure can be criticized on several grounds. First, equilibrium is tacitly assumed if the investigator intends to make inferences based upon two-locus theory. There is no way of knowing whether this assumption is valid without drawing a sequence of samples over successive generations. Some investigators do provide indirect evidence in support of the equilibrium assumption by showing that estimates of D are consistent over geographically separated populations (e.g. Langley *et al.* 1974; Baker 1975).

The second major criticism arises because in natural populations the sampling unit may not correspond to a single random mating population. That is to say, population substructure may bias estimates of D. The value of D which corresponds to the quantity estimated if sampling takes place without regard to substructure, is

$$D = \bar{D} + \text{cov}(p, q) \qquad (5)$$

(Nei and Li 1972; Cavalli-Sforza and Bodmer 1971; Prout 1973), where $\bar{D}$ is the average value of D over subpopulations, cov(p, q) is the covariance in gene frequency at loci A and B over subpopulations, and p and q are the relative frequencies of genes A_1 and B_1, respectively. In this situation $D \neq 0$ may simply arise due to a covariance in gene frequencies over subpopulations and can not be taken as evidence for epistatic selection. The third criticism relates to the assumption of random mating. If deviations from random mating occur, the estimate of D will be biased. This objection can usually be circumvented in *Drosophilia* where gametes can be sampled directly by the use of balancer chromosomes or progeny testing.

Despite the criticisms listed above, most estimates of D from natural populations indicate that $D = 0$ is the usual condition (see Hedrick *et al.*

1978; and Barker 1979 for recent reviews). Here again we must be cautious in interpreting these data, because rather large samples are necessary to reject the hypothesis $D = 0$, when the true population value is $D \neq 0$ (Brown 1975). The power of statistical tests to detect $D \neq 0$ is limited, especially when gene frequencies are well away from ½ (e.g. $p \leq 0.2$, $q \leq 0.2$).

A different approach to searching for stable linkage disequilibrium involves synthesizing populations with known values of D and then following the dynamical behaviour of D_t (where t is time measured in generations). There are several additional reasons for adopting an experimental strategy beyond those already discussed. First, equilibria with $D = 0$ and $D \neq 0$ may be simultaneously stable in two locus models (Karlin and Feldman 1978; Hastings 1981c) and simultaneous stability of $D = 0$ and $D \neq 0$ at equilibrium has also been demonstrated in multilocus simulations (Franklin and Lewontin 1970). This means that a set of sample observations with $D = 0$ does not preclude the existence of simultaneous equilibria with $D \neq 0$. Consequently, a desirable experimental strategy is to synthesize populations with maximal pairwise linkage disequilibria and then to follow the decay process over successive generations. If the initial conditions, D_o, are maximal, then the system should decay to stable points with $D \neq 0$ if they exist. A second advantage of an experimental strategy is that it provides additional information on the processes governing change.

Despite the clear advantages of an experimental strategy, there are few organisms which satisfy the prerequisites of many well mapped genetic marker loci, short generation time and ease of laboratory culture. *Drosophila melanogaster* does meet these requirements and has been the primary experimental organism for studies of multilocus transmission. Cannon (1963) provided some evidence for stable linkage disequilibrium among recessive morphological markers in a long term experimental population of *D. melanogaster*. However, the population was sampled at just three time points so the trajectory of change could not be established. Rasmuson *et al.* (1967) studied the decay of D between the third chromosome enzyme loci esterase-6 and leucine amino-peptidase and found that D went to zero. These loci are more than 50 map units apart on chromosome three and are expected to recombine independently in females. O'Brien asnd MacIntyre (1971) also studied the decay of D between linked enzyme loci in *D. melanogaster*. While some association appeared initially, D ultimately decayed to zero.

In an effort to further investigate the dynamical behaviour of multilocus genetic systems, we synthesized replicate cage populations of *D. melanogaster* with complete pairwise linkage disequilibria over four enzyme marker loci (Clegg *et al.* 1980). The marker loci studied were isocitrate dehydrogenase, *Idh* (3-27.1), esterase-6, *Est-6* (3-36.8), phosphoglucomutase, *Pgm* (3-43.3) and esterase-c, *Est-c*, (3-49.0). Assuming no recombination in males, the average recombination fraction (over sexes) between pairs of these third chromosome loci ranges from 0.11 to 0.028.

Several additional facts about these experiments require discussion before interpreting the results. First, the cages were maintained on a discrete generation regime so that t was known. Second, the initial state was defined by introducing flies with just two of the sixteen possible gametic types, in random mating proportions, into a replicate pair of large cage populations. The gametic types were denoted FSNS and SFSF for loci *Idh, Est-6, Pgm* and *Est-c*; respectively. This initial structure yields complete pairwise linkage disequilibrium with all initial gene frequencies set at ½. To achieve these initial conditions wild type stocks, which had been maintained in the laboratory for several years, were intercrossed. A consequence of intercrossing different stocks is that the initial population will be in linkage disequilibrium for all loci whose relative gene frequencies differ between the parental stocks. Thus, the dynamics observed at the marker loci will reflect the action of selection on many loci. In an effort to control for these background effects, new recombinant gametic types were extracted from the experimental populations, after they had undergone 15 generations of random mating. Two recombinant gametic types (FSSF; SFNS) were then used to initiate two more replicate cage populations. Gametic frequencies were estimated directly by progeny testing sampled males, so that no assumptions about mating structure were necessary in estimating D. Relatively large samples of gametes were drawn (averaging approximately 200 per sample) in every generation during early generations, and then on alternate generations until generation 50, from each cage population.

Despite the fact that two cages were contaminated by migrant chromosomes during the course of the experiments, the results were unambiguous. Estimated sample paths of D_t converged to the neighbourhood of zero for all locus pairs. Fig. 1 illustrates the observed behaviour for the locus pair *Idh-Pgm*. Note that each replicate pair begins with an opposite initial sign of D ($= \pm \frac{1}{4}$), because of the different gametic orientations used to initiate the two sets of experiments. An unexpected feature of the data was the apparent acceleration of the decay of D relative to the expected neutral rate of l-r per generation.

A crude estimate of the rate of decay of D_t can be obtained from the linear regression of the log plot of D_t on t. If the decay process obeyed the neutral dynamic, then the slope of the regression should equal log(l-r). When the slope of the regression was compared to estimates of r, obtained from the reference population (Clegg *et al.* 1979), it revealed an 'effective' rate of recombination approximately 1.8 times the rate expected, based upon neutral theory. Moreover, both sets of experiments gave similar results.

These experiments provide no evidence for stable equilibria with D $\neq$ 0. This does not preclude the existence of such equilibria, because the experiments feature just two sets of initial conditions. Moreover, it is possible that the system could pass through weakly stable equilibria with D $\neq$ 0, if stochastic variation exceeded the domain of atttraction of such equilibria. Nevertheless, the results are contrary to the hypothesis that high levels of permanent linkage disequilibrium are common.

What more can be learned from the dynamical behaviour of this four-

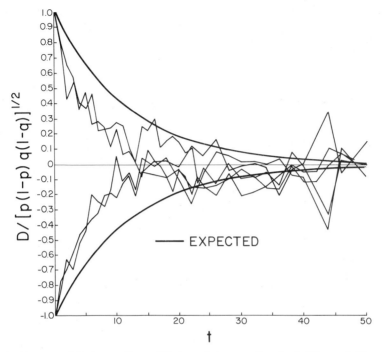

Fig. 1. Decay of linkage disequilibrium between the loci *Idh* and *Pgm*. The trajectories are plotted as the correlation in gene frequencies, $R = D/[p(1-p) \cdot q(1-q)]^{1/2}$, to remove some of the effect of gene frequency change. The expected rate of change of R for neutral genes in an infinite population is shown by the bold curves.

locus system and what factors account for the accelerated decay rates? First, we consider evidence that selection affects the marker loci. There are two indications that selection is important. One indication comes from the gene frequency changes observed at the marker loci over generations. While gene frequencies remain at intermediate values, the gene frequency changes observed in uncontaminated replicates are correlated. This is especially dramatic at *Pgm* (Clegg *et al.* 1980).

The other evidence in favour of selection derives from the time dependent behaviour of the marginal one-locus genotypic frequencies. If we calculate Wright's fixation index, $F = 1 - h/2p(1-p)$, where h denotes the relative frequency of one-locus heterozygotes and p is the marginal gene frequency, we observe that F depends on generation and marker locus. Fig. 2 plots the average behaviour of F (over uncontaminated replicates) for each marker locus, as a function of time.

Initially, F is strongly negative, indicating heterozygous frequencies well in excess of random mating proportions, however as time proceeds F decays towards zero. A reasonable interpretation of these results is that many loci on chromosome three are under selection, and that initially, these loci are in linkage disequilibrium with respect to the marker loci, due

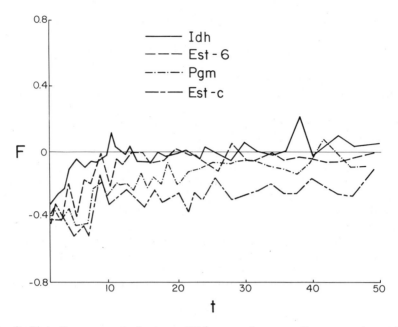

Fig. 2. Plots the average trajectory of F (averaged over replicate experiments) for each locus.

to the way in which the initial populations were constructed. As generations pass, the selected loci become randomized with respect to the marker loci and the observed effect at the marker loci diminishes. The fact that F behaves differently among marker loci suggests that the distribution of selective effects is not uniformly distributed along the chromosome. In particular *Est-c*, and to a lesser extent *Pgm*, appear to be under the influence of strong selection throughout the 50 generations spanned by these data. On the other hand the F statistics for *Idh* and *Est-6* decay to the neighbourhood of zero within the first 15 generations of the experiment. It is important to note that the behaviour of F observed for each marker locus is quite consistent over replicates. The questions we wish to consider next are (1) can elementary models of selection account for the observed results; and (2) what are the theoretical and practical implications of these results?

Dynamics of multilocus systems

Equations (1) describe the dynamics of two-locus systems with selection. General solutions for the time dependent behaviour of this system of difference equations are not available. To gain some insight into dynamical behaviour one must (1) iterate the system of equations numerically assuming particular values for the fitness array $\|w_{ij}\|$ and r (Karlin and Carmelli 1975); (2) study the analogous system of differential equations assuming weak selection (Nagylaki 1974, 1976; Hoppensteadt 1976); or (3) describe the behaviour of equations (1) for simple models of selection in a qualitative framework (Asmussen and Clegg 1982a). We summarize this latter approach, because it is useful for interpreting the experimental results.

The approach employed by Asmussen and Clegg (1982a) involves classifying the dynamical behaviour of D_t into four qualitative regions. These regions are functions of the parameters $\|w_{ij}\|$ and r, and they depend on the point in the gametic frequency simplex at which the dynamical system is initiated. Specifically, D_t is classified into regions where (1) D_t decays to zero at a rate which is greater than the neutral rate, l–r, per generation; (2) D_t decays to zero at a rate slower than the neutral rate, l–r, per generation; (3) D_t decays to a stable point D ≠ 0; and (4) D_t increases for some interval of time t_1, t_2.

Even this qualitative analysis is not possible for two selected loci, begun at an arbitrary point in the gametic frequency simplex. To reduce the problem further, the behaviour of D is analyzed when gene frequencies are in the neighbourhood of their invariant values. To illustrate the kinds of results which emerge from this analysis, consider first the additive viability array (Table 1). A fully polymorphic equilibrium only occurs under this model when both loci are overdominant in fitness. Under these conditions $D_t/D_{t-1} < $ l–r for all t and any initial value D_o, when the two gene frequencies are in the neighbourhood of their equilibrium values. Thus for additive nonepistasis, D decays to zero at a rate which is faster than the neutral rate, when the gene frequencies are in the neighbourhood of a polymorphic equilibrium. This accelerated decay rate is consistent with the experimental results discussed above.

Next consider the symmetric viability array (Table 2). As already discussed, equilibria with D ≠ 0 are possible for this model. The time dependent behaviour of D, in the neighbourhood of the gene frequency equilibrium (p = q = ½), is (Asmussen and Clegg, 1982a),

$$D_t = f(D_{t-1}) \, D_{t-1} \qquad (7)$$

$$\text{where } f(D) = \frac{(1+a)/2-r}{(1+a+b+c)/4 + 4 D^2 E} \qquad (8)$$

Note that D_t can increase if $f(D_t) > 1$. If l–r $< f(D_t) < 1$, D_t will decay at a rate slower than the neutral rate and if l–r $> f(D_t)$, D_t will decay at an accelerated rate relative to neutrality. If E > 0 (positive epistasis) there are two critical values $R_1 = $ ¼ E and $R_2 (> R_1) = $ E/(3–a–b–c) where ½ > r > R_2 implies f(D) < l-r for all D < ¼. Thus an accelerated decay rate relative to neutrality will occur for any initial value D_o (≠ 0), if the epistatic component of selection is suitably small relative to recombination. When E < 0 (negative epistasis) and the double heterozygote is relatively less fit than the single heterozygotes, then for ½ > r > R_2, f(D) > l–r for all D < ¼ (see Asmussen and Clegg 1982a, for a detailed analysis).

Two conclusions relevant to the experimental results emerge from this analysis. First, an accelerated decay of D_t to zero is expected, if the epistatic component of selection is weak relative to recombination. Second, the acceleration phenomenon depends on the sign of E. When double heterozygotes are disfavoured D_t decays to zero at a slower rate than the neutral rate. A natural interpretation of these results is that the acceleration is a consequence of selection increasing the relative frequency of double heterozygotes.

Suppose that many linked loci are selected, as is undoubtedly the case in the experimental work. Will an accelerated decay of D to zero occur and if so, how can these results be reconciled with the simulations of Franklin and Lewontin (1970)? To resolve this paradax we simulated a 93-locus model (Clegg 1978) assuming several schemes of multiplicative selection, including the model of Franklin and Lewontin. The joint behaviour of four neutral loci, in the 93-locus system, with map positions corresponding to the experimental markers observed by Clegg *et al.* (1980), was analyzed. The selection parameter, s, was chosen subject to the constraint that $(1-s)^{89} \approx 0.1$. This choice for the homozygous fitness of a chromosome was based on experimental studies of Tracey and Ayala (1974) and Sved (1975). The decay realizations for D_t in the simulations of Clegg (1978) are indistinguishable from the realizations for the experimental data. D_t goes to zero for all models simulated at a markedly accelerated rate, relative to neutrality. Evidently, the parameterization chosen for the simulations yields a dynamical behaviour consistent with the experimental results. The choice of s per map unit in these simulations was approximately 40-fold less than the parameterization of Franklin and Lewontin. A reasonable conclusion is that the average intensity of selection, in the experimental populations, is well below the level required to maintain permanent linkage disequilibrium.

What are the implications of these findings? First, epistatic selection may accelerate the decay of D to zero, provided E is small relative to r; therefore a rapid decay to zero can not be taken as evidence against fitness interactions among loci. However, it can be concluded that in these particular experiments, fitness interactions are not sufficiently extreme to generate permanent statistical associations at the population level. Since the majority of studies of linkage disequilibrium in large random mating populations also indicate $D = 0$ (Hedrick *et al.* 1978; Barker 1979), it is likely that this conclusion has some general validity. Second, the fact that $D_t \to 0$ rapidly is important in the study of experimental population genetics where an objective is to randomize genetic backgrounds. Of course, very tightly linked loci may still remain associated for long periods of time. Finally, much of quantitative genetic theory assumes that covariances over loci can be neglected in calculating total genetic variances. This, and similar assumptions, may not be unreasonable in the light of these findings.

Theories of associative selection

Two areas of multilocus theory which have fundamental relevance for the interpretation of observed data are the theories of hitchhiking selection

(Maynard Smith and Haigh 1974; Wagener and Cavalli-Sforza 1975; Thomson 1977; Hedrick 1982) and the theory of associative over-dominance (Sved 1968; Kimura and Ohta 1971). These theories posit that the effects observed at a particular locus are a result of statistical associations with other unobserved loci. Two kinds of observable effects are of interest. One effect is gene frequency change monitored over a sequence of generations. The theory of hitchhiking selection asserts that gene frequency change may be due to linkage disequilibrium between the locus observed (assumed not to be the direct target of selection) and a second hypothetical locus undergoing gene frequency due to selection. The second class of effects concerns the observations of heterozygous excess in estimates of genotypic frequency distributions. The theory of associative overdominance claims that heterozygous excess (relative to random mating) is to be expected at a selectively neutral locus on a chromosome with many selected loci, because of the cummulative effect of selection. It also claims that linkage disequilibria between the observed locus and the unobserved selected loci can be expected; however, the associations are generated by the stochastic sampling of gametes. A major distinction between these two theories is that hitchhiking theory is essentially a deterministic theory invoked to explain transient gene frequency changes. In contrast, the theory of associative overdominance is stochastic and directed toward explaining equilibrium distributions.

Both of these theories present profound difficulties for experimental population genetics. Each theory asserts that the process observed is a consequence of linkage and the complexity of the genome. The loci causally related to the selection process are unobserved and potentially unobservable.

Are there useful empirical questions which can be answered within the framework of associative selection? We shall restrict our attention to the dynamical behaviour of experimental systems and hence to the problems of hitchhiking. We begin by developing the elementary theory of hitchhiking (see Asmussen and Clegg 1981 for a more complete exposition). As in earlier sections, we assume two diallelic loci A and B, with recombination fraction r, and we assume that the B locus is selectively neutral. The viabilities at the A locus are W_{11}, w_{12}, w_{22} for genotypes A_1A_1, A_1A_2 and A_2A_2, respectively. Assuming random mating, the gene frequency and linkage disequilibrium variables obey the following dynamic (Asmussen and Clegg 1981),

$$p_{t+1} = \frac{p_t \, w_{1 \cdot t}}{\bar{w}_t} \qquad (9a)$$

$$q_{t+1} = \frac{D_t \, (w_{1 \cdot t} - w_{2 \cdot t})}{\bar{w}_t} \qquad (9b)$$

$$D_{t+1} = D_t \, f(p_t) \qquad (9c)$$

where

$$f(p_t) = \frac{w_{1 \cdot t}\, w_{2 \cdot t} - r\, w_{12}\, \bar{w}_t,}{\bar{w}^2_t} \qquad (10)$$

and where $w_{1 \cdot t} = w_{12} + p_t (w_{11} - 2_{12})$, $w_{2 \cdot t} = p_t (wt21_2 - w_{22})$ and $\bar{w} = p_t\, w_{1 \cdot t} + (1-p_t)\, w_{2 \cdot t}$.

Several important facts regarding the system of equations (9) are (a) p_t changes according to the usual one-locus selection dynamic; (b) $\Delta q = q_{t+1} - q_t = 0$, if $D_t = 0$ or the A locus is at an equilibrium ($w_{1 \cdot} = w_{2 \cdot}$.); (c) D_t ultimately goes to zero; and (d) $f(p_t)$ depends only on the gene frequency variable at the selected locus, in contrast to equation (8).

A complete qualitative analysis of the behaviour of D_t under hitchhiking selection is possible by analyzing $f(p_t)$. The analysis proceeds in the same fashion as outlined for $f(D)$. In particular, $f(p_t)$ and hence D_t can be classified into three qualitative behaviours: (1) $f(p_t) > 1$ and hence $D_t > D_{t-1}$; (2) $1 > f(p_t) > 1-r$ which implies that D_t decays at a slower rate than the neutral rate; and (3) $1-r > f(p_t)$ where D_t decays faster than the neutral rate. Because p_t under equation (9a) converges monotonically to an equilibrium point, the behaviour of $f(p_t)$ can be uniquely described. Asmussen and Clegg (1981) show that the selection intensity (s) must exceed r, under single parameter models of selection (e.g. symmetric overdominance, directional selection) for $f(p_t) > 1$ for any $p_t\varepsilon(0,1)$. They also show that hitchhiking is likely to be most influential when a favoured gene is in low frequency, as would occur when an advantageous mutant enters a population. Conversely, $f(p_t) < 1-r$ for a range of gene frequencies which decrease as r decreases, but which first shrinks and then enlarges as s increases.

Experimental studies of hitchhiking selection

Can hitchhiking selection be empirically investigated? We consider two experimental approaches to this question. The first approach involves studying the behaviour of marker genes scattered over a major portion of the genome in populations subjected to a specific stress environment. The experiments involved synthesizing replicate pairs of cage populations of *D. melanogaster*, where one pair of cages was subjected to ethanol stress, by augmenting the media with 10 per cent ethanol (Cavener and Clegg 1978). Eight enzyme marker loci were monitored over successive generations. In addition, levels of linkage disequilibrium were estimated among all pairs of linked marker loci, for the initial population, and at regular intervals thereafter. The populations were maintained on discrete nonoverlapping generations so that the generation time was known.

One of the marker loci investigated was alcohol dehydrogenase, *Adh* (2–50.1), which might be expected to respond to ethanol stress. Of the remaining seven marker loci, only alpha-glycerophosphate dehydrogenase, α-*Gpdh* (2–20.5), has any known connection to ethanol metabolism.

Consequently, we regard *Adh* as the target locus and we are interested in two questions: (1) is there a differential gene frequency change at *Adh* in ethanol cages as compared to control cages; and (2) is the response specific to the target locus (*Adh*), or do other random markers show a gene frequency response as might be expected under the hitchhiking hypothesis?

The results show a clear and replicated increase in the *Adh-F* allele which continues over 50 generations (Cavener and Clegg 1978; 1981). Of the remaining loci, only α*Gpdh* shows a gene frequency response under ethanol stress. Moreover, linkage disequilibria among marker genes were low initially and remained low during generations when these statistics were estimated. It therefore appears that gene frequency changes only occurred at loci where a potential metabolic connection existed between the stress environment and the enzyme function. The case for a selective response at *Adh* seems especially strong because the *F* allele has twice the specific activity of the *S* allele, and has been shown to increase in other ethanol selection experiments (reviewed by McDonald 1983).

The response at α*Gpdh* is more problematical, but can not result from hitchhiking with *Adh* because D is small between these loci and r is about 0.15 (averaged over sexes). Cavener and Clegg (1981) use the theory developed above to argue that if the change at α*Gpdh* is due to hitchhiking, then the selected locus must be within about four map units of α*Gpdh*. The ability to place quantitative bounds on the hitchhiking hypothesis is important to the extent that it brings this theory within a testable empirical framework.

A different empirical approach to the study of hitchhiking selection involves studying the behaviour of marker genes, in linkage disequilibrium with a linked gene, undergoing strong directional selection. The objective is to ask whether the behaviour at the marker loci can be predicted, based upon the gene frequency change at the selected locus. To investigate this issue Clegg *et al* (1976, 1978) synthesized replicate experimental populations of *D. melanogaster* where the legal genes, Glued, *Gl* (3–41.4) or Stubble, *Sb* (3–58.2) were at a relative frequency of ½, in strong linkage disequilibrium with the marker loci *Pgm* and *Est-c* initially. Maximum likelihood estimates of selection components at the lethal locus were obtained from the extinction curve of the lethal gene, following the methods of Anderson (1969).

Calculations of the expected patterns of gene frequency change at the marker loci, using recombination rates estimated from the reference population and estimated selective values for the genotypes at the lethal locus, differed markedly from the observed results. In particular, the marker loci decreased less in gene frequency than expected and then showed a rapid increase back to intermediate gene frequency levels. These results indicated the existence of other selected genes in the neighbourhood of the marker loci. The results also indicated a substantial epistatic component of selection associated with the centrometric region of chromosome three. Later experiments by Cochrane and Richmond (1980), using the marker loci *Est-6* and *Pgm*, gave a better fit to the expected behaviour based on selection at the lethal locus. It is likely that the distribution of selective values varies along the chromosome. This interpretation gains additional support from the different behaviours of the F statistics shown in Fig. 2.

To investigate further the effects of hitchhiking selection in systems with a lethal gene, Clegg (1978) simulated 93-locus models. Two classes of models were studied, including a model which assumed many over-dominant loci scattered along the chromosome (balance model), and a model which assumed many deleterious recessive genes in repulsion phase (classical model). Based on these simulation results, Clegg (1978) suggested that it might be possible to distinguish between the classical and balance hypotheses from the gene frequency dynamics of marker genes associated with a lethal gene. This suggestion has not been confirmed by more extensive simulations (Turelli, personal communication).

Experiments on the joint behaviour of lethal genes and associated marker genes are informative to the extent that they show how real genetic systems respond to very strong selection. We may conclude that recombination is very effective in separating closely linked genes during episodes of strong selection. The results also show that in random mating systems, hitchhiking selection is only effective if $s > r$, and this will usually require tight linkage.

One class of genetic markers where $r < s$ with major selected genes is nucleotide substitutions. The use of cloned genes, as molecular probes to restriction endonuclease digested DNAs, has revealed that polymorphic fragmentation patterns are common. Perhaps the best studied example is the β-globin gene cluster in man (Antonarakis *et al* 1982; Kazazian *et al.* 1983). This 50 kilobase (kb) region of DNA includes genes coding for embryonic (ε), fetal ($^G\gamma$, $^A\gamma$), and adult (δ, β) globin genes and the pseudogene ($\psi\beta_1$). To date, 12 polymorphic restriction endonuclease sites have been identified in this region. Marked linkage disequilibrium exists among some of these polymorphic restriction endonuclease sites and associated genes. In certain instances hitchhiking selection is implicated and it may be possible to make some deductions about the evolutionary history of major polymorphisms from the context of these associations. To develop this point we consider the β-globin locus in greater detail.

Kan and Dozy (1978) first showed that the β-globin S allele (β^s) (responsible for sickle cell anaemia) was in strong linkage disequilibrium with a polymorphic *HpaI* restriction endonuclease site, about 5kb 3' to the β-globin coding sequence. In particular, they showed that the conditional frequency of the 13kb *HpaI* fragment, given that the individual had β^s, was about 0.8. Later workers reported a somewhat lower conditional association from different US black populations (Panny *et al.* 1981). Because malarial selection in Africa is believed to be of relatively recent origin, the assumed sequence of events was that the β^s mutation arose on a 13kb *HpaI* fragment already polymorphic in the population. As β^s increased in frequency, so did the 13kb fragment, due to hitchhiking selection. Several authors have pointed out that if this is correct, and assuming reasonable estimates of r, s and t, then the conditional association should still be virtually one (Kurmit 1979; Straus and Taylor 1981; Asmussen and Clegg

1982b). While several explanations for the discrepancy are possible, the most likely explanation is a multiple origin of β^s. This explanation has gained further support from a geographic survey of the β^s-*HpaI* association, which showed high linkage disequilibrium among individuals of West African origin, but little or no linkage disequilibrium among individuals from India, Saudia Arabia and East Africa (Kan and Dozy 1980). Thus the pattern of linkage disequilibrium, on a broad geographic scale, contains information on the origin of a major human polymorphism.

Inferences about population structure and population history

In certain cases it may be possible to make inferences about population history based upon the behaviour of D. One situation where geographic gradients of D may be informative arises from the migration and fusion of different populations. When admixture between two populations with different gene frequencies occurs, equation (5) may be written as,

$$D = m(l-m) \ (p_1-p_2) \ (q_1-q_2), \qquad (11)$$

(Cavalli-Sforza and Bodmer 1971) where m and l-m are contributions of populations one and two, respectively to the mixture and where p_i, q_i (i=1,2) refer to the gene frequencies at loci A and B in populations one and two, respectively.

Because D decays to zero at a geometric rate, tightly linked genes are most informative about historical events like population admixture. Degos and Daussen (1974) have examined the geographic distribution of D for the tightly linked HLA loci. Based upon the gradient in D values, they identify potential routes of human population migration in Europe and they postulate the existence of fusion centres characterized by high levels of D. Interestingly, the fusion centres are all close to the Atlantic Ocean, suggesting that admixture was greatest when one population had been driven to the coast. Maps of migration gradients based on D are in rough qualitative agreement with maps based on linguistic and population group analyses. A similar analysis of Pacific populations by Serjeantson *et al.* (1982), also demonstrates the value of D in highlighting regions of possible admixture.

The study of linkage disequilibrium in a geographic context will become increasingly informative as the number of tightly linked polymorphic marker loci increases. This is because processes like admixture, which reflect breeding structure, are homogeneous over loci, unlike selection processes. Consequently, geographic patterns can be tested for homogeneity, over different sets of marker loci, to test hypotheses about such historical processes as migration and admixture. As more molecular markers become available, increasing precision can be expected. With the advent of restriction fragment polymorphisms, like those discussed above for the β-globin gene family, historical inference is likely to become an increasingly important area of application of multilocus population genetics.

Recently, multilocus estimation models have been introduced to the study of plant mating systems (Shaw *et al.* 1981; Ritland and Jain 1981). The basic idea is that as the number of loci increases so does the proportion of uniquely marked gametes in the population. It is therefore possible to identify an increasing fraction of outcross events, because the male gametes received have an increasing probability of carrying marker genes which could not have been transmitted by the maternal parent or by other plants in a local area. Smith and Adams (1983) have exploited this idea to determine the frequency of pollen contamination in seed orchards of Douglas-fir. Ellstrand (1984) has employed multilocus gametes to estimate paternity and pollen flow in populations of wild radish. These applications are especially significant, because they provide a new approach to the study of migration and gene flow, a problem which has often proved intractable in the past.

The pattern of multilocus transmission may also provide some information on the major demographic characteristics of populations. Clegg and Cavener (1982) and Pollak (1984) have studied a mathematical model of two-locus transmission of sex-linked genes in age sructured populations. Expressions for the dynamical behaviour of D_t in populations with overlapping generations were obtained along with asymptotic rates of convergence of D_t to zero. The resulting equations were applied to experimental data on the transmission of pairs of sex-linked genes in replicate cage populations of *D. melanogaster* (Clegg and Cavener 1982). Crude estimates were obtained of the relative life table of the experimental populations based upon the time dependent behaviour of D_t. Pollak and Callanan (1982) have also studied the dynamical behaviour of pairs of autosomal genes in age-structured populations. They show that the time required to reduce D by a factor equal to (1–r) is a good estimate of the generation interval. These results suggest a useful connection between the empirical problem of measuring the demographic characteristics of populations and the pattern of multilocus transmission.

SUMMARY AND CONCLUSIONS

A primary concern of evolutionary theory has been the generality and magnitude of epistasis, or interlocus interactions in fitness. A major reason for this concern is that single locus population genetic theory is unlikely to provide a reliable interpretation of observations and experiments, if interactions are sufficiently strong to lead to permanent statistical associations in multilocus transmission. The population statistic which has received most theoretical and empirical attention is the linkage disequilibrium function, D, which measures the covariance in allelic state among alleles at pairs of diallelic loci. Experimental studies of the decay of D over generations provide no evidence for stable equilibria with $D \neq 0$. Instead, these experiments show that D decays to zero at an accelerated rate relative to neutrality.

Mathematical models, and computer simulations, of the dynamical behaviour of D show that an accelerated decay rate is expected, if the epistatic component of selection is suitably weak relative to recombination. We conclude from these analyses that recombination is a powerful force and permanent statistical associations over loci are unlikely to be a general characteristic of the genetic structure of large random mating populations.

The problem of hitchhiking selection is considered empirically. Experimental work aimed at determining the importance of hitchhiking selection is reviewed in the light of recent theoretical analyses. The theoretical generalization that s (selection intensity) must exceed r (recombination fraction) for hitchhiking to be important is consistent with experimental results. In addition, experiments to detect hitchhiking at randomly chosen loci, in populations subjected to specific stress environments, suggest that most loci are unaffected.

Good evidence for hitchhiking selection can be obtained from molecular polymorphisms very tightly linked to selected genes. The specific case of β-globin alleles in strong linklage disequilibrium with restriction fragment polymorphisms is considered. Historical evidence on the probable multiple origin of the β^s allele can be inferred from the context of these associations. It is concluded that molecular polymorphisms will become a rich source of historical information, because $r \approx 0$ with other major loci implies that associations will persist for long periods of time.

There is a variety of areas where the pattern of multilocus transmission can be exploited to gain insight into other population processes. Specicic cases involving migration, admixture, mating structure and demographic structure are discussed. We conclude that multilocus population genetics is rich in empirical content.

Acknowledgement

Supported in part by NSF grants DEB-8118414 and BSR 8304796.

References

Akin, E. (1982). Cycling in simple genetic systems. *J. Math. Biology*, **13**, 305–324.

Anderson, W. W. (1969). Selection in experimental populations. I. Lethal genes. *Genetics,* **62**, 653–672.

Antonarakis, S. E., Boehm, C. D., Giardina, P. J. V. and Kazazian, H. H. (1982). Nonrandom association of polymorphic restriction sites in the β-globin gene cluster. *Proc. Natl. Acad. Sci. USA,* **79**, 137–141.

Asmussen, M. A. and Clegg, M. T. (1981). Dynamics of the linkage disequilibrium function under models of gene-frequency hitchhiking. *Genetics,* **99**, 337–356.

Asmussen, M. A. and Clegg, M. T. (1982a). Rates of decay of linkage disequilibrium under two-locus models of selection. *J. Math. Biol.,* **14**, 37–70.

Asmussen, M. A. and Clegg,. M. T. (1982b). Use of restriction fragment length polymorphisms for genetic counseling: Population genetic considerations. *Am. J. Human Genet.* **34**, 369–380.

Baker, W. K. (1975). Linkage disequilibrium over space and time in natural populations of *Drosophila montana. Proc. Natl. Acad. Sci. USA*, **72**, 4095–4099.

Barker, J. S. F. (1979). Inter-locus interactions: A review of experimental evidence. *Theoret. Pop. Biol.*, **16**, 323–346.

Bodmer, W. F. and Felsenstein, J. (1967). Linkage and selection: theoretical analysis of the deterministic two locus random mating model. *Genetics*, **57**, 237–265.

Brown, A. H. D. (1975). Sample size required to detect linkage disequilibrium between two and three loci. *Theoret. Pop. Biol.*, **8**, 184–201.

Brown, A. H. D. (1979). Enzyme polymorphism in plant populations. *Theoret. Pop. Biol.*, **15**, 1–42.

Cannon, G. B. (1963). The effects of natural selection on linkage disequilibrium in populations of *Drosophila melanogaster. Genetics*, **73**, 351–359.

Cavalli-Sforza, L. L. and Bodmer, W. F. (1971). *The Genetics of Human Populations*. San-Francisco: W. H. Freeman.

Cavener, D. R. and Clegg, M. T. (1981). Multigenic response to ethanol in *Drosophila melanogaster. Evolution*, **35**, 1–10.

Cavener, D. R. and Clegg, M. T. (1978). Dynamics of correlated genetic systems. IV. Multilocus effects of ethanol stress environments. *Genetics*, **90**, 629–644.

Clegg, M. T. (1978). Dynamics of correlated genetic systems. II. Simulation studies of chromosomal segments under selection. *Theoret. Pop. Biol.*, **13**, 1–23.

Clegg, M. T., Kidwell, J. F., Kidwell, M. G. and Daniel, N. J. (1976). Dynamics of correlated genetic systems. I. Selection in the region of the glued locus of *Drosophila melanogaster. Genetics*, **83**, 793–810.

Clegg, M. T., Kidwell, J. F. and Kidwell, M. G. (1978). Dynamics of correlated genetic systems. III. Behaviour of chromosomal segments under lethal selection. *Genetics*, **48**, 95–106.

Clegg, M. T., Horch, C. R. and Kidwell, J. F. (1979). Dynamics of correlated genetic systems. VI. Variation in recombination rates in experimental populations of *Drosophila melanogaster. J. Heredity*, **70**, 297–300.

Clegg, M. T., Kidwell, J. F. and Horch, C. R. (1980). Dynamics of correlated genetic systems. V. Rates of decay of linkage disequilibria in experimental populations of *Drosophila melanogaster. Genetics*, **94**, 217–234.

Clegg, M. T. and Cavener, D. R. (1982). Dynamics of correlated genetic systems. VII. Demographic aspects of sex-linked transmission. *Amer. Natur.*, **120**, 108–118.

Degos, L. and Dausset, J. (1974). Human migrations and linkage disequilibrium of HL-A system. *Immunogenetics*, **3**, 195–210.

Dobzhansky, Th. (1970). *Genetics of the Evolutionary Process*. New York: Columbia Univ. Press.

Ellstrand, N. C. (1984). Multiple paternity within the fruits of the wild radish, *Raphanus sativus. Amer. Natur.*, **123**, 819–828.

Ewens, W. J. (1979). *Mathematical Population Genetics*. New York: Springer Verlag.

Ewens, W. J. and Thomson, G. (1977). Properties of equilibria in multilocus genetic systems. *Genetics*, **87**, 807–819.

Feldman, M. W., Franklin, I. and Thomson, G. J. (1974). Selection in complex genetic systems. I. The symmetric equilibria of the three-locus symmetric viability model. *Genetics*, **76**, 135–162.

Felsenstein, J. (1965). The effect of linkage on directional selection. *Genetics*, **52**, 349–363.

Franklin, I. and Lewontin, R. C. (1970). Is the gene the unit of selection? *Genetics*, **65**, 701–734.

Hastings, A. (1981a). Stable cycling in discrete-time genetic models. *Proc. Natl. Acad. Sci. USA*, **78**, 7224–7225.

Hastings, A. (1981b). Disequilibrium, selection and recombination: limits in two-locus two-allele models. *Genetics*, **98**, 659–668.

Hastings, A. (1981c). Simultaneous stability of D=0 and D≠0 for multiplicative viabilities at two loci: an analytical study. *J. Theor. Biol.*, **89**, 69–81.

Hastings, A. (1982). Unexpected behaviour in two locus genetic systems: an analysis of marginal underdominance at a stable equilibrium. *Genetics*, **102**, 129–138.

Hedrick, P. W. (1982). Genetic hitchhiking: a new factor in evolution? *Bioscience*, **32**, 845–853.

Hedrick, P., Jain, S. and Holden, L. (1978). Multilocus systems in evolution. *Evolutionary Biology*, **11**, 101–184.

Hoppensteadt, F. C. (1976). A slow selection analysis of two locus, two allele traits. *Theoret. Pop. Biol.*, **9**, 68–81.

Kan, Y. W. and Dozy, A. M. (1978). Polymorphisms of DNA sequence adjacent to human β-globin structural gene: relationship to sickle mutation. *Proc. Natl. Acad. Sci. USA*, **75**, 5631–5635.

Kan, Y. W. and Dozy, A. M. (1980). Evolution of hemoglobin S and C genes in world populations. *Science*, **209**, 388–391.

Karlin, S. (1975). General two-locus selection models: some objectives, results and interpretations. *Theoret. Pop. Biol.*, **7**, 364–398.

Karlin, S. and Feldman, M. W. (1970). Linkage and selection: Two-locus symmetric viability model. *Theoret. Pop. Biol.*, **1**, 39–71.

Karlin, S. and Carnelli, D. (1975). Numerical studies on two-loci selection models with general viabilities. *Theoret. Pop. Biol.*, **7**, 399–421.

Karlin, S. and Feldman, M. W. (1978). Simultaneous stability of D=0 and D≠0 for multiplicative viabilities at two loci. *Genetics*, **90**, 813–825.

Karlin, S. and Liberman, U. (1976). A phenotypic symmetric selection model for three loci, two alleles: the case of tight linkage. *Theoret. Pop. Biol.*, **10**, 334–364.

Karlin, S. and Liberman, U. (1979a). Central equilibria in multilocus systems. I. Generalized nonepistatic selection regimes? *Genetics*, **91**, 777–798.

Karlin, S. and Liberman, U. (1979b). Central equilibria in multilocus systems. II. Bisexual generalized nonepistatic selection models. *Genetics*, **91**, 799–816.

Kazazian, H. H., Chakravarti, A., Orkin, S. H. and Antonarakis, S. E. (1983). DNA polymorphism in the human β-globin gene cluster, in *Evolution of Genes and Proteins*, M. Nei and R. K. Kohen eds., Sunderland, MA: Sinauer Associates, Inc.

Kimura, M. (1965). Attainment of quasilinkage equilibrium when gene frequencies are changing by natural selection. *Genetics*, **52**, 875–890.

Kimura, M. and Ohta, T. (1971). *Theoretical Aspects of Population Genetics*. Princeton, N.J.: Princeton Univ. Press.

Kurnit, D. M. (1979). Evolution of sickle variant gene. *Lancet* i, 104.

Langley, C. H., Tobari, Y. N. and Kojima, K. (1974). Linkage disequilibria in natural populations of *Drosophila melanogaster*. *Genetics*, **78**, 921–936.

Lewontin, R. C. (1964). The interaction of selection and linkage. General considerations: heterotic models. *Genetics*, **49**, 49–67.

Lewontin, R. C. (1974). *The Genetic Basis of Evolutionary Change*. New York: Columbia Univ. Press.

Lewontin, R. C. and Kojima, K. (1960). The evolutionary dynamics of a complex polymorphism. *Evolution*, **14**, 458–472.

Lewontin, R. C., Ginzburg, R. and Tuljapurkar, S. D. (1978). Heterosis as an explanation for large amounts of genic polymorphism. *Genetics*, **88**, 149–169.

McDonald, J. F. (1983). The molecular basis of adaptation: a critical review of relevant ideas and observations. *Ann. Rev. Ecol. Syst.*, **14**, 77–102.

Maynard Smith, J. and Haigh, J. (1974). The hitchhiking effect of a favourable gene. *Genet. Res.*, **23**, 23–35.

Nagylaki, T. (1974). Quasilinkage equilibrium and the evolution of two-locus systems. *Proc. Natl. Acad. Sci. USA*, **71**, 526–530.

Nagylaki, T. (1976). The evolution of one- and two-locus systems. *Genetics*, **83**, 583–600.

Nagylaki, T. (1977). *Selection in One- and Two-Locus Systems*. Berlin: Springer-Verlag.

Nei, M. (1983). Genetic polymorphism and the role of mutation in evolution, in *Evolution of Genes and Proteins*, M. Nei and R. K. Koehn, eds., Sunderland, MA: Sinauer Associates, Inc.

Nei, M. and Li, W. H. (1973). Linkage disequilibrium in subdivided populations. *Genetics*, **75**, 213–219.

O'Brien, S. J. and MacIntyre, R. J. (1971). Transient linkage disequilibrium in *Drosophila. Nature*, **230**, 335–336.

Panny, S. R., Scott, A. F., Smith, K. D., Phillips, J. A., Kazazian, H. H., Talbot, C. C. and Boehn, C. D. (1981). Population heterogeneity of the *HpaI* restriction site associated with the β-globin gene: Implications for prenatal diagnosis. *Am. J. Hum. Genet.*, **33**, 25–35.

Pollak, E. (1984). Gamete frequencies at two sex-linked loci in random mating age-structured populations. *Math. Biosciences*, (in press).

Pollak, E. and Callanan, T. (1982). Convergence of two-locus gamete frequencies in random mating age-structured populations. *Math. Biosciences*, **62**, 179–199.

Prout, T. (1971). The relation between fitness components and population prediction in *Drosophila*. I. The estimation of fitness components. *Genetics*, **68**, 127–149.

Prout, T. (1973). Appendix to Mitton, J. B. and Koehn, R. K., Population genetics of marine pepecypods. III. Epistasis between functionally related isoenzymes in *Mytilus edulis. Genetics*, **73**, 487–496.

Provine, W. B. (1971). *The Origins of Theoretical Population Genetics*. Chicago: Univ. of Chicago Press.

Rasmuson, M., Rasmuson, B. and Nilson, L. R. (1967). A study of isozyme polymorphism in experimental populations of *Drosophila melanogaster. Hereditas*, **57**, 263–274.

Ritland, K. and Jain, S. K. (1981). A model for the estimation of outcrossing rate and gene frequencies using n independent loci. *Heredity*, **47**, 35–52.

Serjeantson, S. W., Ryan, D. P. and Thompson, A. R. (1982). The colonization of the Pacific: the story according to human leukocyte antigens. *Am. J. Hum. Genet.*, **34**, 904–918.

Shaw, D. V., Kahler, A. L. and Allard, R. W. (1981). A multilocus estimator of mating system parameters in plant populations. *Proc. Natl. Acad. Sci. USA*, **78**, 1298–1302.

Slatkin, M. (1972). On treating the chromosome as the unit of selection. *Genetics*, **72**, 157–168.

Smith, D. B. and Adams, W. T. (1983). Measuring pollen contamination in clonal seed orchards with the aid of genetic markers. In *Proceedings XVII Southern Tree Improvement Conference*. Athens, GA: Univ. of Georgia Press.

Straus, D. S. and Taylor, C. E. (1981). Hitchhiking and linkage disequilibrium between hemoglobin S and nearby restriction sites. *Hum. Hered.*, **31**, 348–352.

Sved, J. A. (1968). The stability of linked systems of loci with a small population size. *Genetics*, **59**, 543–563.

Sved, J. A. (1975). Fitness of third chromosome homozygotes in *Drosophila melanogaster. Genet. Res.,* **25**, 197–200.

Thomson, G. (1977). The effect of a selected locus on linked neutral loci. *Genetics,* **85**, 753–788.

Tracey, M. L. and Ayala, F. J. (1974). Genetic loads in natural populations: Is it compatible with the hypothesis that many polymorphisms are maintained by natural selection? *Genetics,* **77**, 569–589.

Wagener, D. K. and Cavalli-Sforza, L. L. (1975). Ethnic variation in genetic disease: Possible roles of hitchhiking and epistasis. *Am. J. Hum. Genet.,* **27**, 348–364.

Weir, B. S. (1979). Inferences about linkage disequilibrium. *Biometrics,* **35**, 235–254.

Wills, C., Crenshaw, J. and Vitale, J. (1970). A computer model allowing maintenance of large amounts of genetic variability in Mendelian Populations. I. Assumptions and results of large populations. *Genetics,* **64**, 107–123.

Wills, C. and Miller, C. (1976). A computer model allowing maintenance of large amounts of genetic variability in Mendelian populations. II. The balance of forces between linkage and random assortment. *Genetics,* **82**, 377–399.

Wright, S. (1931). Evolution in mendelian populations. *Genetics,* **16**, 97–159.

Yamazaki, T. (1974). Organization of linked genes under frequency-dependent selection of minority advantage. *Japan J. Genet.,* **49**, 33–36.

Yamazaki, T. (1977). The effects of overdominance on linkage in a multilocus system. *Genetics,* **86**, 227–236.

Hierarchy and evolution

NILES ELDREDGE and STANLEY N. SALTHE

Recent controversies in evolutionary biology boil down to one central issue: is the 'modern synthesis' (which focuses on a single level of evolutionary dynamics and claims that the neodarwinian paradigm is both necessary and sufficient to explain all evolutionary phenomena – cf. Mayr 1980, p. 1) sufficiently complete to provide an accurate description of the complexities of evolution? Paleontologists (e.g. Gould 1980) and molecular biologists (e.g. Dover 1982) who have questioned both the effectiveness and propriety of viewing the population-level processes of natural selection and genetic drift as the sole important determinants in evolution, have seen the need to amplify evolutionary theory. Meanwhile defenders of the faith (e.g. Ruse 1982) see such mavericks merely as 'problem children' once again stirring up trouble. A prominent theme these days – at least among those who feel the synthesis is too simple and simplistically reductionist – is the perceived need for an evolutionary theory that takes into account the several ontologically-based hierarchies in the biotic realm. We need a hierarchical theory not just because the theories that cover molecules, populations and phyla are too multifarious to fit into a single statement, but more importantly because nature itself is hierarchically arranged. The several concrete proposals of this kind (e.g. Wright 1953, 1964; Gerard 1958; Bertalanffy 1968; Valentine 1968; Bonner 1969; Iberall 1972; Salthe 1975; Conrad 1976; Miller 1978; MacMahon et al. 1978) have for the most part been constructed only from an epistemological perspective. We also observe that, although many of us have talked about the need for a hierarchically structured theory, there has as yet been relatively little solid work towards developing such a theory in detail. We hope, in this paper, to redress the balance a bit (see also Vrba and Eldredge 1984).

Some general aspects of hierarchies

We propose to explore a theory which sees nature as a hierarchy of entities existing at different discrete (or at least quasi-discrete) levels of organization (e.g. Bunge 1979). Recent and current moves in this direction (Valentine 1969, 1973; Salthe 1975; MacMahon et al. 1978; Plotkin and Odling-Smee 1981; Eldredge and Cracraft 1980; Gould 1982; Arnold and Fristrup 1982; Eldredge 1982) all fall short of providing clear, precise and fully explicit formal proposals that will articulate all we know of the evolutionary process, be it ecological or genealogical.

We begin with the assumption that nature is indefinitely complex (Buchler 1966; Wimsatt 1974). We further assume that the hierarchical levels are nested one within the other. This is a requirement, not of hierarchy theory per se (see Pattee 1973; Wimsatt 1974; Allen and Starr

1982), but of the material world that is being represented. Wholes are composed of parts at lower levels of organization, and are themselves parts of more extensive wholes. In principle the world is indefinitely complex (Buchler 1966), but in practice we are concerned in any particular sphere of interest with a restricted range of phenomena, the interactions between which explain most of the data generated by our observations. These phenomena are determined in the first place by our own presence at a given level, which sets their scale, and in the second by our interests. Our theory will be constructed in such a way as to preclude infinite regress in our analyses.

Entities at different levels do not directly interact in the same dynamic process: the forces in a windstorm do not interact with the digestive processes of the animal it drives to shelter. Instead they constrain each other so as to set up the possibilities and limits of what can happen at other levels: digestion is slowed as blood rushes from the gut to the legs of the fleeing animal – that is, its rate is regulated. These constraints (the 'non-holonomic constraints' of Pattee 1977) are most effective across contiguous levels and their importance drops off as the levels involved are increasingly remote: alterations of relationships in the solar system will not affect this animal's digestion even though such alterations may well control the occurrence of storms. This is a statement of the principle of non-transitivity of effects across levels developed at greater length elsewhere (Salthe ms.). Thus, consider that the functioning of your cells directly affects you but cannot directly affect the population of which you are a part (see also Bateson 1972, 1979). Its immediate import is that for any basic analysis no more than three levels (and no fewer) will be required to be considered as interacting in the production of phenomena. Our hierarchy of nature, therefore, is unlike the familiar Linnaean hierarchy of systematics, in which relationships are transitive (Buck and Hull 1966).

Our theory must be capable of representing diachronic (allochronic) process as well as synchronic structure (Piaget 1971). Each level is taken to represent a dynamic system in its own right (Bunge 1979); all processes leading to changes of state can be accounted for by natural laws appropriate to the level in focus together with constraints (Wigner 1964; Pattee 1977) originating at other levels, for the most part the two contiguous levels. Constraints are not reducible to laws – they are different kinds of things (Allen and Starr 1982). One group of these constraints, representing Aristotle's material causes (Montalenti 1974) determines the kinds of processes that can possibly occur at a given level. They emanate primarily from the next level below the one in focus. These have been, together with the lawful processes themselves, the major focus of reductionist science in the Twentieth Century. The other set of constraints is imposed primarily from the level next above that in focus, and represents controls or regulation on the lawful processes being observed at the level in focus (Polanyi 1968). These represent in part Aristotle's efficient, final and formal causes, and made their recent appearance in science with the rise of systems theories in the late 1940s. Further development of this basic triadic system is to be found elsewhere (Salthe ms.), where justification is made for referring to the lower level constraints as 'initiating conditions' and to the upper level constraints as 'boundary conditions' on the process being observed. Boundary and initiating conditions establish a fundamental asymmetry in the hierarchy of nature. Boundary conditions are powerful in being able to exert some measure of control simultaneously over all subsystems contained within the system from which they originate. Initiating conditions, on the other hand, originate within one subsystem and must cooperate with many others in order to affect the supersystem within which they all exist and, hence, they are by contrast 'weak'. Yet initiating and boundary conditions are materially the same thing – they are the results of the transformations effected by the processes occurring at any level. If their effect is upward, they are contributing to the initiating conditions at the next higher level; if their effect is downward, they become boundary conditions on the next lower level. Thus entities at any level face both upward and downward simultaneously, conveying information in both directions – they are the 'holons' of Koestler (1967, 1978).

When we turn to the world to apply a theoretical structure like the one described, we discover the need for further elaboration. The non-transitivity principle, for example, would not be required in a world less obdurate than the actual physical world, where initiating conditions at various levels would not usually intercept boundary conditions traversing the levels from above and *vice versa*. In the real world the entities found at different levels are, although all material, different in kind. If this were not so the world would not in fact be complex enough to require hierarchical representation. Formally, we must note that levels are classes of concrete entities (Bunge 1979). Particular instances of these entities are all individuals (Ghiselin 1974, 1981; Hull 1980, 1981) at whatever level. But the individuals that are found within others as subsystems are members of different classes (levels) which are not, and cannot be, members of the classes (levels) to which the supersystem belongs. Thus, no level has classes (or other levels) as members; all levels have concrete individuals as members, but individuals of very different scale in each case. Thus, there is a hierarchy of nested individuals but not a hierarchy of levels (Bunge 1979) which loose usage (ours included) would sometimes lead one to suppose. The situation is similar to that between taxa and taxonomic categories (Simpson 1961). The relationship between levels is not one of inclusion but of seriation according to rank. Cells are included parts of organisms, but the cellular level is not a member of the organismic level – organisms are. That cells and organisms are different kinds of things is seen when we recall that cells can only affect organisms *en masse* while an organism can affect all its cells immediately and directly; their relationship is not symmetrical – in this context $a = b \ne b = a$. If entities at different levels were the same kinds of things these inequalities would be equivalent.

Different kinds of phenomena have another bearing on our enterprise, this time arising from the kinds of processes we choose to study. The evolutionary process involves both genealogic and ecologic entities. These are as different in kind as species are from ecosystems. Yet a complete evolutionary theory must refer to both kinds of entities. Nevertheless, no

Table 1

The genealogical and ecological hierarchies: the twin process hierarchies of evolution. Arranged so that organisms, the only individual entities common to both hierarchies, are aligned, the concomitant alignment of other sorts of individuals between the two hierarchical systems by no means implies either identity or equivalence.

Genealogical hierarchy	Ecological hierarchy
Codons	Enzymes
Genes	Cells
Organisms	Organisms
Demes	Populations
Species	Local ecosystems
Monophyletic taxa	Biotic regions
(Special case: all life)	Entire biosphere

single nested hierarchy can include both – despite our own initial attempts to integrate the two hierarchies, they are 'incompatible descriptions' to use Pattee's expression (1978). Yet during the history of life ecosystems have provided constraints of importance to species and *vice versa*. Note again that constraint is the characteristic mode of operation of one entitity upon another of different kind. We suggest that the way to ensure that ecosystems may be represented as having an effect upon species without having them in the same immediate structure is to represent nature as a system of parallel hierarchies (Table 1). Wherever a label is found (e.g. 'deme'), processes governed by the laws of nature take place. Between any such labelled levels the only mode of interaction is constraint, either in the form of boundary conditions or of initiating conditions. Thus constraints on processes may come from immediately above in the same hierarchy, immediately below, or from any level (usually higher) in the parallel hierarchy. That is, constraints come in all cases from kinds of entities other than the ones involved in the processes under observation. Thus non-transitivity is the rule only within one hierarchic column. The world so viewed is complex in every conceivable direction and dimension (for metaphysics, see Buchler 1966; for the material world see Mandelbrot 1977) and we must seek the rules of interaction between the different kinds of individuals inhabiting that part of it we choose to study. It is precisely this attitude that will allow us ultimately to integrate, unify and articulate what was formerly (one might almost say 'formally') separate in the so-called synthetic theory of evolution.

The genealogical hierarchy

We might think of evolution as the hypothesis that all organisms are related. Radically different from Dobzhansky's definition (e.g. 1951,

p. 21) and the many subsequent variant forms it has taken ('evolution is change in gene content and frequency within populations' – still in vogue, cf. Harris 1981, p. 2), the notion that all organisms are related is actually a statement of genealogical interconnectedness – half of Darwin's 'descent with modification'. It carries with it the prediction that evolutionary novelties are nested and define nested sets of taxa, of which the taxon 'all life' is a special case. The inclusive taxon 'life' is defined by synapomorphies (evolutionary novelties shared by an ancestor and all its descendants): RNA appears to be such a synapomorphy. Though the notion is firmly established in empirical comparative biology, in principle this particular notion of evolution is refutable.

The actual historical patterns of evolution are nested sets of evolutionary novelties ('synapomorphies') and the congruent hierarchy of nested monophyletic taxa. Vrba and Eldredge (1984) refer to the former as the 'hierarchy of homology' and the latter as taxic components of the Linnaean hierarchy. They further conclude that both of these hierarchies require additional theory for their explanation. Part of such theory must reside in notions of genealogy in the evolutionary process. To put it another way, the taxic and homology hierarchies are historical patterns created by hierarchically organized processes: the genealogical and ecological systems. The elements of the genealogical and ecological hierarchies interact, regulating change within one another, and, as a byproduct, creating the two hierarchies of homology and monophyletic taxa.

The levels of both the ecological and genealogical hierarchies that we consider are defined by various classes of individual entities – individuals in addition to the class of conventionally recognized individual organisms (Hull 1980a). Indeed, some of the recent resurgence of interest in biological hierarchies and their relationship to the evolutionary process (e.g. Eldredge and Cracraft 1980; Ghiselin 1981; Eldredge 1982; Gould 1982; Arnold and Fristrup 1982) stems from the explicit formulation that species can be construed as individuals and not simply as classes (Ghiselin 1974; Hull 1976). It is perhaps better to say that the Linnaean category 'species' is a class, while each taxon considered a biological species (construed as discrete reproductive communities) is an individual. Species in general are kinds of individuals, and thus also a class.

Species are individuals because they are spatiotemporally bounded entities: they have origins, histories and terminations, just as individual organisms do (see Eldredge 1984). Individuals generally have properties unique to themselves, though each one of a pair of monozygotic twins remains an individual in spite of their putative genetic identity. Similarly, all sexually reproducing species differ at least in some of the elements of their Species Mate Recognition Systems (Paterson 1978) – a matter of further genealogical importance. Species-specific properties may be construed as sum-of-the-parts (organismic or demic) properties, or may be 'emergent' – properties of the species as a whole that are not simply the sum of the observed properties of the component demes and organisms. An example of the former may be parameters of ecological niche exploitation: a euryhaline species is euryhaline either because each of its component organisms is physiologically euryhaline, or because geographic variation among allopatric populations sums up to a broad range of salinity tolerances. An example of the latter – a true species-level property – would be the degree to which neighbouring demes actually exchange propagules. This depends on the actual geographical situation and pattern of deme relationships as well as on lower-level phenomena such as population structure and the dispersal ability of the organisms. Being part of the species is not transitive across levels when species are viewed as individuals. In any case, truly 'emergent' 'species-level' properties are not requisite for construing species as 'individuals'; properties unique to individuals of various levels become important only when notions of different levels of 'selection' are considered (Vrba and Eldredge 1984).

What is of interest, however, in defining individuals of any sort is the specification of the 'glue' that provides the cohesion to the spatio-temporally bounded entities. The core of any notion of genealogy is the production of new entities from old – entities, moreover, of like kind (i.e. at the same level). Individual organisms mate and produce new organisms. Species, it is widely alleged, fragment in various fashions to reproduce two (or more) where once there was but one. If species are individuals, what then is the 'glue' imparting cohesion? It is simply the continuing reproductive plexus, the exchange of propagules across demes and the continued interbreeding among organisms – with the resultant production of new organisms.[1] The glue holding a species together is the continual production of lower-level component individuals – demes or organisms. Note that production of new individuals from old may involve precise duplication (exact 'replication' – as in asexual budding or fission) or some degree of novelty: for the moment, the important point is simply the production of new individuals of like kind, whatever the degree of similarity between parent and offspring may be.

We can now ask if the pattern holds at other levels. For example, species occasionally produce new species. And this production of 'new entities of like kind' – new species from old – is the glue that, almost by definition, holds together monophyletic taxa of rank higher than species. Such monophyletic taxa are thus themselves individuals: spatiotemporally bounded entities held together by the continual production of the next lower-level class of component individuals – species. Taxa of rank higher than species, however, do not produce additional entities of like kind, so we have apparently reached the upper level of the genealogical hierarchy with the class of individuals simply labelled 'monophyletic taxa' (see Vrba and Eldredge 1984, for additional discussion of this point).

---

[1] We include 'demes' as individuals within the genealogical hierarchy, midway between organisms and species. As breeding clusters of organisms demes are not equivalent to ecological 'populations'. Introduced by Wright, 'demes' have not fared well as ontological entities of concern to evolutionary theorists. As Vrba and Eldredge (1984) remark, however, to ignore demes in the genealogical hierarchy is to reject out of hand Wright's 'shifting balance theory'. In any case, those who doubt the existence of demes in nature may simply 'delete and close up' that segment of the hierarchy, and see organisms as simply nested within species.

If there are putative individuals – demes, species and monophyletic taxa – above the organism level, we might suppose there are kinds of biological individuals below that level as well. The nucleotide bases are an obvious possibility. Bases are a class of molecule, and indeed 'cytosine' and 'guanine' are classes of bases with 'defining properties'. But within any strand of DNA, each particular instance of a base constitutes an individual. The 'glue' holding each particular base-entitity together comes from the several kinds of forces involved in chemical bonding. And linked base pairs are famous for producing more of themselves. Below the level of bases, the individuals are biochemical entities not (at least as yet) explicitly implicated in the evolutionary process.

Codons (triplet base pairs) encode the amino acids of proteins. The 'glue' holding codons together, it can be argued, is the continual synthesis of the individual base pairs. 'Genes' these days, however, tend to be seen as segments of DNA with introns and exons. There are 'pseudogenes', and 'functional genes' that actually are transcribed and encode a product. There are sections of gibberish DNA and redundant DNA, both within and between 'genes'. Though there are, then, hierarchical aspects to genetic organization and subdivisions of 'genes' themselves have aspects of individuality, it seems more appropriate to view the entire complex DNA segment designated as a 'gene' as the next higher component of the genealogical hierarchy. Genes are held together by the continual production of linked base pairs.

Chromosomes are also possible candidates for the sobriquet 'individual'. They are tolerably discrete during some of the course of the life of a cell and interactions among both homologous and non-homologous chromosomes are important in the elaboration of some gene products, in crossing-over and in large-scale mutation events. On the other hand, chromosomes are not ubiquitous properties in biotic nature, being confined to eucaryotic cells, and it can be argued that the production of new chromosomes from old is reducible beyond the level of the gene down to the level of the base pairs themselves – two points arguing for the exclusion of chromosomes from the genealogical hierarchy. It seems more sensible to go from base pairs to genes to organisms in the genealogical hierarchy.

Organisms are, of course, the paradigmatic example of 'individuals', useful by analogy in exploring the individuality of other sorts of biological individuals. There are, of course, some well known classes of instances where such individuality is not at all clear-cut – such as the separate polyps within a bryozoan or coelenterate colony. Clearly both polyps and colonies are individuals in the sense used here – but neither is an individual of precisely the same sort as an individual *Homo sapiens* (see Williams 1966).

A more interesting problem with organismic individuals is that they constitute the only class of individuals to appear in both the genealogical and ecological hierarchies. An individual *Homo sapiens* organism is a member of a species and has its own genotype – and thus is a member in good standing of the genealogical hierarchy. But each *Homo sapiens* organism also belongs to a population that is a part of an ecological community nested within an ecosystem (our cultural innovations to the contrary notwithstanding) and thus perforce is an equally valid component of the ecological hierarchy. This observation led us for years to pursue, in vain, an attempt to find other exact correspondences between individuals within both the ecological and genealogical hierarchies – obscuring the main point of the present paper: that the relationship between the two hierarchies consists of intertactive effects between individuals found within the two different hierarchies. Individual elements within the ecological hierarchy are largely responsible for the shuffling of properties of individuals within a given level within the genealogical hierarchy – while the reproducing individuals within the genealogical hierarchy determine the very components, the actual interactive biotic players in the game, within the ecological hierarchy.

We pursue the nature of the interactions between the two hierarchies in further detail below. We remain convinced that only organisms provide identical elements in the two hierarchies – but find this situation just a trifle unsettling, if only because it is only organisms that are so easily agreed upon by all to be individuals. Our failure to find other individuals common to both systems may reflect more the difficulty of recognizing other sorts of individuals in the biotic realm – individuals (such as species) which, because they exist in spatiotemporal dimensions very different from those of organisms, are difficult to conceptualize as 'individuals'.

In any case, for the record, the 'glue' holding organisms together is, of course, cellular cohesion, but at base this cohesion depends upon the continual production of proteins elaborated on the basis of the genotype. And continual production of new genomes from old is essential for the continuing existence of any organism. Moreover, organisms are clearly spatiotemporally bounded and of course engage (by a variety of sexual and vegetative means) in the production of new individuals of like kind. There is no quarrel with the status of organisms as individuals!

We have already discussed the ontological status of demes, species and monophyletic taxa as individuals and as components of the genealogical hierarchy. Each particular instance of these classes of individuals – base pairs, genes, organisms, demes, species and monophyletic taxa – is a spatiotemporally restricted entity whose internal cohesion derives from the continual production of new individuals from old at the next lower level. The hierarchy, as depicted in Table 1, is nested.

Genes must reproduce themselves (and elaborate interactive gene products) to keep organisms going. Organisms must produce more organisms to keep demes going, and so on. The nested form of the hierarchy results in a structure forming a series of levels. It is our contention (see also Eldredge 1982; Vrba and Eldredge 1984) that each level of the genealogical hierarchy constitutes a quasi-discrete level of the evolutionary process. Specifically, change at any level reflects the shuffling of properties among next lower level individuals within any individual. We now consider the general aspects of those processes.

PROCESSES OF STASIS AND CHANGE WITHIN THE GENEALOGICAL HIERARCHY

Thus far we have spoken in general terms of two sorts of processes operating within each level of the genealogical hierarchy. The first process is simply the production of more individuals: we need theories of gene replication (and its errors – 'mutation'), production of new organisms (theories of development) and the origin of new demes and species. To some extent, of course, and however inadequate they may as yet be, we have such theories already available.

The second sort of process is the shuffling of lower-level individuals within upper-level individuals. Natural selection – differential reproductive success among organisms within demes – is the paradigmatic deterministic example of such a shuffling process. (Genetic drift is the equivalent-level stochastic shuffling process.) Three levels, minimally, are involved: L_i (the level of the organism), L_{i+1} (the level of the deme), and L_{i-1} (the level of the genome). Put another way, natural selection is a statistical, yet deterministic, process that shuffles the frequencies of the genetic properties of organisms as a function of differential reproductive success among organisms within demes. Note, too, that actual shuffling of organisms – their actual physical as opposed to mere 'genetic' deaths – while no longer a formal requirement for the modern concept of natural selection, nonetheless may be involved in 'natural selection'. Patterns of differential births and deaths of organisms may both be implicated in the sorting processes of natural selection. From the hierarchical point of view, the actual demise of an organism must be reinstated in the theory – obviating a tendency frequently seen in the literature of population genetics to represent the accumulation of change effected by selection and drift as a supposed process rather than a historical record.

We must ask, then, if for any ith level there are similar 'shuffling' processes such that in general individuals are shuffled within the next higher individuals. By analogy with the narrow 'differential reproductive success' concept of natural selection, can we speak in general of the shuffling of properties of L_{i-1} individuals among L_i level individuals within L_{i+1} individuals? 'Species selection' has been proposed as an explicit analogue to natural selection, but at a higher level, where species composition within a monophyletic taxon is being modified through time (Eldredge and Gould 1972; Stanley 1975a). In a recent review of such models Vrba and Eldredge (1984) reserve the term 'species selection' for instances involving true 'species-level' properties – i.e. aspects of species that are 'emergent' and not merely the sum-of-the-parts totality of properties of its component individuals. Species selection in this sense is a shuffling of species – either by differential rate of origin or extinction, or both – within a monophyletic taxon. But note, too, that L_{i-1} individuals (demes in this instance) are also being shuffled. In general, all L_{i-n} individuals within the genealogical hierarchy are shuffled as the ith level individuals are shuffled within L_{i+1}. This is the phenomenon of 'downward causation' (Campbell 1974) discussed further below, in Vrba and Eldredge (1984) and extensively under the rubric of 'regulation' by Salthe (ms.).

It is obvious that one of the two general within-level processes – the production of new individuals – while important in its own right in maintaining the very existence of the next higher level individual, is also one of the sub-components of the other general class of processes active within each level: the shuffling of the L_{i-1} individuals within the ith level individuals. In particular, rate of production of new L_{i-1} individuals is half of the familiar equation $R = S\text{-}E$: rate of increase (R) of new entities (species, say) is equal to rate of appearance (speciation rate – S) less rate of disappearance (extinction rate – E) (Stanley 1979; Vrba 1980). Change in rate of origin of new ith level individuals (ΔS) is thus a component of the general problem of changes (or lack thereof) in state within the ith-level of the genealogical hierarchy.

SHUFFLING: BOUNDARY CONDITIONS, CONSTRAINTS AND CASCADING EFFECTS

We have used the expression 'shuffling' (which may, or may not, result in actual state changes) for differences accruing in the ith level in terms of I-n individuals. The paradigm of natural selection working among organisms within demes to effect generation-by-generation changes in allelic frequencies nicely reveals the general structure of such shuffling within the ith level of the genealogical hierarchy. For such shuffling to occur at any level, there must of course be significant differences among the next lower-level individuals. And there must be continual production of such novelty. The neodarwinian paradigm sees novelty arising essentially from replication mistakes within the genome.

Extrapolating to the ith level, we ask where the differences among species arise, and we see that they come from the different demes and organisms that comprise the species – but these differences, as we have already acknowledged, themselves arise (with the exceptions noted below) at the genetic level. To say that all anatomical differences among elements of the biota ultimately arise at the molecular level is hardly astonishing, but bears repetition here as it is an aspect of relationships within the genealogical hierarchy which is seemingly 'reductionist'. Organisms appear very special to us in part because they carry within them a representation of their relations to other members of their deme and to their wider environment in the form of a genome. This representation acts as a map for the organism as it ontogenetically traverses its various environments. Given this or that environmental input, the norms of reaction of the gene product complexes produce some phenotypic responses within a fairly narrow range of possibilities. We are often impressed by that very narrowness to the extent of forgetting that the distributions of norms of reaction do have significant variability and that choices are made by the organism within that variability as it controls its ontogenetic responses to shuffling (regulatory constraint) from still higher levels. Still, it remains significant that we have not yet discovered any storage of information of this kind at any other level. Now, deme-level characters such as population structure and density, might seem to us to be a direct consequence of this organismic guidebook, but it is not if we think about it carefully. Whatever population structure we may have depends on organismic properties such as vagility, degree of sociality or territoriality, life history and reproductive mode – and these in turn depend upon anatomical and nervous system morphology, which in turn depend upon gene action. There we have the reductionist sequence of lower-level constraints, each giving rise to new upper-level constraints and so on in an indubitable causal chain. But here is at the same time upper-level regulation (downward causation) operating too. Demic structure is a result of the interaction of organismic behaviour within the deme with respect to various environmental variables which serve as constraining contexts. Population structure is itself variable with respect to these higher-level variables: how dense is the population? What other genotypes are present? In what kind of a pattern? And so on. These will impose response patterns in a chain of regulation down to the genetic determinants.

Novelties ultimately arise at a particular lower level, but this fact does not lead to a reductive theory of evolution because change in state – shuffling at the ith level – need have no effect at the next upper level. For example, Dover (e.g. 1982) and other molecular biologists have recently been asserting that there can be a tremendous amount of molecular change within the genome – amounting to virtual turmoil in some cases – with little or no discernible effects on the phenotypes. Put another way, phenotypic stability – such as the protracted periods of stasis advocates of 'punctuated equilibria' claim as general within the fossil record – says nothing of the stability of the genotype: the genotype, too, could be relatively stable, or could actually be changing rapidly (Salthe 1972, 1975). Another example: allelic frequencies can change greatly, with many accumulated phenotypic effects, yet without necessarily causing new species to form.[2] Species turnover might be great, but in relatively stable equilibrium, such that no change in basic numbers or overall 'niche-type' of species occurs within a monophyletic group – e.g. the 'steady-state' mode of macroevolution (Eldredge and Cracraft 1980, ch. 6), perhaps an apt description of mammalian evolution in general since the Oligocene.

Constraints operate, not only from lower levels upward, but also in the reverse direction. Thus, in many cases, if a species becomes extinct so do all its demes, organisms and genes. However, this sequence is not necessarily so simply transitive. It is possible, for example, for a species to become extinct while organisms that were parts of it still exist. Thus, several species of oaks found in the Rocky Mountains extend their ranges into drier and colder northern limits. As we approach this limit we find sexual reproduction curtailed by unsuitable conditions, while at the very limits individual trees stand in isolation, no longer in meaningful contact of any kind with conspecific neighbours, facing the elements alone (Neilson

---

[2] That is to say, species defined as discrete reproductive communities, as we define them here. Species defined simply as classes, diagnosed and recognized on the basis of degree of anatomical modification within a phyletic continuum, are of course, 'evolved' as a mere function of phenotypic modification (see Eldredge 1984). Such a concept of species explicitly denies that species can be considered as individuals and is thus of no interest to us here.

and Wullstein 1981). Now, should some catastrophe selectively eliminate the viable populations of these species to the south leaving only the more northerly individuals standing, the species would be extinct as reproductive communities, demes would be gone, but individual organisms would still hang on for a possibly significant period of time. It is quite possible that this scenario describes patterns of extinction in sessile organisms. This example points out the artificiality of the concept of species extensionally defined (Buck and Hull 1966) as merely the class of organisms taken to be its 'members'. Shuffling of L_{i-1} individuals within the L_i level alters the variation among the L_i individuals – which becomes the raw material for the shuffling going on within the next higher level. But it causes that shuffling only in the restricted sense of the 'material causes' of Aristotle (Montalenti 1974). 'Shuffling' is not symmetrical; it has its downward effects (e.g. individuals at the next lower level being eliminated), but this only sets up constraints (called 'initiating conditions' in Salthe ms.) for shuffling at the next higher level.

Thus inter-level interactions within the genealogical hierarchy are not symmetrical. Two generalizations seem particularly important: (1) shuffling of L_{i-1} individuals within L_i level individuals automatically shuffles all L_{i-n} individuals. (2) Shuffling of L_{i-1} individuals within the ith level produces the variation among the L_i individuals – which becomes the raw material for the shuffling going on within the next higher level. But it does not cause that shuffling. Shuffling indeed is not symmetrical: it has its downward effects, but only sets constraints for shuffling at the next higher level.

The ecological hierarchy

The ecological hierarchy is composed of a familiar series of individuals: molecules (enzymes), cells, organisms, populations, local ecosystems, biotic regions, and, finally, the entire biosphere (Table 1). We will argue that each of these units is a class, any particular instance of which is a historical entity – hence an 'individual' in Ghiselin's (1974) terminology. These individuals are nested to form the hierarchy; the cohesion holding each individual together appears to be the dynamic interactions among the next-lower individuals: it is interactions among organisms that bind populations together, while populations interact to form ecosystems.

It was our original intention to view the abiotic world as a third hierarchy, lying in parallel with the ecological and genealogical hierarchies. Such a position now strikes us as unduly uncomplicated; though the impingement of the abiotic on the biotic world probably would best be analyzed from a hierarchical perspective, in this paper we merely point out that the abiotic world directly affects the biotic realm – far more strongly than the biotic realm affects the abiotic. We also feel that most of the effects wrought by the abiotic world on the evolutionary process are filtered through the ecological hierarchy – though geographic processes of course can affect the genealogical hierarchy directly (as when formerly continuous habitats fragment, a necessary if not always sufficient pre-condition for the fragmentation of reproductive communities – 'speciation').

Turning, then, to the ecologic hierarchy of living systems, we first consider the lowest meaningful level: the molecular. We are inside the cell; there are both organic and inorganic molecules of various sizes, the largest being gene products and multimers of these, the enzymes and structural proteins. There are minute forms of liquid crystalline structure like membranes, phases such as liquids and gels, and sol-gel transitions. Appropriate predicates (referring to dynamic processes) here would be 'reduction', 'oxidation', 'esterification', and 'polymerization'. The amounts of substrates, equilibrium constants and rates of chemical reactions dominate our thinking at this level. We are aware of chemically and physically different regions corresponding, for example, to mitochondria or clusters of microtubules and the boundaries of membranes. Temperature and pH are important boundary conditions. Like all levels above and below it, entities at this level are propelled into activity by energy exchanges, in this case the forming and breaking of chemical bonds. Organic evolutionary change of rather radical amount would be needed to initiate important permanent changes at this level.

We move upward to the organism level.[3] Organisms (as we have already discussed) are the paradigmatic individuals, being the ones we know best. Indeed, we can provisionally use 'organism' for an ostensive definition of 'individual' – otherwise a system whose parts share a 'common fate' (Campbell 1958) or a system whose parts are in reciprocal relationships (Salthe 1982). Miller (1978) treats this level exhaustively. As a summary label for organismic processes we can use 'homeostatic ontogeny'. The predicates 'metabolism', 'physiology', 'excretion', 'senescence', 'ovulation', 'anger', 'intelligence', and the like are appropriate here and would be misplaced or merely metaphorical at other levels. That is, unlike words with more general referents, like 'reproduction', or 'growth', these predicates are specific to this level. Evolutionary change is easily registered here, and, indeed, this is the classical individual wherein organic evolutionary changes were first discovered and tabulated. In this regard the organism in current theory appears primarily as an economic machine adapted to various ways of making a living. (Indeed, many might prefer to refer to the 'ecological' hierarchy as the 'economic' hierarchy). The organism is said to 'reproduce itself' but in our ecological hierarchical framework this has little meaning. As we have seen, reproduction has

[3] We could move to a cellular level in a hierarchy where it would be important for us to distinguish multicellularity as a special condition. We are here trying to locate these discontinuities in the natural system that would be important to evolutionary questions in general. That it might be possible to locate further discontinuities between some of these we have identified is not a remarkable thing. In part, the perspective we bring to our studies and the nature of our problems will themselves influence just how many discontinuities it is useful for us to consider. At one time on the earth there were no multicellular organisms and yet the hierarchy of interactions among living systems was in operation. Both the evolutionary process and our attempts to recognize hierarchical levels can interpolate levels when it becomes necessary to do so – an ontological task for nature, an epistemological issue for us.

meaning only in the context of the genealogical hierarchy; in an ecological context, energy exchange drives the system and the individual organism has a standard thermodynamic history (Zotin 1974).[4]

When organisms of the same kind interact we find ourselves at the population level. Huddling, pecking order aggression, denning up, swarming, schooling, hunting in packs, grooming, nursing, territorial aggression and others are characteristic phenomena responsible for producing our favourite variables at this level – density, numbers, rates of growth, biotic potential, survivorship and so forth. Any of them might be reckoned processes at this level. We have reached a level that many prefer to treat as epiphenomenal (Simberloff 1980). The variables measured here are often treated as mere statistical summaries of the actions of individual organisms. We cannot take that view here and we note that in order to flock together birds of a feather must have a real context in which to do it. (A rejoinder might be that contexts multiply indefinitely. Our reply is that our theoretical orientation and problems will help us identify those that are needed in our work, and it is patent that ecologists throughout this century have ostensively identified the population for us as a real thing – cf. Hutchinson 1978).

If a population is real, where are its boundaries? Like the amoeba of the dispersed phase of the cellular slime mould, its boundaries are in incessant flux compared with that of the typical organism. But contacts between organisms in the population clearly do have spatiotemporal continuity over the years. Whether or not it is an easy practical matter to locate the boundaries of any population is a separate epistemological question which has received scant attention to date. It is usually possible to decide that one is working within one population instead of two and until now that has sufficed. Evolutionary change at this level can result in modifications of the ecological niches of populations.

When we become concerned with the interactions of organisms of different species, as in studies of, e.g. predation, we have moved up to the local ecosystem level, where problems of definition are even more perplexing, giving rise to even greater doubts about the reality of this level by some workers (Engelberg and Boyarsky 1979; Hoffman 1979; Simberloff 1980). Populations – not organisms – interact at the ecosystem level. This is tricky: despite the fact that one might observe a fox killing and eating a quail, it is nonetheless populations that are interacting. This is a matter of theory, and we must recall the principle of non-transitivity. The singular act of a given individual with respect to another of a different species, so vivid to our senses, has no more theoretical import at this level than have the mutual surges of hormones and emotions accompanying mating within

---

[4] Many of the laws of nature, such as the laws of thermodynamics, apply isomorphically across all hierarchical levels (i.e. they pertain severally to each level), and we can see from this that nomological structures are for the most part non-hierarchical in character. Hierarchy is an idiographic concept at heart. Since the grail of reductionism has always been the most general concept, we see again the necessary relationship between that research programme and the one that will emerge from what is being suggested here (see Wimsatt 1976 for an interesting discussion of the relationship between reductionism and hierarchical structure).

two organisms (or the jostling of the liver of the one by the motions of the other) for the population level. When we observe this act of predation we are seeing it through the filter of a theory that is not appropriate in our present context. Then, too, there is the matter of scale. In order to report correctly our observation of this event from the present perspective we must take the trouble to note that 'a part of the predator population is culling a part of the prey population', if, indeed, we choose to report the event at all. But in order to do this with facility we must have a mental paradigm switch. Without that it will be easier for us spontaneously to observe events on our own scale which may be correlated with what is going on at, say, the ecosystem level than to see these latter whole (i.e. holistically) – something that, alas, may not be really possible. Part of the problem of scale concerns time. The relaxation times and 'equilibrium constants' of processes at a higher level like this are considerably longer and larger than those applicable to the organismic events we are familiar with.

The processes, then, that appear to us at this juncture to be taking place at the ecosystem level are predation, interspecific competition, symbiotic interactions, jockeyings for realized niche expansion, variational play on the food web, changes in carrying capacities as these can be derived from biotic interactions (Van Valen 1973) and the like, none observable as discrete events. As with the population, so there is also a problem with discerning the boundaries of a community. One of us has attempted a beginning at this (Salthe 1983) by suggesting that populations with reciprocal interactions (energy and matter flows both to and from each to the other directly or indirectly) are parts of the same community while those with only one-way relationships would be viewed as interacting only indirectly, at a still higher level. We may note that everything is not in fact connected, even indirectly, to everything else (Buchler 1966; Allen and Starr 1982), and, indeed, that the physical impossibility of this has been taken as a source of hierarchical structure in the world (May 1972; Soodak and Iberall 1978). Evolutionary change at the ecosystem level has often been considered from the point of view of changes in community diversity (e.g. Whittaker 1977; Niklas *et al.* 1980) and this may be treated as an instance of the evolution of informational complexity in thermodynamically open systems (Lotka 1924; Margalef 1963; Wesley 1974). Primary succession is a concept of relevance here, and in this light can be viewed as a kind of constitutive change in comparison with the reaction to perturbation known as secondary succession. Some aspects of ecological niche evolution are entrained by these changes as well.

Moving upward again, we come to the level of the regional biotal system. We have reached a level of such unfamiliar scope and of such remoteness from our habitual objects of thought that we will be able to say little at this time concerning processes that are going on there. Whatever discussion has transpired about this level has tended to melt biotic and abiotic factors together, as in the 'biogeographic region' concept of Levins and Lewontin (1980) or the 'biotic province' of Valentine (1973). Thus the presence of a forest in one area influences the humidity of the air in adjacent ecosystems; the humidity is not, *per se*, a biotic factor. In effect, a regional biota has interposed a net of initiating conditions that intercept and modify the flux of humidity about a particular local ecosystem in such a way that leaving the biotal level out of consideration in describing these changes would require us to generate them as fluctuations of still higher-level processes (say, evaporation from oceans) responsible for the humidity in the region to begin with. Wimsatt (1976) has noted that as we proceed upward, levels tend to appear to us increasingly diffuse and less well-defined. In part this is surely an epistemological consequence of our own idiosyncratic presence at a given (lower) level (Allen and Starr 1982), but it may also mean that these higher levels have actually proceeded toward entification at a slower pace, as suggested by Wimsatt.

Another, related, problem here, noted by Valentine (1973), is that it becomes increasingly difficult for us to view processes at higher levels like this as emerging from results of processes at lower biotic (in this case community) levels where these results would be functioning as initiating conditions. Here, it seems to us, the abiotic world becomes even more important. At the higher ecological levels it seems clear that input from the abiotic realm to both initiating conditions is large in comparison with input via initiating conditions by the living systems themselves. Put another way (and as we have already noted), the grand processes carried out by the earth as a whole have as yet been little infiltrated and only trivially influenced by living systems. For a complete description, however, we must reckon with the latter, and to be formally consistent we must do so in such a way that living systems could increase the importance of their contributions during evolutionary time. We are concerned here more with formal system structure than with magnitudes of effects. Thus today on the earth living systems do contribute slightly to the initiating conditions giving rise to the economic (energy flow) processes that take place over vast portions of the earth's surface. In the past there was a time when they contributed nothing, and in the future they may become more dominant (Wesley 1974). If this happens the regional biotal system level will become richer in content and its entities will become more clearly distinct from the upper-level entities of the purely abiotic realm.

These problems are further exacerbated when we begin to consider the total biosphere as a functional system. One troublesome question: to what degree can we today disentangle its processes from those described in the abiotic realm of nature? Also, is the total biosphere system the last level of interest to biologists? The abiotic realm obviously continues beyond the solar system into levels whose relationships to biology are not at this time clear. Probably it will not be any more useful for our purposes to go above the biosphere level at present than it is to go below the molecular.

Interactions between the genealogical and ecological hierarchies

We now consider the relationship between the two 'process' hierarchies – the ecological and genealogical. Both clearly have something to do with evolution. Both, also, have internal dynamics and processes of change intrinsic to them. Both are fundamentally non-transitive and asymmetrical inasmuch as the relationships between levels within each hierarchy are concerned. And we have already noted that organisms are the only entities held in common by the two hierarchical systems. We will argue that the relationship between these two process hierarchies is not one of formal identity of component individuals, but rather an interactive one: components of the ecological hierarchy severally affect individuals within the genealogical hierarchy, and *vice versa*. Such complex interactions mediate and regulate change in both systems. A consequence of this interaction is the historical patterns of the sequential genealogical and ecological histories of life on earth. Genealogically speaking, the related hierarchies of homology and taxa (Vrba and Eldredge 1984) – the two 'historical' hierarchies – form as an automatic consequence of the complex interactions of the genealogical and ecological hierarchies throughout the immense span of geological time.

We have characterized the basic natures and structures of the ecological and genealogical hierarchies separately. Both are composed of individuals, any extant one of which may be sampled at any given moment. Moreover, individuals within both hierarchical systems have histories – however ephemeral, however widely the scale of duration (and spatial extent) may vary. All such individuals are spatiotemporal (hence by definition 'historical' – Hull 1978) entities. All such individuals have internal cohesion: the 'glue' imparting cohesion to individuals within the genealogical hierarchy is the production within the ith individual of new L_{i-1} individuals. In contrast, the 'glue' lending cohesion to all ith level individuals within the ecological hierarchy stems from the energetic exchanges among component L_{i-1} individuals. The interactions among individual organisms provides the cohesion for the population of *Sciurus carolinensis* in Central Park. By the same token, interactions among populations within an ecosystem impart cohesion to that ecosystem.

We are aware of two bodies of work relevant to the concept of two interacting hierarchical structures: the works of Howard Pattee on complex systems (Pattee 1970, 1972, 1977, 1978, 1979 – with Teggart 1925 as an interesting forerunner) and of David Hull on evolving systems (Hull 1980a, 1980b, 1981, based in part on Dawkins 1978). The dualism of these workers also informs our representation. Pattee develops the theme that complex systems characteristically involve the interaction of two very different kinds of entity: dynamic and informational. One of these engages in dynamic processes of a kind frequently described in equations as rate-dependent. Observations of these processes may lead us to formulate 'natural laws'. Classical physical systems contrived by experimental design give the paradigmatic examples. But even here initial and boundary conditions may affect the actual results generated by the operation of the laws of nature. These conditions operate as informational constraints and do not interact directly in the lawfully proceeding process. In geophysical nature such constraints give rise to inorganic energy-dissipating forms such as dust devils, icicles and ocean currents. In general, constraints arise from entities different in scale from those interacting to produce the lawful process at the ith level. These constraints are informational in nature rather than dynamic, and the physical world is produced by this interaction with dynamic systems. What is produced at one level of organization can act as constraints for processes at other levels.

Now, Pattee notes, with the appearance of living systems we find that at the organism level, at least, important aspects of informational constraint have become separated into a special subsystem, the genome, whose major task is to supply information from lower levels to the organism. Our genealogical hierarchy arises from the realization that separate informational configurations in some way analogous to the information entities existing at the cellular level – i.e. genes – exist at other levels, just as do the dynamic, economic, ecological systems they inform (Campbell 1982). Patterns in the genealogical hierarchy guide the processes characteristic of the ecological hierarchy. At the same time these processes actually produce the genealogical patterns, and so the two sorts of entities in the two hierarchies are mutually dependent.

Here we contact Hull's work. He has made a distinction between 'replication', 'interaction', and 'evolution'. In order for evolution to occur, stored information must change on the basis of interaction with the environment. Individuals that evolve must be spatiotemporally extended in time and be capable of allowing their stored information to become modified on the basis of some kind(s) of selection process(es). In order to be selected an individual must be spatiotemporally relatively more restricted in extension than an evolving individual. As a result of shuffling of these kinds of individuals ('units of selection') the more extended individual (the 'lineage') can evolve. Evolution means that the stored information in the lineage will become altered. It does so when other individuals – 'replicators' – replicate the information. We then have three kinds of individuals: replicators, interactors and lineages. Hull leaves open the possibility that each kind of individual may be found at different levels in a complex evolutionary system. As a quick extrapolation to our system, we may note that the genealogical hierarchy is certainly the seat of both replication and evolution, while the ecological hierarchy is certainly the seat of interaction. Beyond that it is difficult at present to go. We find units of selection also in the genealogical hierarchy. Thus species are spatio-temporally more restricted than lineages (monophyletic taxa) and will be shuffled as the taxon evolves. In other words, the two systems are at present only partially congruent.

In general, the genealogical hierarchy affects the ecological hierarchy by supplying the interacting players of the ecological game. There could not be two colour phases of peppered moths as part of the English lichen-moth-pollution-thrush predation system if there were no (1) insects, (2) Lepidoptera, (3) moths, (4) *Biston*, (5) *B. betularia*, (6) local demes of same in nothern England, (7) individual organisms of *B. betularia*, and (8) a genetic system specifying both mottled and melanic forms of colouration. Interactive effects cut across levels between the two hierarchies: the existence (or not) of a two-fold system of colouration in peppered moths has a significant effect on the particular moth-thrush-lichen system in England. But absence of *Biston betularia* altogether would have still greater ramifications – and so on, on up the genealogical hierarchy. No moths at all would have far greater implications for the ecological hierarchy than the loss of this particular colour dimorphism within *B. betularia* in northern England. The higher the level of individual in the genealogical hierarchy, the higher the level in the ecological hierarchy at which its effects will tend to be felt. Imagine a world without insects.

There is no simple equation where lower-level individuals within the genealogical hierarchy affect only lower-level individuals within the ecological hierarchy, and higher-level individuals affect higher-level ecological individuals. But that kind of non-transitive relationship does seem to be the general rule. Consider the historical effect of the extinction (in the Lower Triassic) of bellerophontid gastropods (primitive, bilaterally symmetrical archeogastropods – hence presumably herbivores). Spanning the entire Paleozoic, bellerophontid species, genera and families came and went. Among other habitats, bellerophontids were generally common elements of near-shore muddy-bottom molluscan-dominated communities. When extinction claimed the Devonian *Retispira leda*, other, similar species of *Retispira* took its place in comparable habitats – in similar communities – in the Carboniferous. But extinction of all bellerophontid species, hence genera, families and so on, affected not only all marine biogeographic regions with bellerophontids (i.e. higher-level ecological individuals) – but also forever changed the complexion of each and every small-scale muddy bottom molluscan-dominated local ecosystem. Today *Nassarius obsoletus* (not, incidentally, a herbivore) is all over the intertidal mudflats of Jamaica Bay. But there are no bellerophontids, and have not been in such environments for upwards of 200 million years.

What about the opposite situation: can presence or absence of relatively small-scale individuals of the genealogical hierarchy have large-scale ecological effects? Friends of the snail darter are inclined to think so – and indeed, in some ecological theory (and indeed in some simple if large-scale actual ecological situations – such as the tundra biome) the fate of a single allele may affect the fates of organisms in such a way as to affect transitively the entire ecosystem. Most large-scale ecological individuals, however, seem sufficiently complex and 'robust' that the comings and goings of even individual species have no lasting major impact.

It seems to us, then, that in terms of the effects of the genealogical hierarchy on the ecological hierarchy that we are once again faced with 'downward causation': the larger the genealogical individual, the larger the scale of the ecological individuals potentially affected – and the component smaller-scale individuals nested within the larger ecological individuals will be affected as well. There is no exact equivalence in scale of levels in the two hierarchies, however, and it may be the case that changes in relatively low-level genealogical individuals could have relatively large-scale effects in the ecological system. But, in general, it takes upper-level genealogical individuals to affect larger-scale ecological individuals.

Thus changes in the genealogical hierarchy have the consequence of modifying the composition of individuals (i.e. shuffling them) within the ecological hierarchy. Such changes are 'ecological' (i.e. for any moment in time, they affect the interactions among the L_{i-1} individuals), 'historical' (in the manner we have outlined) and 'evolutionary' – reorganization of individuals within the ecological hierarchy automatically affects the processes of birth and death of individuals within the genealogical hierarchy, thereby changing the information stored there. This is not to say that the only way the ecological hierarchy affects the genealogical hierarchy comes after the genealogical hierarchy has modified the ecological hierarchy: such profoundly two-way interactions of course are chicken-and-egg dilemmas in terms of 'ultimate' cause. Both hierarchies affect each other in complex ways; but in addition, the ecological hierarchy has 'reactive effects' on the genealogical hierarchy simply because it is largely (though not exclusively) through the ecological hierarchy that the abiotic world impinges upon the biota.

Once again, the paradigm of natural selection shuffling allelic frequencies within demes reveals the basic nature of effects wrought by the ecological hierarchy and the abiotic realm on the genealogical hierarchy. 'Selection pressures' in nature (see, e.g., Bock 1979, for an example of such a discussion) are usually identified as such abiotic elements as temperature, pressure, density of photo-illumination and so forth, while biotic factors include both within- and among-species ecological interactions: energy resources and competition for same are perhaps the two most commonly cited sources of 'biotic' selection pressures.

Once again the analogy seems to hold throughout the genealogical hierarchy: the processes of (1) production of new genealogical individuals and (2) the shuffling of L_{i-1} individuals within the ith-level individual (which involves *inter alia* the interplay of the births of new individuals and their deaths) are stimulated and to an important extent regulated by events in the ecological hierarchy. In terms of the 'births' and 'deaths' of new individuals, the effects of the ecological hierarchy on the genealogical hierarchy are easiest to see at relatively high levels within the genealogical hierarchy. Species extinction is an ecological phenomenon springing from extrinsic sources within a biogeographic region. Speciation – more an accident of geography than anything else, as a rule – is profoundly ecological. The recent reawakening of interest in the relationship between niche-width on the one hand, and rates of speciation and extinction (see, e.g. Eldredge 1979; Eldredge and Cracraft 1980, ch. 6; Vrba 1980; Fowler and MacMahon 1982) explicitly seeks to explain differential rates of speciation and species extinction in terms of ecological variables. Vrba and Eldredge (1984) have recently reviewed the various deterministic and stochastic 'shuffling' models (including 'species selection', the 'effect hypothesis', and others). All such models envision the 'shuffling agent' as part of the abiotic and biotic 'environments' – meaning, in most cases, the ecological hierarchy.

Descending the genealogical hierarchy, it becomes more difficult to point to the *direct* effects of the ecological hierarchy. Epigenesis within most non-mammalian organisms – i.e. most of life – is affected (albeit to varying degrees) by external, including abiotic, factors. Cosmic rays alter the genome. But the lower we go in the genealogical hierarchy, the more sheltered the processes of birth and death of individuals becomes. Shuffling processes such as Dover's (1982) 'molecular drive' are seen as wholly intrinsic to the genome itself and are entirely unaffected by the ecological hierarchy.

Thus it is easy to see how relatively large-scale individuals within the ecological hierarchy affect the processes of birth and death of large-scale elements, such as species, within the genealogical hierarchy. And shuffling of species, as we have already argued, leads to shuffling at lower levels throughout the genealogical hierarchy. Thus ecosystems affect genomes by the pattern of 'downward causation' within the genealogical hierarchy. Though there can be direct effects of individuals (at any level) within the ecological hierarchy on lower-level individuals within the genealogical hierarchy (the effect of cosmic rays on the genome being an extreme example), the main effects of ecology on the genealogical hierarchy seem to be filtered non-transitively through species, demes and organisms on down through the lower levels.

Summary: Towards a more complete evolutionary theory

We have presented the bare outline of what we take to be an appropriate structure for evolutionary theory – if various aspects of the hierarchy of nature are to be taken into account by evolutionary theory, as we feel they must. In a nutshell, we have proposed that the hierarchies of homology and taxa are twin historical patterns that emerge automatically from the general process of 'descent with modification'. The deterministic and stochastic processes underlying the production of these patterns, however, are to be found in the cross-level interactions among the various individuals arrayed in two other, dynamic process hierarchies: the genealogical and the ecological.

We have outlined the general nature of the processes going on within each level of both these hierarchies, and specified the general nature of the interactions (effects, boundary conditions, constraints and the like) among levels within both the genealogical and ecological hierarchies. Neither hierarchy turns out to be symmetrical. And we have characterized the general nature of cross-level interactions between the two hierarchies. We have concluded that the process of evolution requires an interaction between the two hierarchies. In other words, few lasting ('historical') changes in the ecological hierarchy can occur without input from the genealogical realm – since it is the genealogical hierarchy, at least in the long run, that supplies the basic 'players' in the ecological hierarchy. The converse is nearly always true too: with processes such as 'molecular drive' among the rare exceptions, little change (and virtually no proliferation at the species level) can be anticipated within the genealogical hierarchy except as a reactive effect to input from the ecological hierarchy. Even genetic drift in the real world must involve some input from the ecological hierarchy.

What we have not done is develop an explicit evolutionary theory *per se*. There are ecologic theories, selection theories, speciation theories, theories of epigenesis and replication of the genome. We have merely tried to suggest how all the various sorts of biological theories generally fit together – and that all are relevant to understanding evolution. It is our conviction that, based on this structural hatrack, paleontologists, systematists, ecologists, population geneticists, developmental biologists and molecular biologists can see more clearly how their data and theories potentially fit in with those emanating from other disciplines – disciplines long accustomed to dealing with different sorts of ontological entities on different orders of scale.

The modern synthesis, it seems to us, has failed to provide a workable (testable) evolutionary theory. Nor did it 'synthesize' except in the most limited ways. We believe this failure reflects a pervasive reductionism, one that saw only organisms as individuals – though of necessity the theory made statements about the next (upper and lower) adjacent levels (especially, and explicitly, by Dobzhansky 1937, cf. p. 13). Epistemologically, the synthetic theory does not address ultra-small or ultra-large scale phenomena – molecules, say, or monophyletic taxa. The ontological view of the biota as hierarchically arranged should have the epistemological consequence of allowing us to develop more fully theories appropriate to the levels of our data – our various sorts of individuals. These theories should be testable because they will be developed with reference to the appropriate individuals. We no longer need try to cram all of the 3.5 billion year history of the 90 + phyla into a single phenomenological level.

Acknowledgements

We thank the following colleagues for stimulating discussion or for having the patience to read the initial draft of this paper: Stephen Jay Gould, David Hull, Marjorie Grene, Neil Landman, Michael Novacek, Ronald Pilette, Elisabeth S. Vrba and our editors, Richard Dawkins and Mark Ridley.

References

Allen, T. H. F. and Starr, T. B. (1982). *Hierarchy: Perspectives for Ecological Complexity*. Univ. Chicago Press, Chicago.

Arnold, A. J. and Fristrup, K. (1982). The theory of evolution by natural selection: a hierarchical expansion. *Paleobiology* **8**, 113–129.

Bateson, G. (1972). *Steps to an ecology of mind*. Ballantine Books, New York.

— (1979). *Mind and nature: a necessary unity*. E. F. Dutton, New York.

Bertalanffy, L. von (1968). Introduction. In *General System Theory* (ed. L. von Bertalanffy), Braziller, New York.

Bock, W. J. (1979). The synthetic explanation of macroevolutionary change – a reductionistic approach. In *Models and Methodologies in Evolutionary Theory* (eds. J. H. Schwartz and H. B. Rollins), Bull. Carnegie Mus. Nat. Hist. **13**, 20–69.

Bonner, J. T. (1969). *The scale of nature: a panoramic view of the sciences*. Pegasus, New York.

Buchler, J. (1966). *Metaphysics of natural complexes*. Columbia Univ. Press, New York.

Buck, R. C. and Hull, D. L. (1966). The logical structure of the Linnaean hierarchy. *Syst. Zool.* **15**, 97–111.

Bunge, M. (1979). *Treatise on basic philosophy*: Vol. 4, A world of systems. D. Reidel, Dordrecht.

Campbell, D. T. (1958). Common fate, similarity, and other indices of the status of aggregates of persons as social entities. *Behav. Sci.* **3**, 14–25.

Conrad, M. (1976). Biological adaptability: the statistical state model. *Biosciences* **26**, 319–324.

Dawkins, R. (1978). Replicator selection and the extended phenotype. *Z. Tierpsychol.* **47**, 61–76.

Dobzhansky, T. H. (1937). *Genetics and the Origin of Species*. Columbia Univ. Press, New York. Reprinted ed., 1982.

— (1984). The ontology of species. In *Species and Speciation*. (ed. E. S. Vrba), Monogr. Transvaal Museum.

Dover, G. (1982). Molecular drive: a cohesive mode of species evolution. *Nature* **299**, 111–117.

Eldredge, N. and Cracraft, J. (1980). *Phylogenetic patterns and the evolutionary process. Method and theory in comparative biology*. Columbia Univ. Press, New York.

— (1982). Phenomological levels and evolutionary rates. *Syst. Zool.* **31**, 379–388.

— (1984). What, if anything, is a species? In *Species and Speciation. (ed. E. S. Vrba), Monogr. Transvaal Museum.*

Eldredge, N. and Cracraft, J. (1980). Phylogenetic patterns and the evolutionary process. Method and theory in comparative biology. Columbia Univ. Press, New York.

Eldredge, N. and Gould, S. J. (1972). Punctuated equilibria: an alternative to phyletic gradualism. In *Models in Paleobiology*, (ed. T. J. M. Schopf), pp. 82–115. Freeman, Cooper and Co., San Francisco.

Engelberg, J. and Boyarsky, L. L. (1979). The noncybernetic nature of ecosystems. *Amer. Naturalist* **114**, 317–324.

Fowler, C. W. and MacMahon, J. A. (1982). Selective extinction and speciation: their influence on the structure and function of communities and ecosystems. *Amer. Naturalist* **119**, 480–498.

Gerard, R. W. (1958). Concepts and principles of biology: initial working paper. *Behav. Sco.* **3**, 95–102.

Ghiselin, M. T. (1974). A radical solution to the species problem. *Syst. Zool.* **23**, 536–544.

— (1981). Categories, life and thinking. *Behav. Brain Sci.* **4**, 269–313.

Gould, S. J. (1980). Is a new and general theory of evolution emerging? *Paleobiology* **6**, 119–130.

— (1982). The meaning of punctuated equilibrium and its role in validating a hierarchical approach to macroevolution. In *Perspectives on evolution,* (ed. R. Milkman), pp. 83–104. Sinauer, Sunderland.

Harris, C. L. (1981). *Evolution*. State Univ. New York Press, Albany.

Hoffman, A. (1979). Community paleoecology as an epiphenomenal science. *Paleobiology* **5**, 357–379.

Hull, D. L. (1975). Central subjects and historical narratives. *History and Theory* **14**, 253–274.

— (1976). Are species really individuals? *Syst. Zool.* **25**, 174–191.

— (1978). A matter of individuality. *Philos. Sci.* **45**, 335–360.

— (1980a). The units of evolution. In *Studies in the Concept of Evolution*. (eds. U. J. Jensen and R. Harre), The Harvester Press, London.

— (1980b). Individuality and selection. *Ann. Rev. Ecol. Syst.* **11**, 311–322.

— (1981). Metaphysics and common usage. *Behav. Brain Sci.* **4**, 290–291.

Hutchinson, G. L. (1978). *An introduction to population ecology*. Yale Univ. Press, New Haven.

Iberall, A. (1972). *Toward a general science of viable systems*. McGraw-Hill, New York.

Koestler, A. (1967). The ghost in the machine. Macmillan, New York.

— (1978). *Janus: a summing up*. Vintage Books, New York.

Levins, R. and Lewontin, R. (1980). Dialectics and reductionism in ecology. *Synthese* **43**, 47–78.

Lotka, A. J. (1924). *Elements of physical biology*. Williams and Wilkins, Baltimore.

MacMahon, J. A., Phillips, D. L., Robinson, J. V. and Schimpe, D. J. (1978). Levels of biological organization: an organism-centered approach. *Bioscience* **28**, 700–704.

Mandelbrot, B. B. (1977). *Fractals: form, chance and dimension*. W. H. Freeman, San Francisco.

Margalef, R. (1963). *Perspectives in ecological theory*. Univ. Chicago Press, Chicago.

May, R. M. (1972). Will a large complex system be stable? *Nature* **238**, 413–414.

Mayr, E. (1980). Prologue. In *The Evolutionary Synthesis*, (eds. E. Mayr and W. B. Provine), pp. 1–48. Harvard Univ. Press, Cambridge.

Miller, J. G. (1978). *Living systems*. McGraw-Hill, New York.

Montalenti, G. (1974). From Aristotle to Democritus via Darwin: a short survey of a long historical and logical journey. In *Studies in the philosophy of biology and related problems*. (eds. F. J. Ayala and T. H. Dobzhansky), Univ. California Press, Berkeley.

Neilson, R. P. (1981). Biogeography of *Quercus gambelli* and *Quercus turbinella* in relation to seedling drought response and atmospheric flow structure. Ph.D. thesis, Univ. of Utah, 128 p.

Niklas, K. J., Tiffney, B. H. and Knoll, A. H. (1980). Apparent changes in the diversity of fossil plants: a preliminary assessment. In *Evol. Biol.* (eds. M. K. Hecht *et al.*), **12**, 1–89.

Paterson, H. E. H. (1978). More evidence against speciation by reinforcement. *S. Afr. J. Sci.* **74**, 368–371.

Pattee, H. H. (1970). The problem of biological hierarchy. In *Towards a Theoretical Biology*. (ed. C. H. Waddington), 3. Drafts. Aldine, Chicago.

— (1972). Laws and constraints, symbols and languages. In *Towards a theoretical Biology*. (ed. C. H. Waddington), 4. Essays. Aldine, Atherton, Chicago.

— (1973). The physical basis and origin of hierarchical control. In *Hierarchy Theory: The Challenge of Complex Systems*. (ed. H. H. Pattee), Braziller, New York.

— (1977). Dynamic and linguistic modes of complex systems. *Gen. Syst.* **3**, 259–266.

— (1978). The complementarity principle in biological and social structures. *J. Soc. Biol. Struct.* **1**, 191–200.

— (1979). The complementarity principle and the origin of macromolecular information. *Biosystems* **11**, 217–226.

Piaget, J. (1971). *Biology and knowledge: an essay on the relationship between organic regulations and cognitive processes*. Univ. Chicago Press, Chicago.

Plotkin, H. C. and Odling-Smee, F. J. (1981). A multiple-level model of evolution and its implications for sociobiology. *Behav. Brain Science* **4**, 225–268.

Polanyi, M. (1968). Life's irreducible structure. *Science* **160**, 1308–1312.

Ruse, M. (1982). *Darwinism defended*. Addison-Wesley, Reading.

Salthe, S. N. (1972). *Evolutionary Biology*. Holt, Rinehart and Winston, New York.

— (1975). Problems of macroevolution (molecular evolution, phenotype definition, and canalization) as seen from a hierarchical viewpoint. *Amer. Zool.* **15**, 295–314.

— (1983). An extensional definition of functional individuals. *Amer. Naturalist* **121**, 139–144.

— Ms. Evolving hierarchical systems: their structure and representation. In press, Columbia University Press, N.Y.

Simberloff, D. S. (1980). A succession of paradigms in ecology: essentialism to materialism to probabilism. *Synthese* **43**, 3–39.

Simpson, G. G. (1961). *Principles of animal taxonomy*. Columbia Univ. Press, New York.

Soodak, H. and Iberall, A. (1978). Homeokinetics: a physical science for complex systems. *Science* **201**, 579–582.

Stanley, S. M. (1975a). A theory of evolution above the species level. *Proc. Nat. Acad. Sci.* **72**, 646–650.

— (1975b). Clades versus clones in evolution: why we have sex. *Science* **190**, 382–383.

— (1979). *Macroevolution*. W. H. Freeman and Co., San Francisco.

Teggart, F. J. (1925/1977). *Theory and Processes of History*. Univ. California Press, Berkeley.

Valentine, J. W. (1968). The evolution of ecological units above the population level. *J. Paleont.* **42**, 253–267.

— (1973). *Evolutionary paleoecology of the marine biosphere*. Prentice-Hall, Englewood Cliffs.

Van Valen, L. (1973). A new evolutionary law. *Evol. Theory* **1**, 179–229.

Vrba, E. S. (1980). Evolution, species and fossils: how does life evolve? *S. Afr. J. Sci.* **76**, 61–84.

Vrba, E. S. and Eldredge, N. (1984). Individuals, hierarchies and processes: towards a more complete evolutionary theory. *Paleobiology*.

Wesley, J. P. (1974). *Ecophysics: the application of physics to ecology*. Charles C. Thomas, Springfield.

Whittaker, R. H. (1977). Evolution of species diversity in land communities. In *Evol. Biol.* (eds. M. K. Hecht *et al.*), **10**, 1–67.

Wigner, E. P. (1964). Events, laws of nature, and invariance principles. *Science* **145**, 995–998.

Williams, G. C. (1966). *Adaptation and natural selection*. Princeton Univ. Press, Princeton.

Winsatt, W. C. (1974). Complexity and organization. In *PSA–1972, Boston Stud. Philos. Sci.* (eds. K. F. Schaffner and R. S. Cohen), **20**, 67–86. D. Reidel, Dordrecht.

— (1976). Reductionism, levels of organization, and the mind-body problem. In *Consciousness and the Brain: a Scientific and Philosophical Inquiry*. (eds. G. G. Globus, G. Maxwell, and I. Savodnik), Plenum Press, New York.

Wright, S. (1953). Gene and organism. *Amer. Naturalist* **87**, 3–18.

— (1964). Biology and the philosophy of science. In *Process and Divinity: the Hartshorne Festschrift*. (eds. W. R. Reese and E. Freeman), Open Court Publ. Co., LaSalle.

Zotin, A. I. (1972). *Thermodynamic aspects of developmental biology*. S. Karger, Basel.

Narrow Approaches to Phylogeny: A Review of Nine Books of Cladism

MICHAEL T. GHISELIN

1. *Phylogenetics: The Theory and Practice of Phylogenetic Systematics.* E. O. Wiley. John Wiley and Sons, New York. 1981. xv + 439 pp. $42.50.

2. *Phylogenetic Patterns and the Evolutionary Process: Method and Theory in Comparative Biology.* Niles Eldredge and Joel Cracraft. Columbia University Press, New York. 1980. viii + 349 pp. $37.50.

3. *Systematics and Biogeography: Cladistics and Vicariance.* Gareth Nelson and Norman Platnick. Columbia University Press, New York. 1981. xi + 567 pp. $49.00.

4. *Phylogenetic Analysis and Paleontology: Proceedings of a Symposium Entitled 'Phylogenetic Models,' Convened at the North American Paleontological Convention II, Lawrence, Kansas, August 8, 1977.* Joel Cracraft and Niles Eldredge, Eds. Columbia University Press, New York, vi + 233 pp. $35.00 cloth, $12.00 paper.

5. *Vicariance Biogeography: A Critique: Symposium of the Systematics Discussion Group of the American Museum of Natural History May 2–4, 1979.* Gareth Nelson and Donn E. Rosen, Eds. Columbia University Press, New York. 1981. xvi + 593 pp. $47.00.

6. *Problems of Phylogenetic Reconstruction.* The Systematics Association Special Volume No. 21. K. A. Joysey and A. E. Friday, Eds. Academic Press, New York and London. 1982. x + 442 pp. $58.50, £31.40.

7. *Advances in Cladistics: Proceedings of the First Meeting of the Willi Hennig Society.* V. A. Funk and D. R. Brooks, Eds. The New York Botanical Garden, Bronx, New York. 1981. xii + 250 pp. $29.50 paper. U.S.A. postage $1.75, elsewhere $2.75.

8. *Advances in Cladistics, Volume 2: Proceedings of the Second Meeting of the Willi Hennig Society.* Norman I. Platnick and V. A. Funk, Eds. Columbia University Press, New York. 1983. xi + 218 pp. $32.50.

9. *Synopsis and Classification of Living Organisms.* Sybil P. Parker, Ed. McGraw Hill, New York. 1982. 2 Vols. xvi + 2,398 pp. $149.50.

In the 1830s Charles Darwin invented phylogenetic classification. He put this innovation to good use during the eight years of research that led to the publication, in 1851 and 1854, of his *Monograph on the Sub-class Cirripedia*, but in that work such terms as 'genealogical tree' could be interpreted as metaphors. It was only in *The Origin of Species* that he predicted that 'Our classifications will come to be, as far as they can be so made, genealogies' (page 486). The difference between this position and that of Darwin's predecessors is so profound as largely to have been overlooked, and the changes that were in order have been slow to come. Repeatedly systematists have reverted to antiquated ways of thought.

Prior to Darwin, biological classification was ahistorical in principle. The very word 'classification' suggests that it means the making of classes, or at least their discovery. A class is a kind of group the members of which, if there are any, share certain defining properties. For example, a bachelor is an unmarried male. A married bachelor is logically impossible, a contradiction in terms. When a bachelor marries, he changes, and ceases to be a member of the class, but the class remains unaltered. In other words, individuals can change, but classes cannot. If species and other taxa are classes, then they cannot possibly evolve. Before Darwin it was generally assumed that biological taxa are no different from the natural kinds of mineralogy or chemistry. Thus in his Empirium Naturae Linnaeus included three kingdoms, Animalia, Plantae, and Lapides. Natural objects could be arranged into groups, but the groups were not conceived of as historical units.

Darwin changed all that. For him, the taxa stood to each other as relatives in a genealogical tree. A tree, however, is an organism, not a class. It is an individual. Like its component twigs and branches, it is a whole made up of parts, not a nested set of similars. Although this was not made sufficiently explicit, the branches or lineages did come to be recognized as real units, or concrete elements, in biological systematics. It was interesting, but irrelevant, that sometimes there was a family resemblance among relatives. In genealogical classification the only thing that counts is filiation, as is clear from the fact that males and females often differ a great deal. The names of taxa are proper names, like yours and mine, and have no defining properties. The name has to be attached to the thing named by an ostensive definition, as with a christening.

Converting a phylogenetic tree into a traditional classification in the form of a Linnaean hierarchy of groups within groups has its difficulties. Imagine, if you will, a tree – make it a rather bushy one with numerous branches. Like the whole tree, any entire branch constitutes an individual. But what of two separate branches? They would hardly constitute a single object or individual. Two separate branches of a phylogenetic tree without the common ancestor form what is called a 'polyphyletic' taxon. Likewise we might consider the portion of a tree from which one or more branches have been removed. Although this seems more like a whole than two separate branches, it has the arbitrary character of a class. Like a tree except for some of its branches, a 'paraphyletic' taxon is one that incorporates the common ancestor but not all of its descendants. Some authors refer to a taxon consisting of the common ancestor and all of its descendants as a 'holophyletic' one. This is less ambiguous than calling them 'monophyletic', which traditionally has meant that the common ancestor is part of the group. Taxa which are not holophyletic are called 'grades'. Two kinds of grades need to be distinguished, according to whether they represent polyphyletic or paraphyletic taxa. A polyphyletic grade would leave out the common ancestor as in Haematothermia (Aves plus Mammalia). A paraphyletic grade would leave out some of ·the descendants of the common ancestor, as in Reptilia. Polyphyletic grades may even consist of several paraphyletic taxa.

Grades have frequently appeared in evolutionary classification systems. One reason for using them is that the categorical rank of a taxon (i.e., whether it is a genus, family, etc.) is able to suggest the 'amount of difference' between a taxon and its relatives. Thus, ranking the human species as a separate family, class, or even kingdom, expresses how different we consider ourselves to be from our poor relations. Amount of difference can be expressed by means of paraphyletic grades, but this means obscuring the relationships. Darwin used paraphyletic grades, but not polyphyletic ones, in his classification of the Cirripedia. Many other systematics however have used polyphyletic grades, favouring what are sometimes called 'horizontal' classifications. These are even less expressive of genealogical relationships.

'Typological' or 'essentialist' approaches to classification treat taxa as if they were classes. More importantly the defining properties of taxa are thought to reveal a metaphysical entity called the 'essence' of the group. Such approaches are often overtly Platonic or Aristotelian in their philosophy. It is hard to reconcile them with any treatment of taxa as individuals or historical units. Since 1859 genealogical classification has had many distinguished advocates. But it has always been opposed by typological alternatives such as the Platonism of Owen, Naef, and Remane. Even within what purport to be Darwinian circles typology has been highly influential. Julian Huxley advocated the use of grades. But perhaps the most typological among the architects of the Synthetic Theory was G. G. Simpson. He was strongly supportive of polyphyletic grades. Indeed he went so far as to redefine 'monophyly' so as to make it virtually synonymous with what everybody else had meant by polyphyly. According to his criterion, Vertebrata would still be monophyletic if Aves were descended from Echinoidea and Mammalia from Crinoidea.

At first Ernst Mayr accepted Simpson's taxonomic philosophy, though they always differed at the species level. Later he repudiated much of it, leading a campaign against typology and recently endorsing the thesis that species are individuals. At the higher levels he has repudiated polyphyletic grades, but not paraphyletic ones. The issues surrounding phylogenetics are clouded, however, by the dispute over phenetics. This was a philosophy of taxonomy that advocated basing classification on something called 'overall similarity'. Nobody has ever given a satisfactory explanation of what this term is supposed to mean, though originally it had something to do with feeding a lot of data into a computer and correlating traits. Numerical taxonomy is alive and flourishing, but the phenetic philosophy is dead. However, in arguing against phenetics, Mayr made a strategic mistake. Instead of rejecting similarity as the basis of classification he claimed that what matters is not phenotypic, but genotypic, similarity. Thus phenotype was confounded with soma, phenetic, and who knows what else. To find essences and similarity we had to examine the Unmoved Mover – DNA.

A rather different approach was taken by Willi Hennig, who elaborated a theory of 'phylogenetic systematics'. Hennig permitted no grades whatsoever, neither polyphyletic nor paraphyletic ones. A Linnaean hierarchy was to express the genealogical relationships clearly and unambiguously. Hennig's approach had the virtue of consistency, but there was a price for it. He wanted to subdivide each group wherever a branch occurred. This meant that there had to be a large number of levels, or categories. The problem became even more difficult if one wished to use the categories to express the amount of difference. The only way to do this would be to leave some groups undivided, and this meant even more categories.

Mayr lashed out at Hennig as well as the pheneticists, and this was not altogether fortunate. Hennig's real opponents were the German typologists, not the American evolutionists. He was against Plato, not Darwin. Mayr called Hennig a 'cladist' (a clade means a branch), by which he meant one for whom organisms are ordered and ranked solely on the basis of branching sequences. Hennig himself did not fit the definition, but the name continues to be used for his followers. The resulting polarity helps to explain why cladism has been associated with attacks on the theory of natural selection.

Two issues need to be kept distinct here. One is the problem of how genealogy should correspond to formal classification. The other is how we ought to study genealogy and historical biology in the broadest sense. When I began to do research on phylogenetics over twenty years ago, it was obvious that traditional classification was of little utility for studying any aspect of comparative biology. What one really needed was a phylogenetic tree and a clear understanding of what had happened in the evolutionary history of the group. Let it be assumed that one could do without a formal classification scheme. Therefore when, in the fall of 1964, I read Hennig's *Grundzüge einer Theorie der Phylogenetischen Systematik*, the topic of formal classification did not interest me very much. As to the second problem, that of how we come to know about phylogenetics, Hennig seemed to offer little that was not obvious to anyone who proceeded simply by asking what had happened to the group of organisms being investigated. For some reason Hennig is given credit for the notion that the useful evidence is shared, derived characters, which he called 'synapomorphies'. It turns out that these are approximately the same thing as the homologies of evolutionary anatomists: i.e., derivatives of some ancestral precursor. Neither did Hennig's approach differ very much from that of the German Platonists to whom he was opposed. In putting specimens together on the basis of morphological homologies and nothing more, Hennig was arguing for a procedure hard to distinguish from that advocated in Remane's *Grundlagen des Natürlichen Systems* or older works from which it was derivative. The main difference was with a concern for biogeography, which reflected a most non-Platonic metaphysics. Be this as it may, Hennig and his followers have perpetuated the myth that the data of phylogenetics have to be limited to morphological characters arranged in a scheme of like-with-like, and nothing else. They have rejected such principles of historical inferences as were developed by

Darwin and Dohrn. Methodologically they remain pre-Darwinian typologists, and even ontologically they are not consistent evolutionists. Therefore the books reviewed here are of interest as much in terms of what has been suppressed as of what is discussed.

The books reviewed here possess a certain earnestness and enthusiasm that is always attractive in a scientific work. I particularly enjoyed the one by Wiley, which explains cladistic methodology very clearly, and is quite effective at rebutting objections to strictly genealogical systems. Among other things he shows how branching sequences can be indicated, not just by division, but by annotation and sequencing, thus reducing the number of categorical levels and furthering stability. Wiley treats the individuality of species as a major theme in his book. As he points out, what really evolve are species: they speciate and become transformed. Genera and higher taxa do nothing whatsoever. He wants to distinguish what he calls 'historical entities' from individuals, on the grounds that higher taxa, unlike species, are not integrated. Thus he arranges the universe as follows:

    Classes
    Historical entities
    Individuals

It seems to me that the following arrangement is more satisfactory:

    Classes
    Individuals
      Historical entities
      Integrated wholes

A more important matter is Wiley's advocacy of the so-called 'evolutionary species definition'. Here he seems inconsistent with respect to the very criterion that leads him to see an important difference between species and genera. He wants to treat groups of clones in addition to sexually-reproductive wholes, as species. This is like creating imaginary marriages for bachelors. 'Agamospecies' are like heaps of leaves that have fallen off the tree that gave rise to them. One of Hennig's basic methodological principles was that what he called syncretic systems are incoherent, confusing fundamentally different kinds of objects. The evolutionary species definition is a vestige of Simpsonism that the cladists should exorcise as soon as possible.

Eldredge and Cracraft likewise present a clear and lucid exposition of cladistic methodology. Beyond that they attempt to develop a new approach to the study of macroevolution. They argue that the work of Simpson and others on that topic has involved an illicit extrapolation from the specific level to higher levels. If organisms and species function as integrated wholes but genera do not, then the higher levels must be decoupled from the lower ones. Upon this foundation they erect an admittedly tentative theory, involving species selection. Long-term changes are explained in terms of differential rates of speciation and extinction, analogously to the differential reproduction of organisms in natural selection. That diversity as it exists has been produced through interactions among species seems thoroughly legitimate, whatever the merits of any particular theory. However, Eldredge and Cracraft entertain scant consideration either of organisms or species as active participants in such processes. Rather we get a picture of ecological and morphological specialization linked to speciation events. It seems to me that Eldredge and Cracraft have gone from a legitimate decoupling of ontological levels to an illegitimate decoupling of epistemological ones. Where it is perfectly reasonable to distinguish among various kinds of things, such as species and genera, it is another matter whether they ought to be treated as if they were not the parts of the same universe. Eldredge and Cracraft dismiss the use of 'scenarios', by which is meant hypothesis about events that occurred in the past, as 'story-telling'. We are admonished to deal with a hierarchy of characters and nothing else, and only intrinsic ones at that. This excludes biogeography and ecology, and considerations of function and adaptive significance. But, as one might have anticipated, the scenarios are smuggled back in when an attempt is made to flesh out the model with discussions of real organisms. Eldredge and Cracraft are really interested in evolution, and it makes sense that they should ask what actually has happened and why, in spite of methodological pontifications.

Nelson and Platnick's *Systematics and Biogeography* is more extreme, divorcing systematics from evolutionary theory altogether, and occasionally sniping at natural selection. The philosophy is mainly one of idealistic morphology argued by means of preposterous abuses of language. They explicitly endorse typology (p. 328). In support of this position they assert that natural taxa (lineages or holophyletic groups) have 'defining properties'. This implies that natural taxa are classes, not individuals, a point which is obscured somewhat by their use of the term 'set'. According to logic as it is explained in the current textbooks, properties can be used to describe individuals, but not to define them. Nelson and Platnick however claim that the synapomorphies of a group are indeed defining. Thus, 'legged' is supposed to be defining of Tetrapoda. Therefore, a legless tetrapod would be a contradiction in terms. Snakes, of course, are tetrapods, so they must have legs. Where are they? The answer we are given is that there are two 'character states': 'legs present' and 'legs no longer present'. Snakes have legs of the second kind. I mention in passing that this kind of sophistry is by no means an isolated phenomenon. The literature on systematics abounds in verbal confusion about privative characters and 'negative things'. It should be emphasized that defining characters are necessary, not contingent. If the Tetrapoda are by definition four-legged, then any tetrapod that ever has lived, ever will live, or even possibly could exist, must possess four legs. A statement about what was true as a matter of historical fact is no defining property. If I was bearded yesterday, I am still me if I shave, and I would still be me if I had not been bearded yesterday. As good typologists Nelson and Platnick have to treat the world as inhabited by nested sets of characters, not by organisms, populations and lineages. Evolution is conceived of, not as a succession of generations in which one kind of organism replaces another, but as transformation of characters. As they profess, at least, to believe in evolution, Nelson and Platnick are hard-pressed to develop a coherent essentialist philosophy.

That taxa are historical units, not classes, implies that they must always occupy some definite position in space and time. This makes biology, like geology and linguistics, an historical science, and one of its major goals is to reconstruct the history of life on earth in all of its aspects. Or so one might think, but many cladists have taken a much more restrictive view of things. With respect to the fossil record, Nelson and Platnick repeat the claim of such idealistic morphologists as Remane that all it gives us is more specimens for strictly formal comparison. The claim is insiduous, partly because the role of fossils in the study of evolution has been so grossly misrepresented by paleontologists themselves. Unfortunately, although we are told what role fossils do not play, we are not told what roles they do play. The treatment of biogeography is much more substantial. Among the advantages to Hennig's approach to classification is that it does not conflate similarity with propinquity of descent, and in biogeography all that matters is genealogy. A phylogenetic tree ought to be an ideal instrument for the study of geographical distribution. The places where evolutionary events have occurred ought to be part of the scenario. By plotting trees on a map, the various speciations and other events may be correlated and explained. This allows geology and biology to become a single, unified science, with the two lending each other mutual support. However, many cladists, including Nelson and Platnick, have a somewhat different attitude. They want to use an approach called 'vicariance biogeography'. If several groups of organisms display the same pattern of distribution, it is reasonable to infer that the same causes have been operative. In vicariance biogeography the basic cause is the subdivision of biotas due to successive origins of barriers. The breakup of Gondwanaland is a good example. Branching sequences correspond very nicely here. The zeal for such an approach has led to attacks on what is called 'dispersal biogeography'. Given hindsight it is easy to see that a lot of error resulted from unclear thinking about such matters and that bad phylogenetic methodology was part of the difficulty. However, Nelson and Platnick give us a warped view of what went on, blaming Darwin and Wallace for the notion that populations have moved around much more than in fact they have. They forget that both Darwin and Wallace were profoundly impressed with insular biotas, where the effects of both colonization and local diversification are particularly striking. They neglect to tell us that Darwin and Wallace knew about faunal breakup and interchange due to the rise and fall of land and sea-levels. They seem unaware of the fact that it was Darwin who first proposed a great Pacific continent as part of his theory of coral reefs. It never occurs to them that the data were biassed toward more recent events, and that Wallace freely acknowledged the possibility that a southern connection might explain older ones. Nor do they tell us about the *ad hoc* character and other failures of land-bridge theories which Darwin and Wallace opposed. Finally, it seems odd that the ultimate success of plate tectonics is not seen as a justification for scenarios. Indeed, we can only look forward to the time when biogeography will provide us with a narrative account of what actually happened, and not just a pattern of nested taxa and nested areas.

Five of the books reviewed here are based upon meetings. The one edited by Cracraft and Eldredge includes some criticisms of the cladists, but most of this is not particularly effectual. Boucot argues that much of what is claimed as new had been known all along, the difference being largely a matter of jargon. He points out (p. 204) that the cladists 'show little concern for anything other than pure morphology'. It should be pointed out that 'pure morphology' means morphology in the strict definition of that term. It has nothing whatever to do with function, only with formalistic schemes. In the same spirit Bretsky (p. 155) says that cladism 'may be perceived as a reactionary movement, negating the training of students to look at organisms not as static morphologies out of museum drawers or sent in by a field geologist for identification, but as once-living creatures moulded by the demands of a particular environment'. Indeed the cladists in this volume devote much effort to justifying such a thanatological approach. Cracraft repeats the myth about Darwin's views on saltation that was created out of whole cloth by the advocates of the punctuated equilibrium theory. Gaffney lashes out at the Synthetic Theory as well. Here as elsewhere Eldredge treats adaptive scenarios as if they were a bad thing.

True to form, the introduction to the volume on vicariance biogeography edited by Nelson and Rosen tells us that Darwinism is 'a metaphysical and not a true science because its basic statements about the natural world are framed in a way such that a given prediction will always be realized'. The book claims to be a critique, but it is more of a beatification. Nonetheless it contains some very instructive material. Among these is a paper by Brundin, one of the first to apply Hennig's techniques to biogeography. Brundin criticizes the approach of Croizat and those who claim him as prophet. Brundin argues that dispersal is a fact to be dealt with, something that has to be taken into account if we are to have a complete picture of what has happened. A more doctrinaire cladist such as Platnick has to reject dispersal because it cannot be detected using his methodology. Again and again we find truth being subordinated to technique. Croizat's paper makes it abundantly obvious why virtually nobody took him seriously until the cladists came along. He tells us that Darwin was 'a good observer, but, alas, an indifferent thinker'. When one finds that one's views differ from those of someone else, one ought to find out what the issues are and consider the case on its merits. It never occurred to Croizat that Darwin, right or wrong, had perfectly good reasons for concluding what he did. Had he known what these were, Croizat might have presented a better case for his own views.

The volume edited by Joysey and Friday comes much closer to a substantive confrontation between cladists and others. The article by Charig represents a relatively moderate evaluation by one who is not a cladist. Charig finds much merit in cladistic techniques, and admits that his own work had been slipshod. He finds it objectionable that the cladists redefined the term 'monophyly' to mean what many now call 'holophyly'. He makes the very good point that 'monophyly' and 'polyphyly' have to do with origins, 'paraphyly' and 'holophyly' with composition. Forey tells us that scenarios are undesirable. On the other hand Meeuse shows the utility of ecological scenarios and Butler that of physiological ones.

Patterson's essay on 'Morphological characters and homology' is thoughtful and interesting, but contains serious logical mistakes. He tries to show that homology and synapomorphy are synonymous, and there is much truth in what he says. A synapomorphy is diagnostic of a holophyletic taxon, and so is an homology. But this does not mean that the two terms are strictly equivalent. Homology statements are ordinarily made in the context of comparative anatomy, and are restricted to correspondences between parts. Synapomorphy is a more general term for unique innovations present in the common ancestor. Thus synapomorphies could be attributes of entire organisms, or even geographical ranges. He also fails to understand the relation of correspondence, and therefore wrongly treats homology as a kind of similarity. The mistake here is evident when we realize that the relation of correspondence is transitive, whereas that of similarity is intransitive. If A is homologous to B, and B is homologous to C, then A must be homologous to C. But if A is similar to B, and B to C, A and C could be quite different. Brothers are similar in respect of being male siblings, but that does not make brotherhood a subset of similarity: a brother can be quite unlike his sister. Patterson tries to establish that consistency is the real criterion of homology. He rejects complexity, because some homologues are simple. But all this establishes is that complexity is not the only criterion of homology. In the same spirit he tells us that 'belief in, or knowledge of, evolution is superfluous to homology analysis'. The mere fact that some aspects of homology can be treated apart from the evolutionary context does not imply that all of them should be. This insensitivity to context, be it evolutionary, functional, ecological, or textual, is a rampant vice among cladists.

The two volumes of proceedings of the Willi Hennig Society meetings discuss a wide variety of topics. In the first of these, Brooks tells us in a theoretical paper that what is called the weighting of characters is not legitimate. Then he and his collaborators provide a fine example of weighting in a study on freshwater stingrays and their parasites. For example they use the rectal gland, which has atrophied, as evidence for a former marine ancestry. Here we have an application of a traditional canon of evidence in evolutionary comparative anatomy. Such use of vestigial structures is not acceptable in orthodox cladism. Again, scenarios keep reappearing where they are useful in solving interesting biological problems. When scientists talk out of both sides of their mouths, attend to what they do, not what they say.

In the second volume parsimony is discussed at length. The basic rationale to parsimony in phylogenetics is that one should hypothesize no more convergence than is necessary to explain the data. Given enough *ad hoc* hypotheses, one can justify virtually any tree. All one need do is find a little evidence in support of one's own hypothesis and explain away the evidence for its competitors. The trouble with cladistic techniques is that they underestimate the amount of parallel evolution that has occurred. Phylogenetics with minimal parallelism is like astronomy with the least number of epicycles. Granted no other criterion, it is the best one can do. In this the cladist and their philosopher supporters (Brady and Sober) agree. Yet it can easily be forgotten that scientists may have other options besides parsimony. We might invoke additional evidence, and different criteria. In astronomy, perhaps, we might try a heliocentric universe, ellipses instead of circles, and the mechanics of Newton or Einstein. In biology we might substitute the scenario for the cladogram, and the anatomy of Darwin for that of Oken.

An article by Hull entitled 'Karl Popper and Plato's metaphor' is particularly relevant. Throughout the volumes here reviewed, cladist authors appeal to aspects of Popper's philosophy for justification. Hull argues that they are mistaken in one important respect. By the testing of theories Popper meant what are called universal statements. This would mean, again, statements about classes, but taxa are not classes. Therefore although statements about taxa might be about several things (hence general or universal in form) they are not strictly universal. This is a very important distinction because it helps to differentiate between historical generalizations and laws of nature. Contrary to what some authors, such as Mayr, have claimed, there are indeed laws of nature in biology. But these are laws about classes of biological entities, not about individual ones.

The whole scope of Popperian philosophy is germane here, for the cladists seem largely to have missed the point. In the course of my early research on phylogenetics, certain pheneticists told me that what I was doing was not legitimate. The logic of many discussions on invertebrate phylogeny left much to be desired as well. Therefore I read great stacks of books on logic and philosophy, including the works of Popper. In the light of that background I read the works of Darwin, and found that corpus a superb illustration of Popperian principles. My book *The Triumph of the Darwinian Method* explains these matters, especially with respect to Darwin's barnacle monograph. As is well known, Popper misunderstood the theory of natural selection, but later acknowledged that he had been mistaken. Anti-evolutionary authors, including cladists, find it convenient to overlook what really went on here. Instead of understanding both Darwin and Popper, they misinterpret both. Time and again they do the precise opposite of what Popper rightly advises scientists to do, and their so-called Popperianism degenerates into mere slogans used to badger their opponents.

The cladists have deliberately and openly, as well as implicitly, endorsed typology, or what Popper calls 'essentialism'. If any philosopher who ever lived has been opposed to essentialism in all of its guises, it has been Popper, whose *Open Society and Its Enemies* is one long diatribe against it. Popper takes an 'evolutionary approach' to knowledge, one modelled upon natural selection. For him, definitions are unimportant, because knowledge is of real objects and laws of nature, not of essences. Popper is thus a realist. But the cladists, like many other systematists, are phenomenalists at heart: they want to classify appearances, not things. Hence their classifications are nested sets of characters, not descriptions of the underlying historical order.

For Popper, knowledge is provisional, always subject to criticism. One of his basic themes is the rejection of inductivism as a basis for scientific methodology. He favours instead a hypothetico-deductive approach. The truth does not arise out of the data. Rather, bold conjectures are tested against data, and refuted. In this he rightly appeals to the procedure of Einstein and Darwin. There is a problem here, because, as Hull points out, what Popper had in mind was primarily the testing of hypothesized laws of nature. But Popper maintains that even 'facts' have a hypothetical character. What gets treated is not just a law, but an entire hypothetico-deductive system. An effort to work upward from particulars to generalities will not succeed, because the very 'facts' are uncertain. Yet such an inductivist programme is precisely what the cladists advocate when they ask us to divorce systematic research from all considerations of evolutionary mechanism. We are supposed to wait until the historical pattern is known, and only then, if ever, consider process.

Popper argues that scientific hypotheses must be subject to refutation, and with this the cladists claim to agree. But by insulating their so-called theories from any but a very limited range of data, they do the precise opposite of what Popper had in mind. All we are allowed as evidence is formal synapomorphy schemes – no consideration of ecology, physiology, or mechanism is deemed licit. According to Popper, the way to test an hypothesis about history is to see if it is contradicted by some law of nature. If events of a certain kind never happen under any circumstances, they obviously never occurred in the past. This is the basic rationale for much of historical geology, but cladists seem unwilling to profit from the accomplishments of Lyell. Yes, there are some problems here. We might get stuck with a 'false law', just as we might get stuck with a 'false fact'. But this evades the issue. The only way out is to treat everything, without exception, as hypothetical.

Cladistic techniques often give ambiguous results. Different data imply different genealogies. Usually this is the result of parallel evolution – derived conditions have evolved more than once. As the cladists see it, the only permissible solution under such circumstances is to opt for the most 'parsimonious' tree, in the sense of the one that invokes the smallest number of changes. One cannot use one's understanding of the organisms to decide which changes have occurred more than once. This is called 'character weighting' and is not allowed. We are forbidden, for example, to say that a vestigial part represents the ancestral condition, or to consider what would be physiologically advantageous in a new environment. We are told that invoking multiple changes means an *ad hoc* hypothesis – even when we know that multiple changes have in fact occurred. Again, the Popperian philosophy can be invoked against such views. Popper clearly distinguishes between *ad hoc* hypothesis, intended to preclude refutation, from auxiliary hypotheses, which enrich the system and narrow down the range of acceptable possibilities. There need be nothing *ad hoc* in phylogenetics about invoking stratigraphy, biogeography, genetics, embryology, or ecology. Popper calls not for naive parsimony, but for stringency.

The metaphysical dogma that systematics proceeds by correlating characters leads to legitimate empirical evidence being discarded because it does not fit in with methodological fiats. A good example is DNA hybridization, which theory suggests and experience has shown can be a very useful technique. Eldredge and Cracraft (p. 48) reject it, because it does not distinguish primitive characters from derived ones. As good Popperians we ought to refute something here. How does DNA hybridization work? It uses a mode of inference similar to that of isotopic dating, in which a substance changes from one kind to another, and the proportion of the two is a measure of time elapsed since the origin. In DNA the initial condition is that of the ancestral population, in which for practical purposes the homologous parts of the DNA are identical. After speciation, changes occur such that the proportion of non-identical homologues increases. The proportion of non-identical homologues is a function of the time that has elapsed since speciation, and the tendency to hybridize is a good index of it. The technique may, perhaps, measure absolute time, but relative time is enough to give branching sequences. The technique works. It works because, in spite of cladist animadversions, in phylogenetic research we need not merely put similar objects together. Any procedure that allows us to discriminate between lineages ought to be acceptable.

All this is symptomatic. Cladistic philosophy treats the universe as if it were something other than a whole. Every character is treated as if it lived in a little world all its own; this in spite of the fact that the existence of but one true phylogenetic tree for the whole of life is one of the basic premises. Whatever the merits of phylogenetic analysis, we also need synthesis. The various branches of knowledge must cohere and lend each other mutual support. In setting up an extreme dichotomy between pattern and process, we lose the advantage of what Hennig called 'reciprocal illumination'. Evolutionary biology without phylogenetics is like physics without astronomy. Phylogenetics without evolutionary biology is like astronomy without mechanics.

The last volume under review here was not intended as a work on cladism, but as precisely what the title says it is, a synopsis and classification of living organisms. It is an excellent and authoritative survey of taxonomy as it is currently practised. The editor has done an outstanding job of coordinating the effort. I am not sure whom to blame for some deletions (the collembolans and terrestrial triclads are missing) and misplacements (dorid nudibranchs among the gymnosomatous pteropods), but in a work of such magnitude one cannot hope for perfection. In one sense, however, the book is about cladism. It ends with an essay on taxonomic principles by Bock, one of the leading Simpsonists. I fear he has undertaken a rear-guard action in defence of error. This feeling was confirmed when I read various sections from the point of view of one who desired to gain a better understanding of the evolution of life. Time and again I concluded that we are well off to the extent that genealogy is understood and expressed. A good example is Bock's arrangement of the birds. He divides them into three superorders:

Impennes
Palaeognathae
Neognathae

The Palaeognathae, as the name suggests, are an archaic branch, including the ostriches. The Neognathae constitute all other birds, with the exception of penguins, which in spite of their neognathous jaws and their close relationship to one group of Neognathae (the order Procellariiformes) are placed all by themselves; this because they are highly modified in adaptation to aquatic life. One would think that they could be placed, if not within the Neognathae as a group coordinate to the Procellariiformes, at least in sequence before or after the Neognathae. An analogous arrangement of the Mammalia makes equally good sense, but fortunately is not given:

Prototheria
Cetacea
Metatheria
Eutheria

Nonetheless, Bock does tell us, in the text, what the relationships are thought to be. His account of avian systematics is highly informative and useful. Such is not the case for many of the other groups, even where the phylogenetics is reasonably well understood. Often we are given no idea what evidence is used in erecting the classification. In some cases the treatment of a group conceals relationships for no good reason. Consider, for example, a group I have worked on, the opisthobranch gastropod family Runcinidae. It is split and treated as an order, when it is closely related to one branch of the order Cephalaspidea. The higher-level taxonomy of opisthobranchs has degerenated into a kind of list, a lot of orders with no indication of relationships. Other groups are in even worse condition. Where one might have tried at least to place relatives next to each other, time and again we find the taxa not in a biological sequence, but in an alphabetical one. The cartoonist Sheridan Anderson once published a calendar with the months arranged alphabetically, from April to September, but he was joking. The non-classification of prokaryotes taken from *Bergey's Manual* is absurd, but not funny. At least we are spared the kingdom Protista, which would have turned Plantae and Animalia into polyphyletic grades. Perhaps most disturbing, I came away with the distinct impression that many of the authors have no idea what the scientific merits of one arrangement or another might be. In consequence we are forced to accept the opinions of so-called authorities. Systematics would be far better off if the evidence upon which such judgments are made were clearly stated in such a fashion that inter-subjective evaluation is possible. This is what many cladist authors evidently mean when they have argued that systematics ought to be a science, not an art. This does not put it strongly enough. Deciding what is true on the basis of something other than logic and fact is not art – it is mere pseudoscience.

The various factions among systematics have often behaved more like theologians than scientists, turning to philosophy to rationalize their prejudices and dispose of their competitors. By an artful combination of dogmatism with respect to one's own position and scepticism with respect to the others, anything can be justified. To some it matters little whether such arguments are coherent or not. But to the rest of us it is far from trivial. We biologists have problems to solve. In order to solve those problems we need the data of phylogenetics, as reliably acquired and as effectually presented as possible. To this end we need a clear understanding of the basic principles. The search for such understanding is the proper office of philosophy in science. All else is obfuscation.

Index